The Theatre of Form and
the Production of Meaning

The Theatre of Form and the Production of Meaning:

Contemporary Canadian Dramaturgies

Ric Knowles

ECW PRESS

The publication of *The Theatre of Form and the Production of Meaning*
has been generously supported by the Canada Council,
the Ontario Arts Council, and the Government of Canada through
the Book Publishing Industry Development Program.
This book has been published with the help of a grant from the Humanities
and Social Sciences Federation of Canada, using funds provided by
the Social Sciences and Humanities Research Council of Canada.

CANADIAN CATALOGUING IN PUBLICATION DATA

Knowles, Richard, 1950–
The theatre of form and the production of meaning:
contemporary Canadian dramaturgies

ISBN 1-55022-399-2

1. Canadian drama (English) – 20th century – History and criticism.★
2. Drama – Technique. I. Title.
PS8177.K56 1999   C812'.5409   C99-931992-2
PR9191.5.K56 1999

Cover design by Guylaine Régimbald.

Cover photo by Michael Cooper. Photo shows the set for *Lion in the Streets*,
by Judith Thompson. Produced by Tarragon Theatre in 1990.
Set design by Sue LePage.

Interior design by Yolande Martel.

Printed by AGMV l'Imprimeur, Cap-Saint-Ignace, Quebec.

Distributed by General Distribution Services,
325 Humber College Blvd., Etobicoke, Ontario M9W 7C3.

Published by ECW Press,
2120 Queen Street East, Suite 200,
Toronto, Ontario M4E 1E2.
www.ecw.ca/press

PRINTED AND BOUND IN CANADA

To Christopher
with love

Criticism must think of itself as life-enhancing and constitutively opposed to every form of tyranny, domination and abuse; its social goals are non-coercive knowledge produced in the interests of human freedom.

— Edward Said, *The World, the Text, and the Critic* (29)

Contents

Acknowledgements

Research and scholarship are collaborative enterprises in ways that are not always visible, particularly at this historical moment, when the individual ownership of knowledge is unfortunately privileged in an increasingly professionalized academy. Like all my work, this book has benefited from the support, advice, and scholarship of others; in fact, it would not have been possible without their collaboration, which includes, of course, the contributions acknowledged in the notes and the list of works cited as well as the hard-to-identify contributions attributable to the kinds of intellectual osmosis from which we all benefit. But it also includes direct personal debts that need to be acknowledged. The most general of these, though far from the least important, are to the memberships of those scholarly organizations that are far too infrequently acknowledged as the places where scholarship happens, ideas are exchanged, and mutual encouragement is supplied to those of us, particularly in theatre studies, who can otherwise feel as though we are operating in incapacitating isolation. For me, these debts are most profoundly to my always generous colleagues in the Association for Canadian Theatre Research and Shakespeare Association of America. Similarly, virtually all scholarship is indebted to the forums provided for the circulation of ideas by scholarly journals; many of the chapters in this book have developed in one way or another and in varying degrees out of ideas first floated in *Theatre Research International*, *Atlantis*, *Dalhousie Review*, and *Australasian Drama Studies*, and I am grateful to their editors for the opportunities that they provided.

At the same time, and more directly, I'm fortunate not to be operating in isolation, thanks especially to the generosity, intellectual curiosity, informed enthusiasm, and friendship of my colleagues in drama studies at the University of Guelph, particularly Alan Filewod, Harry Lane, and Ann Wilson. I am also indebted to many of my students and former students at Guelph, particularly Mayte Gomez, Jennifer Harvie, Ted Little, and Michael McKinnie, for their curiosity, criticism, and, on occasion, direct collaboration, and to Martin de Jong for all of those things as well as his work as a research assistant at a time when I didn't even know that I would be writing this book. And I'm indebted to my current research assistant, Sheena Albanese, particularly for her assiduous checking of my quotations against their sources (any remaining errors, of course, are mine). The outstanding collections at the University of Guelph theatre archives, together with the help of the former archivist, Nancy Sadek, and her staff, were indispensable. I received similar support from Peter Smith, Rebecca Scott, and the staff at Playwrights' Workshop Montreal.

I am indebted, too, to the College of Arts at the University of Guelph and its dean, Carole Stewart, for the administrative leave after a long term as the chair of drama (and a blessedly brief stint as acting dean), leave that allowed me to get this book under way and without which it would not have been possible.

Finally, and most importantly, I am deeply indebted to the challenges, support, friendship, and (always) constructive criticism that I have received on this project over the years from Hélène Beauchamp, Susan Bennett, Cindy Cowan, Barbara Hodgdon, Michael Keefer, Karen Knowles, Ed McKenna, Jenny Munday, Richard Plant, Rob Nunn, Denis Salter, and especially Christine Bold and Skip Shand. And, above all, I want to express my deep debt, years ago but with abiding importance, to Sandy Leggatt.

★   ★   ★

Chapter 4 first appeared in *Contemporary Issues in Canadian Drama*, edited for Blizzard Press by Per Brask; chapter 7 first appeared in *Theatre Research in Canada/Recherches théâtrales au Canada*. They are reprinted here with both permission and gratitude. I am grateful to Blizzard Press, and Anansi/Stoddart, respectively, for permission to reprint the passages from Michael Hollingsworth's *The History of the Village of the Small Huts* on pages 135–37, John Mighton's *Scientific Americans* on page 220, and John Krizanc's *The Half of It* on pages 227–28. This book has been published with the help of a grant from the Humanities and Social Sciences Federation of Canada, using funds provided by the Social Sciences and Humanities Research Council of Canada. I am extremely grateful for their support and that of their anonymous readers.

Introduction
The Politics of Dramatic Form

The form of it. That's all. The form of it.
— George F. Walker, *Nothing Sacred* (90)

"THE THEATRE of Form and the Production of Meaning": what does that mean? Form, at a time of psychoanalytical, Marxist, materialist, and gendered readings of bodies, performances, and productions, seems curiously old-fashioned as a topic, interest in which has been superseded by structuralist and then post-structuralist analyses in what seemed for a time an exponentially increasing frenzy of successive theoretical approaches. And indeed my approach in the chapters that follow draws upon and shares something with many current theoretical positions: where appropriate, I dip into (but try not to appropriate or oversimplify) Freud, feminism, Frye, and Foucault; raid Bakhtin, Barthes, Blau, and the Bible; detour to the historiography of de Certeau and the film theory of de Lauretis, the ethnography of James Clifford, and the cultural theory of Raymond Williams; and finally, if briefly, draw analogies from quantum mechanics.

All this may seem rather scattershot, or even dilettantish, so here I want to outline the thread that (I hope) ties the book together. My interest in "the theatre of form" is an interest in dramaturgical form (inherited generic organizing systems) and structure (the ways in which plays are put together),[1] but not for their own sakes — that is, my interest is a materialist one focused on dramaturgical form and structure *as* theatres, or forums, for the social negotiation of cultural values, or what my title calls "the production of meaning." My project, carried out in the context of the analysis of some contemporary English Canadian dramaturgical forms, structures, and strategies,[2] is, in a sense, to politicize form, to examine form itself as a material agent of cultural affirmation (or reproduction), on the one hand, or cultural intervention, on the other. I want, in the construction of Raymond Williams, to move from formal analysis to formational analysis (*Politics* 79), to develop what he calls a "sociology of forms" (*Culture* 143), and to ask what cultural work is done by different dramatic forms and different dramaturgical structures, whatever the subject matter or thematic content of the works in which those forms and structures are developed or deployed. In a sense, I will be analysing form and to a lesser extent structure as the "unconscious" of the plays under discussion, which may or may not be at odds with their "conscious" subjects, themes, or points of view.[3]

The politicization of form is not a new project. As early as 1928, Bakhtin/Medvedev, in *The Formal Method in Literary Scholarship: A Critical Introduction to Sociological Poetics*,[4] critiqued the work of the Russian Formalists and attempted to articulate an aggressively "sociological poetics" that amounted to a rapprochement between Marxism and formalism. They note, moreover, that the European Formalists themselves "strove to attribute deep ideological meaning to form" (49). Their attempt to link formalist and Marxist approaches was repeated, explicated, and expanded by Tony Bennett in *Formalism and Marxism* in 1979 and further extended by Fredric Jameson in *Marxism and Form: 20th Century Dialectical Theories of Literature*, in which Marxist interpretation is considered to reveal the latent *content* of form: ideology. Williams comes closest, however, to illuminating the project of this book in two essays published in the collection *Problems in Materialism and Culture*, in which he develops the idea of "a structure of feeling" (22). Williams argues in "Literature and Sociology" that (literary) form is essentially an organizing view of the world:

> And it is just this element of organization that is, in literature, the significant social fact. A correspondence of content between a writer and his [sic] world is less significant than this correspondence of organization, of structure. A relation of content may be mere reflection, but a relation of structure, often occurring where there is no apparent relation of content, can show us the organizing principle by which a particular view of the world, and from that the coherence of the social group which maintains it, really operates in consciousness. (23)

In another essay in the collection, "Social Environment and Theatrical Environment," Williams identifies as "still the central inquiry" an approach that delves into "the relations between forms and social formations, crucial everywhere in art but in drama always especially central and evident" (147).

Finally, Herbert Blau articulates clearly the relationship of form to meaning as I understand it when he introduces the useful concept of a "structure of expectation" in the theatre, a structure that, I would argue, is fundamentally dramaturgical:

> The meaning I am talking about is not . . . that of the play, the dramatic text, nor of the characters within the text, nor even that of the actors. . . . [W]hat I am referring to is a deeper contestation with the ideological power behind the text . . . ; that is, the structure of expectation, social and political, from which it emerges and which is likely to be reproduced even in the corporeality of performance. . . . (77)

My concern in analysing some Canadian dramatic forms and the structures of some contemporary Canadian plays, then, is to look in one direction at what for Williams are "the relations between forms and social formations" and what for Blau is the relationship between form and meaning. My concern is to examine the role of dramatic form, and of play structures, as material agents in shaping (rather than simply reflecting) both consciousness and social formations. I am particularly interested in the degrees to which *structural* innovations, through what Victor Shklovsky and his colleagues, the Russian Formalists, called "making strange" (Lemon and Reis; Shklovsky), cannot only, as for Shklovsky, help us to see the familiar more clearly but also allow us to see differently — to see the *un*familiar — and therefore, through changing our perceptual constructions of the world, serve the project of changing the social formation itself.[5]

Seeing differently — or, perhaps, seeing difference — is both a concept and an activity not unlike what Althusser, in his essay on "Freud and Lacan," calls "misrecognition" but identifies with (centrist) ideological formations:

> Since Copernicus, we have known that the earth is not the "centre" of the universe. Since Marx, we have known that the human subject, the economic, political or philosophical ego is not the "centre" of history — and even . . . that history has no "centre" but possesses a structure which has no necessary "centre" except

in ideological misrecognition. In turn, Freud has discovered for us that the real subject, the individual in his unique essence, has not the form of an ego, centred on the "ego," on "consciousness" or on "existence" . . . [and] that the human subject is de-centred, constituted by a structure which has no "centre" either, except in the imaginary misrecognition of the "ego," i.e. in the ideological formations in which it "recognizes" itself.

It must be clear that this has opened up one of the ways which may perhaps lead us some day to a better understanding of this *structure of misrecognition*, which is of particular concern for all investigations of ideology. (219)

All recognitions — including, of course, those instantiated by Althusserian interpellation — are in some sense misrecognitions in the context of what must be seen as an *un*stable social formation, and I am concerned here with strange makings and misrecognitions of a somewhat different sort from Althusser's, misrecognitions that serve both to "make strange," and therefore denaturalize and destabilize dominant ideological formations, and to "try on," as it were, new fits between dramatic forms and (always) emerging consciousnesses and social formations.

Why bother to undertake a politicized reading of dramatic form? Do I really believe in the power of contemporary theatre in Canada to produce dissent or effect change? Well, yes, if anything can (though perhaps not on its own). As Sue Ellen Case has argued,

In the age of television, computer languages and communications satellites, the production of signs creates the sense of what a person is, rather than reflects it (in the traditional mimetic order). The mode of cultural production is reversed: signs create reality rather than reflect it. This condition means that artists and cultural theorists may be the activists and revolutionaries. Modes of discourse and representation may replace the Molotov cocktail. (132)

Case may be too sanguine, but in Canada the arts are among the few avenues left open for counter- or antihegemonic critique, particularly as universities and schools have increasingly, and increasingly openly, become arms of governments, their faculty classified as civil servants and their students openly constructed as industry trainees. And theatre is, of course, the most social of the arts, the most potentially immediate in its effects, and in some genres and venues the least easily contained.[6]

This potential of theatre is revealed perhaps less in the occurrence of occasional neoconservative and homophobic moves to repress a company such as Toronto's Buddies in Bad Times — which, in terms of economic impact and audience size, surely verges on social insignificance — than in the fact that the theatre company has *survived* such attacks and has even expanded, moving in the fall of 1994 to its new home at 12 Alexander Street (which formerly housed George Luscombe's left-wing Toronto Workshop Productions) and establishing itself as North America's largest queer theatre. Recognizing, as Peter Stallybrass and Allon White have demonstrated, the degree to which the socially marginal is often symbolically central to a given culture, it is important to note that the *symbolic* importance of Buddies in Bad Times — as of other similarly disruptive companies across the country (e.g., Calgary's similarly beleaguered Maenad Productions) — far exceeds any immediate impact that its work might have in fomenting revolutionary or even socially subversive sentiments in a particular audience. Also significant is the *cumulative* impact of the company's work — or the cultural work performed by the company's discourse (which includes its shows, its press releases, its symbolic and physical presence in the city, as well as the counterdiscourse produced by its opponents, particularly those in authority). All of this suggests that, like other such theatres, Buddies in Bad Times plays a kind of crossroads role in contemporary Canadian cultural life[7] and that theatre, even on the small scale at which such a company operates, can play a significant role in shaping the social formation.

★   ★   ★

This book is divided into three parts, the first of which, entitled "The Dramaturgical Inheritance: Versions and Perversions," attempts to identify and interrogate the two dominant, inherited traditions of contemporary Canadian dramaturgy, naturalism and modernism, with their respective structural reliance on time and space. It examines versions, variations, and finally *per*versions of those traditional forms in some contemporary plays, and it analyses the degree to which these versions and perversions reproduce, affirm, destabilize, or undermine currently dominant social forms and values. Recognizing and analysing the ways in which inherited form and generic tradition operate as what film theorist Rick Altman calls a "cultural machine" (6 and passim), controlling social formations, constructing social subjects, and containing possible questionings and challenges, this section also looks at ways in which perversely *staging* the machine — foregrounding the formal "givens" — can construct form itself as a theatre in which cultural value can be contested, negotiated, or redefined. It is not incidental to my project here that all of the versions and perversions analysed in this discussion of the dramaturgical inheritance were written by whites — members of what Guillermo Verdecchia has called the "Saxonian community" (40) — or that all of the *versions* — the reinscriptions — were written by straight white men, for whom the inherited forms were presumably least problematic.

Parts 2 and 3, respectively entitled "Beyond Naturalism" and "Beyond Modernism," examine the cultural work performed by structural experiments emerging from naturalist and modernist models, again focusing on time and space respectively. The epilogue gestures toward attempts to merge temporal and spatial organizational principles in plays that look to contemporary, post-Newtonian scientific models, quantum mechanics, and chaos theory. The works discussed in these sections were produced by writers and theatre workers of a wider range of races, ethnicities, genders, and sexualities than those of part 1, people who have a stake in challenging or revisioning ways of seeing that are implicitly or explicitly authorized by Canada's dominant classes and cultures. These sections include considerations of some relatively recent dramaturgical experiments that move beyond the inherited forms underlying naturalist and modernist dramaturgies and attempt to analyse the kinds of affirmative or interventionist cultural/ideological work performed through these structural innovations. Not all of these innovations are altogether new — collective creation, environmental theatre, and metatheatre, for example, have been around for a long time — but they have not been treated in criticism or in the theatrical repertoire as a central part of the inherited dramaturgical tradition *in Canada*, and in any case they are newly created in their specific post-1970 Canadian contexts. These sections range widely in theoretical approach and somewhat less widely in geographical "coverage" within Canada, and like the first section they make no claims either to being comprehensive in theoretical approach or in the selection of plays or to being consistent in style or point of view. Indeed, the critical approaches, within the theoretical context outlined here, and the deliberately divergent structures and styles of writing in each chapter of parts 2 and 3 and the epilogue, are developed in negotiation with the scripts themselves as explorations of the kinds of cultural work performed by the plays. The plays chosen seem interesting to me for the purposes of politicized dramaturgical analysis. They are also (often) plays that I have seen performed within their original social and cultural contexts.[8] I make no claim for the "centrality" of these texts to a national tradition (though I have attempted to choose plays that are published, available, and in most cases taught); I do not want to suggest that they will perform the same cultural work in every context of production (quite the contrary); and I have no wish by choosing them to construct or reconstruct a Canadian dramatic canon. Finally, of course, my accounts and constructions of these texts, social and dramatic, are necessarily those of a culturally and historically determined reader. They will, however, serve as explorations of some of the ways in which dramaturgical form and structure in contemporary Canada have served as theatrical forums for the production, reproduction, negotiation, and reformation of the social order.

It is important, I think, to include here a brief note on the styles and structures of this book and of the chapters that follow. In keeping with the tensions between global theory and local practice, and those between inherited forms and invented styles and structures that are the subjects of this study, I have tried to provide both a "global" frame for the argument and a "local" variety of styles and structures that change considerably in the chapters according to subject matter and subject position. The "global" is embedded most clearly in introductory sections such as this one, and in the epilogue, in which the relationships between temporal, spatial, and space/time structures and naturalism, modernism, process, and politics are articulated. The "local" is perhaps more disruptive and discontinuous: some chapters, such as those on the inherited forms of naturalism and various resistances to them that treat time as process, dwell on a limited number of plays and on structures that develop in leisurely ways through the temporal organization of cause and effect, creative process and theatrical product; others, such as those focusing on modernist and post-modernist organizational principles that rely on iconic imagery or on the dehistoricizing iconographies of spatial organization, survey more briefly a wider range of "imagistic" plays that can more easily be conjured up through brief gestures toward iconographies or spatial strategies that resist both history and development. Finally, each chapter attempts to adopt a voice appropriate to its subject, and, although "objective" and monologic authority is avoided for the most part, the style of the book deliberately ranges from positioned description to dialogue.

PART ONE

The Dramaturgical Inheritance: Versions and Perversions

I

Aristotle, Oedipus, and the Bible:
Forms of Naturalism

Everyday life can be stubbornly non-Aristotelian when it tries.
— Alan Read (51)

ARISTOTLE, Oedipus, and the Bible have a great deal to answer for. In Canada, their combined influence — mediated through the popular reputations and canonical stature of Aristotle, Freud, and *Oedipus Rex*; through the modern, structuralist criticism (including biblical criticism) of scholars such as "our own" Northrop Frye; and through secondary and post-secondary school Shakespeare as taught by English teachers raised on A.C. Bradley — has shaped the dramaturgical unconscious of most playwrights, directors, theatre critics, and theatre audiences of the generation that witnessed the rebirth of Canadian drama in the late 1960s and early 1970s. This is the same generation that produced and celebrated plays such as David French's *Leaving Home* and *Of the Fields, Lately*, Michael Cook's *Jacob's Wake*, and a host of other works in the tradition of poetic naturalism that continues unabated, if no longer unchallenged, even today. In the first part of this chapter, I will consider the ways in which this inherited and essentially conservative dramaturgical unconscious has frequently served to undermine or contain the social concerns and criticisms that constituted the conscious thematic "content" of many of the plays of this generation, including plays by Cook, French, David Freeman, William Fruet, Larry Kardish, and other representatives of the school of "selective naturalism" — "an impressionistic method with strict and fascinating formal controls" — that Urjo Kareda celebrated in his famous 1972 introduction to French's *Leaving Home* (viii).

Most Canadians of my generation, the one whose arrival at adulthood coincided with the resurgence of Canadian drama in the late

1960s and early 1970s, were schooled on neo-Aristotelian concepts of tragedy as represented by Francis Fergusson's 1961 introduction to the Butcher translation of *Aristotle's Poetics*. Fergusson links Aristotle, Sophocles, implicitly Freud, and explicitly Frazer's *The Golden Bough: A Study in Magic and Religion* in a master(ful) narrative/interpretive account of what he introduces as "the most fundamental study we [sic] have of the art of drama" (2). Fergusson concentrates on Aristotle's linking of dramatic action with character motivation in the (neo-Freudian) working out of "a natural history of the psyche's life" (13), on the overriding need for unity and closure in dramatic structure,[1] on the definition of character as "habitual action" (22), and on the concept of catharsis ("the purgation of the passions of fear and pity" [33]).[2] He also stresses the supposed universality of a linear plot structure that consists of complication and denouement, divided by a climax and turning point, or reversal. Fergusson insists that this structure "has to do, not with the dramatist's vision, but with the *means* of making any action clear and effective in the theater" (20), as he attributes to Aristotle belief in the related "Greek notion that the fine arts have no end beyond themselves" (32). The combined effect, of course, is to deny form or structure any ideological weight or cultural coding, treating them as neutral and value-free tools and thereby denying theatre the possibility of having any direct impact on consciousness or the social order.

For Canadian high school and university students who became the playwrights, directors, critics, and audiences of the 1970s and beyond, the requisite linkage of action with motivation, the neo-Aristotelian concepts of unity of action and characterization, and the deployment of reversal and recognition as universal dramaturgical techniques — together with the notion of the necessary nobility of a central tragic hero with a fatal "tragic flaw" — became virtually second nature after four or five years of drilling in classrooms in which the study of Shakespeare's tragedies was obligatory. As students, it didn't occur to us to ask why, if a tragedy had to have a single, central, tragic hero, we had so much trouble agreeing on just whose tragedy *Julius Caesar* was or precisely where, if the play had to have a turning point, it occurred. We became experts, however, at demonstrating that all of these characteristics were somewhere "in" the plays that we studied, since those characteristics were definitive of dramatic "greatness" and the plays that we studied were by definition "great" (or why would we be studying them?). That students of directing are to this day taught in textbooks how to find rising actions, climaxes, turning points, and denouements "in" any play that they take on is an indication of how pervasive, and how pernicious, such concepts have been.

"Classical" tragedy, with whatever recalcitrance Shakespeare's sprawling and populist plays fit the mould, was of course not the only object of study in those 1960s classrooms. We also examined and learned to apply our knowledge of dramatic form to a number of naturalistic dramas and "domestic tragedies" (almost always American, almost always including *Death of a Salesman*), to debate whether they were "really" tragic, since their central characters, whom we learned to call "anti-heroes," were just common men (sic) rather than Aristotle's noblemen. And this exercise paid professional rewards later on for many of us, as is evidenced not only in the dramatic structures and stagings but also in the early critical reception of plays such as *Leaving Home* and *Of the Fields, Lately*, which were inevitably compared with the (implicitly "greater") plays of Miller, Williams, and O'Neill, often through the application of the dramaturgical template learned in school. Thus, Ed Jewinski in 1976 could "classify" *Leaving Home* as "a descendant of the modern domestic tragedy, such as *Death of a Salesman, Cat on a Hot Tin Roof*, or *A Streetcar Named Desire*" (93), in an article arguing that "French, no less than many another modern playwright, such as Miller, Osborne, Williams, or Pinter, presents us with the little man . . . [but] utilizes the 'hero as victim' in his own unique way" (92). Jewinski concludes, however, that "the import of a father as the head of a household, confronted by the decline and collapse of his family, . . . can never really gain truly tragic proportions — at least in modern drama" (94).[3]

Jewinski's focus on the figure of the father in *Leaving Home*, read in the context of what was almost universally referred to as the "coming of age" of Canadian drama in the early 1970s, hints at another interesting phenomenon: the complicity of neo-Aristotelian dramaturgies with (the popular reputation of) "the Oedipus complex" as articulated by Freud and of both with the teleological nationalist narrative of Canada's cultural maturation. R.W. Bevis comments in a review of *Leaving Home* and Freeman's *Creeps* published in 1974 that "Both Freeman and French are young playwrights who seem to have difficulty treating father-figures with understanding" (90); Edward Mullaly, also writing in 1974, comments wittily that "Hopefully, *Of the Fields, Lately* will not only allow French to free himself from his father, but also from Arthur Miller" (132). Indeed, a series of father-and-son plays in the early 1970s, together with the coming-of-age-of-Canadian-drama rhetoric of writing such as Kareda's introduction to the published script of *Leaving Home* and the nationalist manifestos of Canadian playwrights, theatre companies, and journals (e.g., *Canadian Theatre Review*) of post-centennial-celebration Canada, displays not only a certain anxiety of influence but also a kind of national dramatic oedipal crisis seemingly congruent with the dramatic forms and traditions at hand.[4]

Aristotle's use of *Oedipus Rex* as a model, and Fergusson's much more exclusive focus on that play in his introduction to *Aristotle's Poetics*, could not fail in the 1960s and 1970s to conjure up popular understandings of Freud's reading of Sophocles's play in *The Interpretation of Dreams* (362–65) and his theory of the Oedipus complex,[5] which are inscribed in the narratology of naturalistic drama in the period and informed both psychological approaches to directing and the psychologized readings of audiences, reviewers, and critics.[6] The Oedipus complex, in its positive formulation, identifies the male child's desire for his mother, desire that must later be transferred to an appropriate "object." In its negative form, the mother is desired, while the father is identified as the rival. In *The Interpretation of Dreams*, Freud analyses *Oedipus Rex* as the playing out of an unconscious (and archetypal) oedipal fantasy existing not only in the text but also in the author's and audience member's (or reader's) minds. The play that has come to serve as the dominant dramaturgical model in the Western theatre, then, has as its "deep structure" a crisis consisting of the male subject's unconscious or repressed desire (for the mother) or aggression (against the father), followed by a resolution that begins with the recognition of inappropriate desire (or feelings of guilt), and finally the displacement of that desire to a normative, socially acceptable other.[7]

Freud's French follower and explicator, Jacques Lacan, extended Freud's work into the realm of language, arguing that the unconscious, like the conscious, is discursively constructed and that the resolution of the oedipal crisis coincides with entry into the symbolic order (in Peggy Phelan's coinage, at "what the Bible calls the Fall and Lacan calls the Mirror Stage" ["Reciting" 29]). At this point, according to Lacan, the human subject is constituted *as* a subject by his or her relinquishing of experiential access to "the imaginary," or what Julia Kristeva calls the semiotic, pre-oedipal "fullness of being" (which precedes gender divisions), and accepts, in exchange for access to "fullness of meaning," or language, subjection to the law of the father (Lacan 1–7; Kristeva, *Desire* passim).[8] As a discursive field, then, the dramaturgical structure that derives from the combined Aristotelian and Freudian/Lacanian readings of *Oedipus Rex* (what Herbert Blau resonantly calls "the reproductive structure of the oedipal drama" [89]) functions to inscribe a psychosocial norm, serving what Gramsci calls hegemony, Althusser ideology, and feminists patriarchy.[9]

The alliance between neo-Aristotelian and neo-Freudian narratives is complemented and completed by work related to Fergusson's now surprising focus, in his introduction to *Aristotle's Poetics*, on Gilbert Murray's reading of Frazer's *The Golden Bough*. The application of Murray's analysis of "the ritual forms of Greek tragedy" is restricted to tragic form, and Fergusson pays little attention to Aristotle's own brief and fragmented discussion of comedy (59–60).[10] Nevertheless, this work serves as a basis for the structuralist and anthropological criticism of Northrop Frye and C.L. Barber — partly by way of the structuralist anthropology of Claude Lévi-Strauss — and in part had the effect of extending the application of the composite formal tradition that I have been sketching beyond tragedy primarily into the realm of comedy, with which it seems the most congenial (Frye, "The Argument of Comedy," *A Natural Perspective*; Barber, *Shakespeare's Festive Comedy*), but ultimately into virtually any literary genre, ritual formation, or social structure (Frye, *Anatomy of Criticism*). This critical tradition — which, largely through the influence of Frye, became a staple of high school and university instruction in Canada in the 1960s and 1970s — found in all literature an interrelated and ultimately self-referential structure of myths and archetypes that were most fully represented by the Bible (Frye, *The Great Code*, *Words with Power*) and that echo the seasonal rites of death (tragedy) and rebirth (comedy) played out in what are seen to be archetypal "primitive" and Christian religious rituals (Barber 3–57; Frye, *Anatomy* 131–242). The effect of allying this school of criticism with the conflated oedipal tradition of Aristotle and Freud, of course, was to further naturalize the structures and social impacts of reversal, recognition, and social adjustment by articulating and thereby naturalizing parallel structures in seasonal cycles and in religious rituals; by further universalizing those structures in a self-contained, self-reflexive, and ahistorical totalizing narrative; and by providing all-encompassing systems of symbols, drawn from sources in religions as well as nature, in which any part served metonymically to conjure up the totalizing whole.

For Frye, famously (and as discussed in chapter 2), literature has no social referent, but it does have a social and cultural impact, as Michael

Bristol has pointed out, in the "reconciliation of private subjectivity with a social totality" (175).[11] What Aristotle did for tragedy, then ("taming" the fears that it conjures up, in Elin Diamond's formulation [392]), Frye did for comedy, at the same time as he elevated the comic form — and the symbolic structures that he associated with it — to the level of a generic master code for "all literature":

> The mythical backbone of all literature is the cycle of nature, which rolls from birth to death and back again to rebirth. The first half of this cycle, the movement from birth to death, spring to winter, dawn to dark, is the basis of the great alliance of nature and reason, the sense of nature as a rational order in which all movement is towards the increasingly predictable. . . . Comedy . . . is based on the second half of the great cycle, moving from death to rebirth, decadence to renewal, winter to spring, darkness to a new dawn. (*Natural Perspective* 119, 121)

The comic structure, then, is fundamentally based on a vision of renewal and reconciliation. The cultural work that it performs, like that of Aristotelian catharsis, is purgative in that it involves the expulsion of irrational or "unnatural" legalism in order to reinstate rather than overthrow the old order (renewed):

> the irrational law represents the comic equivalent of a social contract, something we must enter into if the final society is to take shape. The irrational law, also, belongs to that aspect of nature which appears, in other contexts, rational, centered in the inevitable movement from birth to death. As the end of the comic action usually reconciles and incorporates its predecessor, what corresponds to the irrational law has been internalized, transformed to an inner source of coherence. (127)

Ultimately, as Malcolm Evans has pointed out, "Frye's discourse . . . inscrib[es] moral and aesthetic certainties as a meta-mythology which occupies a historical void" (81).

Barber's work, closely associated with that of Frye, derives more directly than Frye's from that of Murray and the Cambridge anthropologists on whom Fergusson's introduction relies so heavily. For Barber, the central (comic) structural principle of literature is saturnalian release, the expression and expulsion of surplus desire that allows for individual reconciliation to the "rational" constraints of society. As Bristol notes, then, in spite of the genuine threat to order that festival, carnival, or saturnalia can pose, "Subversion, for Barber, remains a strictly private and parochial moment of defiance that in the end affirms the very order it pretends to uncrown or overthrow" (183).[12]

To summarize, variations on patriarchal, socially affirmative dramatic and narrative structures (and their mutually affirmative social formations and structures of consciousness), while they have dominated the Western world since Aristotle first articulated them in *The Poetics*, were (for various social and cultural reasons) particularly influential in Canada in the years following the centennial celebrations of 1967.[13] Reversal and recognition of a unified, preexisting subject were seen to provide, through empathy with central characters, a satisfying and socially affirmative purging of potentially disruptive emotions, allowing and inscribing a *return* to (reversal) and *recognition* of a preexisting social "norm." This narrative is based on a reading of the dramatic structure of Greek tragedy, particularly of *Oedipus Rex*; it is parallelled and reinforced in both tragedy and comedy by what Frye and other structuralist critics have articulated as the (symbolic) biblical narrative (as the seasonal narrative of *re*birth and *re*newal and the ritual patterns "discovered in" most Western religions and so-called primitive rituals), moving from Old Testament God the Father through a reversal to the birth of Christ; and, finally, it is the basis of the contemporary psychological narrative first articulated by Freud as the Oedipus complex and practised in psychotherapy as (in part) a way to produce a normative, stable subject. This Aristotelian/oedipal/biblical narrative, then, has become the standard structural unconscious of dramatic naturalism in Canada as elsewhere, and the meanings and ideologies that it inscribes, fundamentally conservative and patriarchal (imitating as it does the rising action, climax, and return-to-status-quo falling action of the male orgasm and focusing as it does on the male experience), constitute the primary and affirmative social impacts of the plays that use it, whatever their (conscious) themes or subject matters.

In this chapter, I first want to look at the (symbolic) structures of David French's *Leaving Home* and *Of the Fields, Lately* and Michael Cook's *Jacob's Wake* — which, in a parallel development, have been constructed in Canadian theatre history as "seminal" plays in the oedipal drama of the maturation of Canadian theatre and Canadian nationhood — as versions of the formal dramaturgical tradition that I have been describing. I also want to look at the ways in which George F. Walker's

Love and Anger and *Nothing Sacred* and Judith Thompson's *Lion in the Streets* and *White Biting Dog* "pervert" those symbolic structures, thereby making possible a questioning of some of the values that they inscribe. Where French and Cook for the most part *employ* those structures in ways that naturalize them (French relying most heavily on the oedipal narrative, Cook on the biblical version), Walker and Thompson *foreground* and problematize the Aristotelian, oedipal, and Christian narratives around which their plays are openly and self-consciously structured. French's and Cook's plays make implicit claims to "universal" significance and transcendent insight into the "human condition" (by implication unchanging and unchangeable); Walker's and Thompson's, I will argue, make it possible to question the transparency of the dramatic lenses through which we typically see and *construct* those "truths," and they thereby inscribe the possibility of seeing things differently, constructing *different* "truths," and just possibly providing for change in consciousness and in the social formation itself.

★   ★   ★

David French's first two plays, *Leaving Home* and *Of the Fields, Lately*, first produced at Tarragon Theatre and directed by Bill Glassco in 1972 and 1973 respectively, are perhaps the clearest examples in Canadian theatre of the use of neo-Aristotelian structures to play out oedipal coming-of-age dramas in the implied contexts of Frygian and biblical symbolic structures (French claims that there were only two books in his family home: the Bible and *The Book of Common Prayer* ["David French" 237]). As naturalistic domestic dramas about father-son relationships and the traumas of "leaving home," moreover, these plays have consistently been compared with those of Miller, Williams, O'Neill, and others (French, "David French" 235; Jewinski 92–93; Mullaly 132–33; Perkyns, *Major Plays* 479–80), to which they clearly seem to be indebted (though French himself has acknowledged only Williams ["David French" 241]). Both plays focus on the relationship between Jacob Mercer, late of Newfoundland, and his son, Ben, who has grown up in Toronto, and both involve supporting subplots that reinforce the resonances of what Jerry Wasserman calls "the oedipal twists and turns" of the narrative line (160).

Each play emerges from a sensibility that is profoundly Christian, and each is informed by the symbolic structures that Frye and others have observed in the Bible:

ZIMMERMAN: The epigram [sic] [to *Of the Fields, Lately*] is an excerpt from a Biblical verse about a forgiving and merciful God. It is preceded by: "As a father pities his children, so the Lord pities those who fear him." In *Of the Fields, Lately* the son assumed the paternal role when, in looking back, he was able to be forgiving.

FRENCH: Yes, in that play the son leaves home to save his father. He really has come to some kind of understanding. I always felt that *Of the Fields, Lately* is a deeply religious play. That is not something new in my work. I think that my plays are moral in the sense that they are life-affirming. In fact, the more I write the more religious I get.

ZIMMERMAN: In my end is my beginning. (French, "David French" [interview with Zimmerman] 307)

Both *Leaving Home* and *Of the Fields, Lately* also employ the familiar linear Aristotelian structures of reversal and recognition. Although French claims not to "map out" a structure before writing, he is conscious that a play "always has to move forward. . . . [E]very line of dialogue has to reveal character and push plot and create atmosphere, etc." (310). French's more or less unconscious deployment of a neo-Aristotelian naturalistic form, then, as a kind of common sense or given of dramatic structure, can perhaps be seen to allow the ideological coding of the form to function hegemonically, to speak through or past the conscious intentions of the playwright.

The central action of *Leaving Home* is the conflict between Jacob and his oldest son, the eighteen-year-old Ben, frequently reported to be just like his father. The conflict begins with Ben's failure to invite his father to his high school graduation and culminates in Jacob's climactic beating of Ben with a belt. The basis of the conflict, sexual rivalry over Ben's mother, Mary, constitutes the play's barely suppressed unconscious, which surfaces occasionally in Ben's comments to his brother or mother — "Either Dad goes, or I do" (22) — but most often in a series of jealously ironic comments by Jacob — "That's one t'ing about Ben, Mary. He won't ever leave you" (24) — that occasionally rise to direct confrontation:

BEN (*He rips open his shirt*): I still haven't got hair on my chest, and I'm still not a threat to you.

JACOB: No, and you'm not likely ever to be, either, until you grows up and gets out from under your mother's skirts. (30)

JACOB: It's high time, my lady, you let go and weaned him away from the tit!

MARY (*angrily*): You shut your mouth. There's no call for that kind of talk!

JACOB: He needs more than mother's milk, goddamn it!

BEN (*shouting at JACOB*): What're you screaming at her for? She didn't do anything!

JACOB (*a semblance of sudden calm*): Well, listen to him, now. Look at the murder in his face. One harsh word to his mother and up comes his fists. I'll bet you wouldn't be half so quick to defend your father. (27–28)

The play's opening line, spoken to Ben by his mother, is "Did you bump into your father?" (4).

This oedipal action is underscored by the subplot, a rehearsal for the impending wedding of Ben's younger brother, Bill, to his supposedly pregnant sixteen-year-old girlfriend, Kathy. Kathy is the daughter of Minnie, a widowed former girlfriend of Jacob's in Newfoundland, who shows up for the wedding rehearsal with her new boyfriend, the humourless, silent, but well-endowed embalmer Harold. Kathy is said to have been "kind of stuck on her father, you know" (71), she recognizes that Harold would "like to hop in the sack" with her (65), and her relationship with her mother parallels that of Ben with Jacob, also culminating in a climactic fight (76–77).

This oedipal action is the surfacing less of a conscious theme — and French himself never refers to it in interviews — than of an unconscious, formal connection — the return of the repressed — that feminist theorists and others (notably Teresa de Lauretis and Roland Barthes) have seen as the necessary link between narrative form and masculine, oedipal desire. Barthes views narrative as a monologic, conquering force and notes that "it may be significant that it is at the same moment . . . that the little [male] human 'invents' at once sequence, narrative, and the Oedipus" (*Image* 124). He argues elsewhere that "The pleasure of the text . . . is an Oedipal pleasure (to denude, to know, to learn the origin and the end)" (*Pleasure* 10), in a passage that echoes French's description of his "cathartic" pleasure in the writing of *Leaving Home* ("David French" 246).[14] In *Alice Doesn't: Feminism, Semiotics and Cinema*, de Lauretis explores in more detail the connections between oedipal desire and narrative. Beginning with the observation that "sadism demands a story, depends on making something happen, forcing a change in another person, a battle of will and strength, victory/defeat, all occurring in a linear time with a beginning and an end" (Mulvey 14), de Lauretis demonstrates that the linear narrative constituting Aristotelian "action" is governed by a (sadistic) oedipal logic. According to her, such a narrative is situated within the system of exchange instituted by the incest prohibition, in which women function as both sign and object of exchange, represent the fulfilment of narrative promise, and are positioned as object, objective, or obstacle in relation to the male subject (140).[15]

Not surprisingly, *Leaving Home* concludes with a sentimental exoneration of both Ben and Jacob, of the patriarchal family, and of narrative itself (in that its final moment is a comforting retreat into nostalgic story) while finally placing responsibility for the play's and the men's problems firmly with Mary. Not only does Ben himself blame her — "you set the example, Mom, a long time ago. When we were little" (95) — but also critics of the play, recognizing as always the character's steadfast and selfless service to the men, have tended to agree with him. As Richard Perkyns says, "At the same time as she brings the two sides together, she can be seen as instrumental in unintentionally driving a deeper and more lasting wedge between them" (*Major Plays* 482).[16]

Of the Fields, Lately deals with the return of Ben after two years to find his father recovering from a heart attack that has kept him from working. Like the central action of *Leaving Home*, that of this sequel employs the crisis-to-climax-to-resolution action of neo-Aristotelian tragedy, positions Mary as an object of exchange between the two men, and places the responsibility for their renewed quarrel squarely with her: "You mean he almost died and you didn't tell me?" (30). This play deals less with Ben's oedipal desire for his mother, however, than with his guilt over the death of his father, which, again, is echoed in the play's subplot when Ben's Uncle Wiff suffers similar remorse at the death and funeral of his wife. Unlike *Leaving Home*, too, *Of the Fields, Lately* is structured as a memory play, its central action framed as Ben's memory/narrative of events leading up to his father's death — events that, in his mind at least, began with his unconscious wishes from the time that he was a child. The play opens in an ahistorical present that the stage directions call Limbo, from which Ben addresses the audience, clearly indicating at the outset that the play is about "two men":

> It takes many incidents to build a wall between two men, brick
> by brick. Sometimes you're not aware of the building of the wall,

and sometimes you are, though not always strong enough or willing enough to kick it down. It starts very early, as it did with my father and me, very early. And it becomes a pattern that is hard to break until the wall is made of sound brick and mortar, as strong as any my father ever built. Time would not level it. Only death. (1)

Ben goes on to recount "one such incident," in which he slighted his father at a baseball game, introducing the incident as "the emotional corner-stone of the wall between us" (1) and preparing the audience for the play's central action, which climaxes in his decision to leave home once again, in effect saving his father's dignity while sentencing him to death.

Framing the play as a memory/narrative allows French to suggest the cyclical action of seasonal narratives — "in my end is my beginning" — in which the son, "set free" by the father's death (112), begins the cycle anew and structurally reinforces the culturally affirmative and ahistorical universality of *plus ça change*. . . . However, intriguingly, the memory-play structure also mimics the process of psychoanalysis. French has said that writing *Leaving Home* and *Of the Fields, Lately* was to some extent an exercise in autobiography and was therapeutic for him:

At that time in my life I was a very angry, frustrated, violent person. I knew it had a lot to do with the frustrations that I felt towards my family. And in a way writing was very therapeutic. I wanted to get rid of all that pain I felt inside me about that, which is what I did in the writing. I got rid of most of it with *Leaving Home* and I got rid of a lot more of it with *Of the Fields, Lately*. ("David French" [interview with Zimmerman] 306)

Similarly, Ben is presented in the second play as bringing to the surface, for therapeutic reasons, the history of and motivation for his guilt and finding cause to forgive both his father and himself. However, as Althusser points out in his essay on "Freud and Lacan,"

the Oedipal phase is not a hidden "*meaning*" which merely lacks consciousness or speech — it is not a structure buried in the past that can always be restructured or surpassed by "reactivating its meaning": the Oedipus complex is the dramatic structure, the "theatrical machine" [Althusser is quoting Lacan] imposed by the Law of Culture on every involuntary, conscripted candidate to humanity, a structure containing in itself not only the possibility of, but the necessity for the concrete variants in which it *exists*, for every individual who reaches its threshold, lives through it and survives it. In its application, in what is called its practice (the cure), psychoanalysis works on the concrete "effects" of these variants, i.e. on the modality of the specific and absolutely unique nexus in which the Oedipal transition was and is begun, completed, missed or eluded by some particular individual. These *variants* can be thought and known in their essence itself on the basis of the structure of the Oedipal *invariant*, precisely because this whole transition is marked from its beginnings in fascination, in its most "aberrant" as well as in its most "normal" forms, by the Law of this structure, the ultimate form of access to the Symbolic within the Law of the Symbolic itself. (215–16)

In terms of its social effects, then, French's employment of a psycho-analytic frame within an oedipal structure works like the operations of fate in Greek tragedy: that is, it works to reify the Law of the Symbolic, to universalize the (male) oedipal experience, and to deny the relevance of contextual variables and immediate social contexts, together with the potential for "variants" or human agency to produce changes that are formally precontained.[17]

French's plays were greeted at their premieres — at the height of 1970s Canadian nationalism and the early years of the alternative theatre movement in Canada — by an ecstatic "that's us" (see Johnson, "Is That Us?") and by warm praise for their accurate naturalistic represen-tations of Canadian life. In their first productions, then, the plays served the counterhegemonic agenda of Canadian nationalism well, "affirming for audiences," as Richard Plant says, "The authenticity — the Canadian-ness — of their own lives" (23). At a time when, as Amanda Hale puts it, "the boys were frustrated" (81) and Canadian drama was attempting to demonstrate its mature ability to employ the dominant dramatic forms and to break free from the tyranny of its cultural "fathers," these plays were objects of pride, proof that "we" were worthy of dramatic representation too. As Hale also points out of Canada in the 1960s, however, politically alternative movements, particularly post-colonial-nationalist ones, often neglect or exclude issues of gender, class, or race, and in the end, given the inherited, culturally affirmative structures of prominent plays such as *Leaving Home* and *Of the Fields, Lately*, it is not surprising that "the great male revolution of the Sixties and Seventies did not improve the status of women [or other Others] in theatre" (83).[18]

★   ★   ★

While the underlying biblical symbolic structure plays a secondary or even tertiary role in French's plays, in Michael Cook's 1975 play, *Jacob's Wake*, which takes place on the Easter weekend, it is the dominant organizing principle. And while any disruptive potential in *Leaving Home* and *Of the Fields, Lately* is conventionally contained by the plays' formal unconscious, in *Jacob's Wake* some elements strain against containment by the symbolic structure, pushing at the boundaries of the form and opening faults for renegotiation.

In spite of Cook's claim, as represented by Brian Parker, that "plays occur to him not in the form of Aristotelian 'action' but poetically as 'a series of images, dramatic scenes, and circumstances,'" and in spite of Parker's remark that "The obvious difficulty he [Cook] has in organizing his work [is] perhaps his most serious defect as a dramatist" (22), *Jacob's Wake* is an extraordinarily tightly structured play, "Cook's best shaped," according to Ray Conlogue ("Chilling Dance"). It *is* tightly structured, moreover, precisely in terms of the neo-Aristotelian template discussed above — Cook has said that he was trying in this play "to write a classic tragedy as much as one can in the Twentieth century" ("Michael Cook" [interview with Wallace] 163), and he refers elsewhere to "the crisis and the catharsis which makes the tears flow, which brings the release" ("Michael Cook" 228). In any case, the play is complete with rising actions, complications, and climaxes, together with the minor variation of a considerably foreshortened denouement (of which more below). And, like *Leaving Home* and *Of the Fields, Lately*, the play has consistently been compared with classics of the genre of poetic naturalism: *Long Day's Journey into Night* (Anthony 210; Parker 39), *The Glass Menagerie* (Anthony 210), *Juno and the Paycock*, and, perhaps surprisingly, *Heartbreak House* (Perkyns, *"Jacob's Wake"* 159–62), among others.

Jacob's Wake, moreover, employs a familiar oedipal narrative of father-and-son conflict, repressed desire, transference, and the exchange of (long-suffering) women. The various strands of the play's plot, telling the stories over three (de)generations of the Blackburn family's descent from patriarchal Newfoundland heroism to what is constructed as feminized (and mainland-influenced) corruption and cowardice, all hinge on repressed (or *un*hinged) oedipal desire, as the larger drama-turgical structure of the *play* hinges on the playing out of a particularly sadistic and "masculist" oedipal logic. Cook himself describes the play's situation as follows:

> The Old Sealing Skipper upstairs, his son, Winston, living on welfare, a man of critical sensibility and conscience trying to drown his despair in drink and sardonic wit; his three sons, a politician, a bar-owner, and a religious maniac, and his wife, Rosie, the real power, dominant, yet rarely forceful, secure, without confusion, mother-image constant in the face of disaster, relying upon instinct not intellect . . . to hold her family together. And Aunt Mary, Winston's sister, prim, old-maidish, a schoolteacher, struggling to preserve her dignity in a disruptive house. Outside, the storm becomes a living thing, which threatens and finally engulfs them all. ("Michael Cook" 227)

Among the characters of the older generations, the oedipal plotting is most clearly articulated by the Skipper, who dreams of the "tumble" he once would have had with his daughter-in-law, Rosie (84), a woman who "knows how to comfort an old man" (61); by Winston, who wishes that he could have been the son his father wanted (which, as Rosie reminds him, would mean being dead); and by Mary, who wishes that her father *were* dead. Among the younger generation, the oedipal structuring is represented by the religious Brad, who substi-tutes God for a lost father and religious ecstasy and guilt for a thwarted sexuality; by the politician-son Wayne, whose relationship with his Aunt Mary is both perversely sexual and clearly maternal and who plots to institutionalize the Skipper; and by Alonzo, the son most like his father, who calls plaintively to his mother from his bed and is told by Winston that "What I does is between yer mother and meself, and don't ye fergit it" (51). The play's theme song, which resonates throughout and is heard on a radio at one point (62), is the William Whiting hymn "Eternal Father, Strong to Save."

Cook has hinted that the play's portrait of Winston, its central char-acter, father *and* son, can be read as "self revealing" ("Michael Cook" [interview with Wallace] 168), and, as for French, writing the play seems to have been a way of working through and controlling his own past and present struggles, which are configured in his accounts as oedipal. In his contribution to *Stage Voices: Twelve Canadian Playwrights Talk about Their Lives and Work*, he claims to "write about people I know, including myself," people whom he sees as pursuing "a staggering path toward God!" ("Michael Cook" 217). But God in his work is consistently a stern and awful father, a transcendental signifier to be approached with reverence and fear through language and the (phallic) pen. In the same essay, which includes an account of the archetypally oedipal Hamlet as a playwright, Cook whimsically hopes that "Perhaps there will come a time when I'll create a universe of characters from whom I can be completely detached. Like God. Or Robertson Davies" (215). He also provides a lengthy autobiographical account of his unremembered mother (211) and his anguished father — for whom he expresses great admiration and claims to have written the line, reminiscent of most of his plays' heroes, that "the bravest people I know are the ones who endure." Cook's account of his relationship with his father ends, however, "when my schooling was arrested, abruptly, at the age of fifteen when I was thrown out, and I was at last able to be free" (212). In the immediate wake of this account, and in a passage that evokes precisely the atmosphere of *Jacob's Wake*, Cook tells of becoming a writer as a way to gain access to the symbolic order, because "words are power. And power in this instance meant survival, allowing for a protective shield which warded off the worst excesses of an often brutal and savage and violent life. A life, however, not without light" (213).[19]

Cook's worldview, as represented in *Jacob's Wake*, is congruent with this narrative, and Cook admits that "confrontation with a relentlessly hostile environment," "survival," and living in a land in which "one's history is continually being washed away in front of one's gaze" are "exactly what I'm writing about" ("Michael Cook" [interview with Wallace] 158). "Ironically," he continues,

> it's the women who are survivors in this country. They don't fight the landscape as the men do but accept it in a deeply-felt, feminine way; men fight an heroic confrontation that can only end one way. The women just go on. They have much more in common with the sea in a very real sense. They hate it for what it does, but they are resigned to it. Men like the skipper in *Jacob's Wake* charge into it, teeth bared in a Viking-like sense: we will enter the storm with the boat burning. The social processes, the humanizing processes, are the preserve of women. (158)

The social realm, like the play's women, can only survive with patience, with endurance, and with no hope of change.[20]

If the neo-Aristotelian and oedipal forms perform their anticipated affirmative function as the essentially conservative dramaturgical unconscious of *Jacob's Wake*, then that role is both reinforced and, to some extent, rendered renegotiable by the prominence in the play of its mythicobiblical symbolic structure, which increasingly surfaces for the audience to the level of conscious, and consciously shaped, meaning. The occasion for the play is the return home of the Blackburn progeny for Easter weekend (the action takes place on Maundy Thursday and Good Friday), and it is chock full of biblical symbolism that ranges from the playing of hymns to the naming of places (Trinity, Trinity Bay [85]) and characters — Brian Parker has pointed out the Old Testament resonances of Skipper Elijah's sacrifice of his son, Jacob, and of Elijah's apocalyptic apotheosis (39). There are similar resonances to the names Rachel (Elijah's wife) and Sarah (the lost daughter of Winston and Rosie). Perhaps more prominent, however, are recurrent images of crucifixion (especially 77, 86, and 119) and apocalypse (explicitly 42, 50, 60, 67, 69, 70, 107, 109, 111, 112, 135, 138), both of which surface early in the action and increase in prominence throughout, to climax together with the play at precisely 3:00 p.m. on Good Friday (132), when the storm howls, the power fails, Wayne as minister of the environment sells the island's last fifty thousand acres of standing timber to the Japanese, the government collapses, the dead rise from their beds/ graves, and, with *"three loud, imperative knocks at the door"* (135), all hell breaks loose.

That the play reaches its tragic climax with a symbolic conjuring up of the crucifixion is not unusual; in fact, such a symbolic structure is pretty much de rigueur in post-Frygian, structuralist critiques of tragedy. What is surprising, perhaps, is that not only does the action not reach (or even point toward) the promised Easter Sunday resurrection and reconciliation but also the almost absurdly overstated biblical symbolic structure conflates the crucifixion with the apocalypse, leaping directly from a foreshortened spring to deep winter, from the death of Christ to the (reiterated) "Day of Judgement" or "Apocalypse" (constructed as *"a release, an orgasm"* 67), with no apparent opportunity for reversal or recognition, atonement or rebirth, and virtually no new dispensation.

Jacob's Wake is a strange beast, notable for something more than its failure to slouch toward any recognizable sort of Bethlehem. Canonized by inclusion in course curricula across the country as well as the major national drama anthology (see Wasserman), the play has not been notably successful in the theatre and, in fact, has often conjured up from critics images of disaster in keeping with its own final scene. Myron Galloway, reviewing the premiere for the *Montreal Star*, referred to the play's ending as "copping out," "an hysterical, non-realistic fantasy," of which "the moral seems to be the goblins will get you if you don't watch out" (189). Audrey Ashley, panning the play as a whole, famously described the conclusion as "one of the most ludicrous cop-outs in the annals of Canadian theatre" (190). Strong language. The play's academic success is perhaps not surprising, for *Jacob's Wake* contains a lot of symbolic grist for the pedagogical mill. But what can be made of the almost hysterical response of critics to its premiere — a response not notably repeated when the play was remounted in 1986 and reviewed by Ray Conlogue as "one of Cook's most moving" ("Chilling Dance")?

I suspect that part of the problem was the perennial one of plays from "the regions" being produced outside their points of origin — a problem exacerbated here by the fact that *Jacob's Wake* premiered outside Newfoundland. Another part of the problem may have been the fact that Cook himself, as he says, was "very much an outsider" in a Newfoundland culture that he saw as "not only threatened, but doomed" ("Michael Cook" [interview with Wallace] 157). As a "chronicler" of the death throes of a way of life (157), and as one who felt that "everyone there has to come to grips . . . individually" with that struggle rather than resisting its terms (165), Cook was not notably positioned to intervene directly in the culture of the province or to be accepted critically either within or without a culture that served as his artistic raw material. At the same time, however, as a self-styled rogue Irishman with a background in the British army, Cook *was* in a potentially productive (versus reproductive) liminal position in 1975, when *Jacob's Wake* was first produced, in relation to the cultures of both Newfoundland and the rest of Canada — and the play was notably (and oddly) first produced at the Festival Lennoxville in English Quebec. If Cook's "chronicling" of a dying culture can be seen to be essentially reproductive, particularly given his reliance on Aristotelian and oedipal structures, then his doing so from a marginal perspective, using an aborted formalism that employs, grotesquely exaggerates, and overtly distorts the cyclical structure of "the greatest story ever told," can perhaps also be seen to sow the seeds of disenchantment. In any case, *Jacob's Wake* provoked anxiety in the form of a critical response from mainstream newspaper critics as hostile and excessive as the Newfoundland culture that the play constructs. The playwright's own explanation for his critics' problems with the play, in fact, sounds surprisingly poststructural: "I like mixing forms" (167).

Ultimately, though, however liminal Cook's position, and however disruptive the play's ending may have been to critical comfort, *Jacob's Wake* comfortably embodies, for the most part, the essentialist-humanist views of its author. "Despairing of social change, . . ." Cook in this play as elsewhere celebrates a "human spirit" best revealed through its capacity to suffer heroically and tragically mankind's (sic) universal and inevitable fate (166) — its "universality" signalled in part by the placelessness that it achieves outside its originating culture. It would take more radical deconstructions of traditional dramaturgies before Canadian theatre could break from inherited patterns and engage in more thoroughly and more culturally specific (or "particularist"[21]) interventionist dramaturgical strategies.

★　★　★

Aristotelian *peripeteia* and *anagnorisis* derive from an analysis of a specific kind of drama in a specific historical place and period reflecting specific ideologies; as analytical tools, however, they have been adapted, reconsidered, interpreted, and used with universalist claims throughout the history of Western dramatic criticism, with the result that these structures and the ideologies that they embody have remained privileged, in Canada as elsewhere. In his discussion of Shakespeare's "problem comedies," Northrop Frye points to survival and deliverance as underlying factors in the "unifying social ideologies" of all cultures, and he sees these dominant "myths of concern" reflected in Aristotelian reversal and recognition:

> We notice that some words in religion, such as "conversion" in Christianity or *paravritti* (turning around) in Buddhism, or "revolution" in political ideology, emphasize the fact that one thing necessary is a reversing of the normal current of life. Other words, such as "enlightenment" or "salvation," emphasize rather the sense of recognition that accompanies this process. Reversal and recognition, then, seem to be structural principles outside literature. . . . (*Myth* 13)

It is clear from this account that, as structural principles that function to affirm "unifying social ideologies" in the realms of literature, religion, and politics, reversal and recognition, like conversion, revolution, enlightenment, and salvation, are linear and dialectical concepts that invoke social containment and dramatic closure. And, as Frye remarks elsewhere,

> as far as his main historical influence goes Aristotle points straight ahead. He worked out the organon of a deductive logic . . . and provided a technique for arranging words to make a conquering march across reality, subjects pursuing objects through all the obstacles of predicates, as the Macedonian phalanxes of his pupil Alexander marched across Asia. (*Great Code* 9)

Frye's argument and his metaphors strongly suggest that the ideological weight and endurance of reversal and recognition as structural principles — particularly as articulated by Frye and other modernist critics and as inherited by Canadian students, scholars, critics, theatre professionals, and audiences — render them difficult to avoid completely and useful only through active and creative perversion as shaping structures for those interested in alterity, contingency, or heterogeneity.

In the introduction to *Endangered Species: Four Plays* (1988), Margaret Hollingsworth claims to have written the short, experimental plays "out of perversity" (7). Although she makes the comment in passing, it strikes me as a good starting point for a discussion of what I think of as "the dramaturgy of the perverse" in a number of contemporary Canadian plays, including the plays by George F. Walker and Judith Thompson on which I focus next.

The definitions cited for "perverse" in the *Oxford English Dictionary* range from "selfwilled or stubborn (in error)" to "untoward, froward; disposed to go counter to what is reasonable or required; hence, wayward, petulant, cross-grained." For "pervert," they include "to mis-apply, misconstrue, wrest the purport of." As a structural principle, perversity may usefully be seen as a revisioning of Aristotelian *re*versal (and recognition) as well as an intertextualist (or "interstructuralist") rejection of modernist purity, clarity, and self-containment (as we will see in chapter 2). Unlike the more familiar concept of *sub*version, however, the perverse is not simply arranged in an oppositional (and therefore affirming) relationship to the dominant. Perversion is dialogic in Bakhtin's sense,[22] more variously disruptive and less simply reactive than the concept of subversion suggests.

As a structural device, the perverse revisions the romantic and post-romantic conceptions of unified subjectivity and of unified character and action. It focuses on the *constructed* nature of identity; it displaces the symbolic authority of structural principles such as reversal and recognition; and, while acknowledging and employing engagement with character, plot, and dramatic ritual, it disrupts the complacent, voyeuristic, oedipal, or ecstatic satisfactions and containments provided by dramatic catharsis.

Among the clearest and most prominent contemporary Canadian examples of the creative perversion of neo-Aristotelian dramaturgy are the plays of George F. Walker, in which what he calls "the Walker twist"[23] replaces reversal as a structural principle; in which recognition, at the least, is a more complex and less comfortable concept than in more traditionally linear dramatic structures; and in which the satisfaction of closure is rarely provided. Indeed, if Walker follows any tradition, then it is that of dramaturgical perversity as established by Christopher Marlowe, that most "wayward, petulant, cross-grained," and unsettling of the Elizabethans, whose plays have disturbed drama critics almost as much as his life and opinions disturbed Elizabethan authorities. Walker's *Zastrozzi*, in fact, in its unimpeded and unreversed rising action, echoes the structure of Marlowe's *Tamburlaine*, in which expectations based on the Christianized Aristotle of the *de casibus* tradition are aroused and, together with all sense of poetic justice and dramatic containment, disappointed. Like Marlowe in *Tamburlaine*, *The Jew of Malta*, and *Dr. Faustus*, in which religious, legal, and political authority as well as classical dramatic structure are both invoked and denaturalized, Walker neither rejects nor revises (nor, as he consistently insists, parodies[24]) neo-Aristotelian structures; rather, he perverts them, using them in ways that acknowledge their cultural authority while fracturing and misusing it.

The final scene of Walker's *Love and Anger* uses a trial, perhaps the most conventional of dramaturgical devices for the achievement of reversal and recognition, but it does so in a most unconventional way. Near the end of the play, the publisher of a sensationalist newspaper ("a fascist rag" [21 and passim]) is kidnapped and tried by a lapsed lawyer on the charge of being evil before a makeshift judge who has just escaped from an institution where she was confined as a practising schizophrenic — a condition that the play posits as more normal in its response to the world than the well-adjusted balance of its capitalist "greedy pricks."[25] The trial in *Love and Anger* is inconclusive, there is no reversal in the play's action, and, in spite of the central character Petie Maxwell's best intentions, there is no revolution in the play's plot. But there are fissures in the play's legal and philosophical systems based on binary opposition and "objectivity"; there is the beginning of a new community among the play's variously marginalized characters; and there is a "twist" to the proceedings that is characteristic of Walker and of the dramaturgy of the perverse, which (as I see it) typically *foregrounds* the expectations of its audience in order to disappoint, disrupt, or fracture them. There is also an implied rejection of the concept of "recognition" as the self-discovery of a unified subject, especially in the characterization of the schizophrenic Sarah, who emerges as the unlikely hero of the play.[26] "Character" in this play comes to mean something close to a series of temporarily adopted subject positions that are continually subject to reversal but allow for no final or permanent recognition of an essential self.

If Walker's *Love and Anger* productively perverts the neo–Aristotelian structures of reversal and recognition, then his *Nothing Sacred* (1988) does something similar with the oedipal narrative that it borrows from Turgenev's novel *Fathers and Sons*. Like David French before him, but characteristically with more ironic self-awareness, Walker seems to be conscious of the role of his play in working out his own father-child relationships:

> It's funny that I'm writing about Bazarov at this time because I read *Fathers and Sons* when I was 17 years old, and I related so strongly to that character then. That I should get around to writing about him when I'm 40, and still relate to him so strongly, is odd because I'm no longer just a son; I'm a father, too, and I have to come to grips with that, to understand that as well. ("Looking" 27)

Walker's anxieties of influence, however, although they echo those of French and Cook in the oedipal pleasures of writing the plays, are considerably and refreshingly free of real angst. The program notes to the 1994 revival of *Nothing Sacred* at Toronto's Wintergarden Theatre quote his 1988 account of writing the play: "Do you know the feeling you have when you hear a song or read something and say, 'Oh, I wish

I'd written that'? Well, I wished I'd written *Fathers and Sons*. So I did. . . . It was very liberating." It is not surprising, given both this tone and the play's title, that *Nothing Sacred* treats its oedipal model with something less than reverence; nevertheless, its perversions are not without purpose or seriousness, and its (re)structuring of the narrative of generational conflict might usefully be seen as *anti*-Oedipal in Deleuze and Guattari's sense.

The play is structured around fathers and stories of fathers, with most of its central male characters at one time or another measuring themselves against their fathers or father substitutes, mostly constructed as authority figures (army doctors, military men, gentlemen farmers, or, among the play's peasant and working classes, bailiffs and one's betters). Thus, Bazarov and Arkady rebel, if not always against their actual fathers, whom they know love them, then at least against "the Law of the Father" and the institutions that it represents and reproduces; conversely, the brothers Kirsanov and Pavel struggle and fail to maintain the traditional societal and familial order represented by their father:

> PAVEL: Remember the way father conducted his business . . .
> KIRSANOV: Business? Father was a general in the army, Pavel.
> PAVEL: The business of his life. He conducted it with dignity. He behaved well because he knew what he came from. And he knew what he came from was respected. And so it followed that he showed respect. . . . Remember the holidays. Each holiday marked by the same traditional routine. It gave you strength. It gave you memory . . . Oh I ruined that part of my life myself. Ruined any chance to have a real family. I got carried away by love. . . . Does everything turn dark in this world, Nikolai.
> KIRSANOV: Yes. Darkness. Then . . . what?
> PAVEL: Death. . . .
> KIRSANOV: I know now that I wanted a wife and child to live for. Too late though. (87–88; three-point ellipses in original)

The oedipal failures of these characters are accompanied, moreover, by some intriguingly Freudian resonances. To both his shame and his comfort, Kirsanov, for example, has fathered a child with the daughter of his former housekeeper, Fenichka, and he deflects (or transfers?) his concerns from one kind of flow (of desire) to another: "I should have just said something affectionate to her. Fenichka I love you. I love you

Fenichka. Just like that. . . . So it's up to me. All right then I'll do it . . . [*He starts off*] But not now. I have to supervise the distribution of fertilizer" (61; three-point ellipsis in original). When he calls to her later and she asks "What?" he can only answer "Nothing" (61).

"Nothing" is an important word in this play. It may seem like special pleading to recall in this context that the word in early modern English could mean the female genitals.[27] But there does seem to be a link in the play between an obsession with fathers, with inappropriate, absent, or threatening objects of desire, and with "nothing," which, as the title tells us, is "sacred." Kirsanov's apparent death wish in the passages above is linked, of course, to his supposed failure to assume appropriately the role of the symbolic father and to his inappropriate obsession with "nothing." In addition, the obsessive and fetishistic love of Pavel for Anna Odintsov's mother, now transferred to Anna herself,[28] is explicitly linked — in the passage quoted above and elsewhere — to a failure of (re)production on his part — reproduction in the biological sense and in at least two social senses: capitalist production (surplus value) and the reproduction of his father's traditional order. Pavel's story, moreover, is structurally parallel to that of Bazarov, who as a nihilist, of course, has a different investment in "nothing."

Unlike the plays by French and Cook analysed above, in which father-son relationships figure so prominently and women play minor, exchange, or brokerage roles, *Nothing Sacred* concerns itself with the psychological struggles of its characters only peripherally, or perhaps perversely, preferring to critique the *socially* repressive role of "Oedipus"[29] as it plays itself out in the class struggle. Apart from occasional moments in which Pavel elicits a perverse sympathy, his psychological malaise is seen for the most part to be less sympathetic than simply pathetic.[30] Walker, like Deleuze and Guattari before him, conjures up Oedipus as a psychological complex primarily to mock it and the authority that it has been granted. Socially, however, the play presents a serious criticism of Oedipus, whose myth (as Deleuze and Guattari have demonstrated) has served to reinforce the dominant order by inhibiting the *an*oedipal flows of desire and production and creating docile subjects (in both psychological and social senses) and workers.

The play opens with the savage beating of a peasant by Kirsanov's bailiff, a representative of law who later admits to enjoying the process: "I don't know why. I didn't make human beings. Human beings enjoy beating other human beings. That's a fact" (58). The bailiff also argues, in an evocative conflation, that, if left unbeaten, the peasants will "rob you blind. They'll get drunk and do damage to the machinery. They'll eat their children . . ." (58). Throughout, the play offers criticism of surplus production — most notably as embodied in the sartorially and otherwise superfluous Pavel; of class divisions both explicit and implicit — Bazarov, for example, insists that Kirsanov's "problems regarding his feelings" for Fenichka are in fact "problems . . . about class. His class. Her class" (40); and of oedipal social institutions, including the family:

> BAZAROV: Why do people think that what goes on in a family is somehow beyond the criticism of society in general. Is a family above the civil law? No. Then should it be above the natural law, the laws of behaviour?
> ARKADY: Only when those laws are being imposed by a man who is not only outside the family but outside of society as well. (64)

In the final scene, the dying Bazarov — killed accidentally over a matter of archaic "form . . . That's all" (90; ellipsis in original) — speaks of the reciprocal love between himself and his parents, making it clear that *his* brand of revolutionary nihilism (versus Pavel's fetishistic "nothing") is neither oedipal nor pathological. The scene and the play conclude when Bazarov's last words, "You are the . . . ," spoken to the play's assembled servants and peasants and failing to be the play's final words, are completed by the very characters whom Bazarov sees as "the future." Perverting the tradition of giving the play's last words to its most noble characters, *Nothing Sacred* ends with the servant, the bailiff, and the two peasants planning their future to the accompaniment of Anna Odintsov's laugh of *"light joyful recognition"* (99).

★   ★   ★

Although Judith Thompson has a very different dramatic sensibility than Walker, she employs a Walker-like series of twists in the construction of a representative scene in her play *Lion in the Streets*, a scene with oedipal resonances that also explicitly conjures up yet disappoints the Christian iconography of death and (explicitly baptismal and/or confessional) rebirth. The scene begins with the decision of David, a frivolous young waiter, to enter a church "on a whim" on his way home from work. Once inside, he encounters an elderly priest who, for his own reasons, sees "the hand of God" in the decision, and both David and his confessor review their separate pasts in search of "turning points" that will help them to "make sense" of their lives and forgive one another. The different and isolated "recognitions" at which each character arrives are precipitated by twists in the dialogue that draw attention to the subjective nature of the stories that they construct for themselves and through which they see and interpret the world. Their stories are profound and engaging, yet there is even less sense here than in Walker's plays of a unified or essentialist view of the individual: the scene concludes with David's (mis)recognition, though he is clearly alive, that his sacrificial drowning as a child, a turning point in his confessor's life, not only happened but also was "nice" (42). The "identities" of the characters in the scene are not unified, and they seem here as elsewhere to be contingent on the changing stories that they tell of themselves and one another. The audience's authority as readers, moreover, is consistently undermined, their interpretations of the action undergoing revisions that parallel those of the characters.

In this scene, far from using a single reversal of action to produce recognition and catharsis, Thompson employs an extremely unsettling series of reversals, and a series of shifts in the grounds for our engagement, to lead to an expansion of consciousness and an enlarging if dislocating sense of the multiple choices presented by and continuously contained within (but not *by*) the fictional action. The deterministic worldview reflected, extended, and authorized by Aristotelian linearity and closure is disrupted — perverted — in a structure that employs familiar signposts but is unsettlingly discontinuous because it refuses to resolve itself into a single dominant fiction.

The overall structure of *Lion in the Streets* is equally discontinuous and unsettling. As a "relay play," in the words of the playwright,[31] it reveals fragments from the lives of a series of characters, with one character from each scene carried into the next in a seemingly arbitrary way and the whole held together by the linking presence of a young Portuguese girl, Isobel, whose rape and murder prior to the play's action(s) are hinted at throughout and recounted just prior to her apotheosis at the end. The relay structure, the "through line" provided by the character of Isobel, and the Roman Catholic iconography of sacrificial redemption, however, serve more perversely to create than comfortably to satisfy an audience's expectations for logic, containment, and catharsis. If the ending is genuinely redemptive, then it is perversely so in that its final lines, in the face of the horror and anguish cumulatively revealed and evoked by the play, are a call to the *audience*, beyond all causal or structural logic, and beyond the frame of the play, to engage in a subjective act of faith and to "*take* your life" (62).

In her earlier play *White Biting Dog*,[32] Thompson went further in her perversion of neo-Aristotelian dramaturgy and of overt and eccentrically applied religious and oedipal iconography. According to her, the play was written as an experiment in the use of a traditional linear cause-and-effect plot.[33] The entire redemptive action is precipitated by the white dog's speaking to the central character, Cape Race, who is about to jump off Toronto's Bloor Street Viaduct (a bridge high above the Don Valley, which cuts diagonally across the city), and telling him to save himself by saving his father from death. The play's oedipal plot reaches its anticipated climax at the end of the first act, when Cape and his mother, Lomia, acknowledge their inability to feel "anything" "for others." They kiss, touching tongues, after which Cape tells her that he wants to "bash and bash and bash and bash and bash" her head against the wall (56). The second act moves toward a conclusion in which the sacrificial love of Cape's new lover, Pony, and his father, Glidden, seems to result in a kind of reversal and recognition. Lomia discovers that she is "so, so — sorry for having . . . I *really* am sorry!? (can't believe it herself) Me! I — am" (100; ellipsis in original); and Cape is moved to scream in anguish, acknowledging that "We're not . . . WORTH . . ." and wondering (to the audience?), "Do you think it will make . . . any . . . difference?" (108; ellipses in original).

The religious symbolism that might traditionally accompany such a plot is fully worked out but almost grotesquely overstated, as is the perversely clear rendering of Cape's (adult) oedipal crisis. Thompson builds an elaborate and interconnected series of symbols, verbal links, and visual associations between the white dog/god and the two redemptive characters, Glidden and Pony. They range from Lomia's pet name for her husband ("Pooch") to Pony's association with "the Kirk" (Kirkland Lake) and her graphic but suspect[34] account of her eating (and regurgitating) an unholy communion — a trinity of frozen dachshunds (92–94). All of this serves to denaturalize and highlight the constructed nature of the redemptive fiction that we witness, as when Glidden's entrance at the end of the first act *"on all fours with a big bone in his mouth"* twists what ought to be the play's turning point a notch too far (57). The perversion of the oedipal action and of the play's Roman Catholic iconography similarly works to disrupt the authority of the symbolic order in its representation of any but a contingent and

constructed truth. The play's resolution, without questioning the valid-
ity or value of such constructs, is made contingent on the audience's
conscious production of meaning, becoming a model less of what *is*
than of what we *make*.

In these plays, then, Walker and Thompson have not eschewed
inherited dramaturgical traditions — powerful traditions and symbolic
structures are there to be used — nor have they, like French and Cook,
presented versions of those structures that serve primarily to restrict
their plays' abilities to break from the realm of merely reproductive or
culturally affirmative ideological coding. *Love and Anger, Nothing Sacred,
Lion in the Streets*, and *White Biting Dog* manage, in their different ways,
to foreground and denaturalize their inherited structural principles
together with their ideological weights, and they thereby succeed in
perverting those structures and opening up, again in their different ways,
the disruptive possibility of genuinely productive cultural intervention.

2

Modernism and Its Containments

Nothing has significance. Everything has significance. Between these two extremes, one sweats.

— Herbert Blau (44)

THE SECOND inherited tradition, which (re)surfaced in the Canadian theatrical "renaissance" of the late 1960s and early 1970s simultaneously with the neo-Aristotelian, oedipal, and biblical dramaturgies examined in chapter 1, is the modernist one. From Newfoundland to British Columbia, playwrights from Michael Cook to Tom Cone experimented with modernist forms and aesthetics. In Toronto, while the poetic naturalism of the Davids French and Freeman proved to be the economic, critical, and dramaturgical mainstay of Tarragon Theatre (Freeman's *Creeps* opened at Factory Lab but moved to Tarragon Theatre when its director, Bill Glassco, founded the latter in 1971), playwrights at The Factory Theatre Lab and Toronto Free Theatre consciously drew for their models on the traditions of European modernism. Although these "experiments" rarely received the critical acclaim of their Tarragon Theatre counterparts — indeed, the use of modernist models tended to be derided as derivative rather than celebrated as daring[1] — in some ways they have been more productive as starting points than the poetic naturalism of French, particularly for playwrights such as Michael Hollingsworth and George F. Walker, whose earliest work was sparse, austere, inscrutable, and akin to the archetypally modernist tradition of Genet, Ionesco, and Beckett — the tradition that Martin Esslin invented by labelling a diverse group of modernist plays "the theatre of the absurd."

If the generation of Canadian playwrights, audiences, and critics of the late 1960s and early 1970s was raised in secondary school on the mainstream dramaturgical diet outlined in chapter 1, then the same generation learned to equate the "contemporary" and the "experimental" with this so-called theatre of the absurd. Gestures toward theatrical contemporaneity in secondary school curricula during the 1960s would rarely have gone beyond *Waiting for Godot*, which partly for that reason has earned its canonical reputation in North America as the archetypal modernist play. In universities, any course called "An Introduction to Drama" would almost certainly have ended with Beckett, as did more advanced courses in "Modern Drama," in which students learned that the appropriate "avant garde" reaction to the realist schools of Ibsen, Chekhov, and (early) Strindberg — expressionism and surrealism had little impact in the schools or theatres of English Canada — was to adopt the structures and strategies of *The Bald Soprano, Zoo Story, Waiting for Godot, Endgame, The Maids, No Exit, The Homecoming,* or *Rosencrantz and Guildenstern Are Dead.* In studying these plays — and in linking them with a garden-variety existentialism derived from selected essays and short novels by Sartre, Camus, and Keirkegaard — what that generation (my generation) was likely to learn was that, in terms of dramatic structure, there really was "no exit" and that, in the "thematic" terms of a pop-philosophical, individualist, existential angst in which existence agonizingly precedes essence, "hell is other people." Not much room for cultural intervention there.[2]

The structural feature that these plays share is a peculiarly modernist form of closure, in which form is considered not a forum but a structuralist end in itself. It is not accidental that Russian Formalism developed in the context of constructivism in the arts or that structuralist criticism, including the Canadian variety best represented by Northrop Frye, developed within the (internationalist) context of modernist movements in the visual arts, fiction, poetry, and criticism (notably the poetry and criticism of T.S. Eliot).

For the modernist critic and artist, art is nonreferential and non-representational, and it functions within its own separate realm, satisfying its own internal and disinterested standards of logic, clarity, integrity, and autonomy. Frye has famously asserted, for example, that "Shakespeare [as transhistorical and transcultural exemplar of the artist] has no values, no philosophy, no principles of anything except dramatic form" (*Natural Perspective* 39).[3] Modernist artistic practice is most usefully understood, in this formulation, through (explicitly detached, objective, and pseudoscientific) structuralist analysis, and the work of art, the "product," exists as a kind of "in-itself," creating a realm of experience that is either indifferent to life or a substitute for it. In either case, the work is self-contained and, by external standards, inscrutable.

For the modernist, structure can be seen as the (conscious) construction of independent, self-sufficient artifacts — art for art's sake — as the artist creates by imposing the coherence of order on the chaos of recalcitrant, "unruly" existence (typically gendered female), producing bright, clear, jewel-like kernels of inscrutable truth from the (meaningless) garbage heap of the natural, threatening, and feminine world. The "one" who sweats in the epigraph to this chapter, then, is the (individual male) artist whose "sweat" is exerted in the heroic struggle to contain (or do away with) the threat, sweat (and other living and leaking bodily functions and fluids), and subjectivity of a slippery pre- or asymbolic "other," gendered female in this construction, "killing" it into the unchanging realm and purity of "art" (Gilbert and Gubar 14 and passim). In the epigraph from Herbert Blau, however, sweat is also the equivalent of the "crack" that Leonard Cohen finds in the "everything" of the epigraph to part 2. As Terry Eagleton says, "the body can never be fully present in discourse" (97). And there, for the modernist, is the rub. If, as Lacan claimed, the symbol is the death of the thing (see Eagleton 97), the living and sweating bodily "thing" is the dis-ease that threatens the symbol(ic).

Where I dealt in part in the first chapter with dramatic structures that represented or played out oedipal *crises*, then, in this chapter I want to deal with the struggle to *maintain* oedipal resolutions through the imposition of form in the face of unruly and disruptive feminine and/or bodily threats, which might enact the breakdown of the oedipal resolution that is *constitutive* of unified dramatic form (not to mention masculinity).

In drama — or at least in the plays of what Blau calls "the classical avant-garde" (177) — this modernism manifests itself most often as the construction of plays around unresolved but carefully balanced conflict; circular plotting that, unlike the seasonal/biblical plotting discussed in chapter 1, involves endless reproductive repetition — the reproduction of the plays' own opening circumstances — rather than the rebirth or renewal (and thus historical continuation) of an old order; and the construction of the plays themselves as symbols rather than the employment of symbolism and symbolic structures as signifiers that refer to some larger signified or signs that conjure up an external referent. (Thus, Peter Brook can describe Beckett's archetypally modernist plays as "symbols in an exact sense of the word . . . : a true symbol is hard and clear" [64]. Beckett's plays "stand on the stage as objects," Brook says, and "we get nowhere if we expect to be told what they mean" [65].[4])

The retreat from application, representation, and (psychological or perspectival) depth that these modernist dramaturgies enact can also be seen as a retreat from social and political responsibility into a realm of "pure" form or pure aesthetics; or as a retreat into "pure" philosophy or metaphysics as objectless speculation engaged in for its own sake, as exercise; or perhaps most seriously as a dehumanizing of the work that leaves it open for appropriation by other ideologies of purity, including, most famously and frighteningly, fascism. The links between fascism and modernism are lucidly explicated in Fredric Jameson's *Fables of Aggression: Wyndham Lewis, the Modernist as Fascist* (though Lewis's Canadian sojourn and his 1954 "Canadian" novel, *Self-Condemned*, are often forgotten) and in Frank Kermode's *The Sense of an Ending: Studies in the Theory of Fiction* (93–124).[5] The links between fascism, modernism, and patriarchy, as we will see below, are the explicit subjects of Margaret Hollingsworth's *Poppycock* and Michael Springate's *Dog and Crow*.

The early absurdist plays of George F. Walker and Michael Hollingsworth, the Beckettian one-act plays of Michael Cook, and Tom Cone's explorations of modernist forms drawn from painting all emerged in Canada between 1971 and 1976 and presented recognizable if often inventive variations on familiar European modernist models. Thus, Hollingsworth's *Strawberry Fields* (1973) and *Clear Light* (1973) — although, because of their tendency toward violence, scatology, and sexual "perversity," they have most often been discussed in terms of Artaud and a theatre of cruelty-style catharsis that, in its ideological effects, is like its Aristotelian counterpart (Hancock) — are perhaps best seen as typically modernist theatrical *images*, however violent, images that, to paraphrase Archibald MacLeish on poetry, do not *mean* but simply *are*.[6]

Cook's Beckettian plays, *Tiln* (1971) and *Quiller* (1975), are similarly memorable less for their language, themes, or characterization than for their riveting images: of *Tiln* as a self-appointed god of light, accompanied by the screeching of gulls, moving through a land- and seascape peopled only by Fern, who is buried to the neck in a barrel of brine and dying in a lighthouse at the edge of an apparently empty universe; and of *Quiller* in his dilapidated longjohns on the stage of his clapboard house/coffin arguing with and cajoling the Lord or anyone else who passes by.

Walker's earliest plays, *Prince of Naples* (1971) and *Ambush at Tether's End* (1971), have been described by Chris Johnson in "George F. Walker: B-Movies beyond the Absurd" as "exercise[s] in the theatrical techniques of the Absurd" and compared, respectively, with Ionesco's *The Lesson* and Beckett's *Waiting for Godot* (90, 89–90). Renate Usmiani, like Johnson, interprets these plays as making "a negative statement about the human condition" (37). But neither Johnson nor Usmiani engages in any detailed structural analysis or comments on the significance of Connie Brissenden's observation that "the characters George [Walker] creates seem to hang suspended in space, and they [the plays] are all set somewhere and everywhere" (Introduction ix). The combination of existential despair with the lack of specific social referents and the use of an essentially closed formal model seem to replicate the modernist self-containment of the theatre of the absurd. Even in these plays, however, Walker's characteristic irony creates a formal fissure indicative of the discomfort that Canada's most modernist playwrights have frequently felt with the form. *Ambush at Tether's End*, closely modelled on *Waiting for Godot*, works structurally, as does its model, to contain signification and resist referentiality, but it nevertheless inserts at its outset the self-consciously sardonic premise that "evasiveness is next to godliness" (89) and insinuates the possibility of human choice or agency by creating a portrait of Max's *conscious* (if posthumous) manipulation of Galt and Bush, the play's Vladimir and Estragon characters. In *Prince of Naples*, similarly, there are moments that rely on a self-consciousness — about interpretation and inscrutability (64), about phrases such as "existential conundrum" (72), about the play's own use of Nietzsche (the titular "Prince of Naples" [74–75]), about the theatre (99), and about the 1960s (78–79) — that serves structurally to open the play outward in a way that the metatheatrical references in Beckett, which tend to fold the audience into the play's modernist enclosure, do not.

The references to the 1960s in *Prince of Naples*, in fact, place the 1971 play in a historical moment when existential angst was a popular component of the "disaffection among young adults" that the Local Initiative Program (LIP) and Opportunities for Youth (OFY) grants that funded Factory Lab and other alternative theatres were created by government in part to reduce (Johnston, *Up* 7). The same 1960s disaffection also ultimately points toward Walker's more direct engagement with his society in his later plays. Overall, however, the ideological work performed by these plays is culturally affirmative, serving to deflect disaffection into an existential inertia in which audiences are directed to "suffer" (Walker, *Ambush* 89) or, as in Walker's *Zastrozzi* and the best "art-for-art's-sake" tradition, "occupy yourselves" (55).

★ ★ ★

The modernist concern with form has led several Canadian playwrights, many of whom were educated outside Canada and the reach of the educational constraints discussed so far, to work from models in the visual arts or music, in which purely formalist preoccupations are less likely to be muddied by the kinds of social interactions and immediacies that the theatre invites. As early as 1974, Vancouver's expatriate American Tom Cone experimented in *Cubistique*, as the play's title indicates, with staging cubism. In *Beautiful Tigers*, his 1976 companion play to *Cubistique* (although *Beautiful Tigers* is not cubist, Christopher Dafoe suggests that they are "two acts of the same play" [13], and they have been staged as such), Cone incorporates the construction of a Rousseau painting into the action, which concludes with the painting's completion as its final tableau. Although Cone's work has been compared, not inappropriately, with that of Harold Pinter (Jenkins 111), the more obvious comparisons are those made by Dafoe to Virginia Woolf's *The Waves* and Edward Elgar's *Enigma Variations* or perhaps to the ouevres of Pablo Picasso, Eric Satie, or, as Robert Wallace suggests, poets such as Robert Creeley (see Cone, "Tom Cone" 31). In any case, these short and tightly structured "chamber plays" (Dafoe 10) are perhaps best seen as structural exercises, self-consciously employing the one-act format because of its very restrictiveness (Cone, "Tom Cone" 36). And, as for most structuralist works, it can be said of most of Cone's plays, as Dafoe said of *Herringbone*, that "It occupies the stage as if it owned it and it must be played as if it meant everything and nothing, which it does" (12).

Cone himself claims that *Cubistique* — which recounts the Henry Jamesian relationship in 1920s Paris between a young American woman and her older and more sophisticated European friend — is about the relationship between its two female characters rather than about form ("Tom Cone" 35). The play is most notable, however, for its intricate and elegant dancelike design and for its interpretive inscrutability. In his introduction to Cone's *Three Plays*, Dafoe, significantly, says little about the plot, characters, or themes of the play but describes it as "static" and "abstract," noting that "Repetition and curious juxtaposition are employed to stunning effect and the use of music and unusual word formations increase[s] the air of mystery and perplexity" (10–11). The relationship between the women, in fact, is treated as a series of patterned actions and reactions in which the characters not only seem to be interchangeable but also do perform themselves and each other over the course of a circular action. The play ends precisely as it begins, except that the women have traded lines and positions.

It is not incidental that this play, like much modernist art, employs the representation of (interchangeable but inscrutable) women as the subject of its formalist explorations. The play opens and closes with an image that, through the use of a "pencil" lighting effect, fragments, freezes, and overlaps the features of the two women. The effect is designed to *"suggest a cubist image of two sides of one face"* as the onstage male pianist plays music "from a composer of that period, preferably from Satie's piano compositions" (Cone, *Three Plays* 17). In following the conventions and expectations of modernism and its representation of women, this iconic framing image is representative of the play itself: in fragmenting the bodies, psyches, and narratives of the women, *Cubistique* has the effect of denying its women subjectivity, "killing them into art," in Sandra Gilbert and Susan Gubar's phrase, and presenting the characters as aesthetic objects in relation to both the observing male pianist and the audience. Cone himself has described his audiences as "voyeurs" ("Tom Cone" 40). As in most modernist painting — and most precisely in the paintings of Picasso — "woman" here occupies the position of Other in relation to a male spectatorial subject position, which is not incidental for modernism but in fact makes representation (and the consumption of representation) possible if (agonizingly for the modernist) never complete.

Indeed, the inscrutability of the represented women of *Cubistique*, like that of *Hamlet*'s Gertrude or Leonardo's *Mona Lisa* in Jacqueline Rose's analysis of T.S. Eliot's responses to those works, operates at the point of contact between modernist form, structuralist literary analysis (with its "particularly harsh type of literary super-ego" [102]), and psychoanalysis. For the structuralist, as Rose notes, "Eliot's essay [on *Hamlet*] suggests that the question of the woman and the question of meaning go together" (97–98); that the enigmatic in art and in "woman" (as Other) is both seductive and threatening, leading to the "mystification (or fetishization) of the woman which makes of her something both perfect and dangerous or obscene (obscene *if not* perfect)" (100); and that in both drama and psychoanalysis the oedipal drama, which allocates subjects to their sexual places, can never be ultimately resolved. This failure of representation, finally, "suggests that what is felt as inscrutable, unmanageable or even horrible for an aesthetic theory which will only allow into its definition what can be controlled or managed by art, is nothing other than femininity itself" (101). In *Cubistique*, in fact, it is not only the inscrutability but also the polymorphous sexuality of the women that is staged, ordered, aestheticized, and depersonalized — virtually disembodied. Rose concludes that "Writing which proclaims its integrity, and literary theory which demands such integrity (objectivity/correlation) of writing, merely repeat that moment of repression when language and sexuality were first ordered into place, putting down the unconscious processes which threaten the resolution of the Oedipal drama and of narrative form alike" (102).

In Cone's *Beautiful Tigers*, representation, consumption, and the relationship of the artist to his (sic) (raw) material are explicitly at issue. Set in the studio of Picasso himself in 1908, the play features Picasso, his model and lover Fernande Olivier, Gertrude and Leo Stein, Alice B. Toklas, Guillaume Apollinaire, the chef Felix Potin, Michel (an accordionist), and the imminent arrival of Henri Rousseau for his surprise birthday party. As the characters prepare a meal and a live reproduction of Rousseau's painting *Yadwigha's Dream*, they drink and discuss from their respective positions as artist, writer, model, critic, chef, and patron of the arts the various roles played by one another as well as by genius, sponsorship, inspiration, and application in the construction of both the omelette and the work of art. Ultimately, after considerable debate and in response to Felix's urging, "Go . . . let him love you" (100), the painting and the play are completed simultaneously when Fernande disrobes and takes up the pose of the nude Yadwigha, transforming herself (or allowing herself to be transformed) from raw material into (art) object and completing the representation.

Although the conclusion to *Beautiful Tigers* at first seems thoroughly to transform the work of (making) art and the woman into closed and inscrutable objects for consumption, the play is fractured as *Cubistique* is not when Felix breaks the frame to talk to the audience (from whom he elicits responses), by the characters' conflicting views of the (cultural) work performed by the aesthetic object (including the interpretation of the work by its audience), and above all by the play's representation of the work of art in the process of construction. The structural imposition of aesthetic closure at the end of the play, moreover, cannot entirely contain or control the impact of the work on its consumers, and

Rousseau's response to it, like that of the theatre audience, is left open. Finally, in spite of the self-enclosed absence of social reference constructed by art about making art, there seems to be a *staging* here of the difficulty of imposing modernist form. The possibility that the Other — the woman — will resist containment, refuse representation (Fernande's reluctance to take her "proper place" in the design makes her a threat to the play's and the painting's oedipal resolution), threatens the (male) artist who is busy trying to construct unities and creates anxieties about fragmentation and female duplicity (or multiplicity). The lengths to which the play goes to achieve its formal closure — the completion of "the work" — can be read as the exorcism of a fundamental anxiety about the role of art, the "use" (including consumption) of its "raw" material, and the participation of the modernist work of art in the subjugation of women. Perhaps Cone was referring to such moments when he told Robert Wallace that, although he is "not a political writer," he loves "to play the fault line" ("Tom Cone" 35, 38).[7]

★   ★   ★

Writing of *Cubistique* in his introduction to Cone's *Three Plays*, Christopher Dafoe says that "The play passes through the mind like a piece of complex music, evanescent, beautiful and provoking. It has great poise and a kind of tart beauty" (11). As a self-confessed "great fan of chamber music," Cone consciously structured his 1978 play, *Stargazing,* "in the way that a quartet would be written," and he is always conscious of "how the movements work from beat to beat" ("Tom Cone" 39). In this, his dramaturgy is related less to that of the painterly Lawrence Jeffery than to that of Michel Tremblay (see Wallace and Zimmerman 40), John Murrell, and, more recently, Tomson Highway, each of whom relies heavily on structural principles drawn from music, considered by many to be the "purest" because the least representational of the arts. As Walter Pater famously said (in reference to the late-nineteenth-century symbolist aesthetic), "all art aspires towards the condition of music" (106). Jamie Portman and others have noted Cone's affinity to Tremblay in this regard (see Wallace and Zimmerman 40), noting that Cone might appropriately be said to "score" rather than write his plays, and Tremblay's reliance on musical structures in plays such as *Les Belles Soeurs*; *Forever Yours, Marie-Lou*; *Bonjour, là, Bonjour, Albertine in Five Times* (discussed below); and *Sainte Carmen of the Main* is legendary, leading Tremblay, indeed, to work as a librettist for operas such as *Nelligan*, based on the life and work of Quebec's most famous (and most musical) symbolist poet.

In many ways, *Les Belles Soeurs* is the first in a miniseries of plays in Canada and Quebec that revolve around the representation and orchestration (manipulation?) of a group of women in a musically patterned dance within which the tensions, passions, and injustices that are the plays' subjects function primarily as formal devices that arouse carefully correlated and choreographed responses in order to balance them against others, resolve them, or otherwise contain them. Murrell's *Waiting for the Parade* is a case in point. Like much of his work, the play is structured like a chamber opera, in which dances and songs alternate with group scenes, solo "arias," recitatifs, and scenes of formal move-ment. Thus, for example, an opening dance in *Waiting for the Parade* (7–9) is followed by Catherine's monologue (9), which precedes a scene of orchestrated movement around bandage-rolling (10–15) accompanied by a choric refrain ("I can't stand that woman" [10, 11, 13, 14]), after which the "frame" is closed by another monologue (by Marta) and a song (15–16). And so on. As in *Les Belles Soeurs*, but with more elegance than anger, the structure is dramatically effective and aesthetically pleasing, but it serves, finally, not only to objectify the women as fragments, incoherent in themselves, of an overall design but also to reduce the play's serious issues — such as racism — to dramatic postulates in a formal pattern.

Perhaps it is the capacity of the form for the comfortable contain-ment of potentially disruptive social concerns that accounts for the success and popularity of plays such as *Waiting for the Parade* and Highway's *The Rez Sisters*, which contains elements of both the Murrell play and *Les Belles Soeurs*. Highway was trained as a classical pianist and gained his early dramaturgical experience by working with James Reaney, a student of Northrop Frye whose dramatic work has been extensively analysed by Gerald Parker in the context of formalist European modernism and painters such as Paul Klee. Highway has talked of "applying sonata form to the spiritual and mental situation of a street drunk" (qtd. in Wigston 8), and, as Alan Filewod has argued, this formal conservatism can potentially admit the "colonizing gaze" of a non-Native audience that, playing the roles of both liberal and consumer, is thereby let off the hook ("Averting").[8] Arguably, however, in the case of Highway, the presence of the androgynous Nanabush, the Native trickster figure in the otherwise all-female cast, represents a problematizing structural fissure that destabilizes the representation, though — from the point of view of a non-Native audience — the containments provided by the (in this play) male artist-surrogate are difficult to distinguish from those of the pianist in *Cubistique*. In any case, the passions, opinions, and tragedies of the represented lives of the play's Native women, contained within a comic quest narrative and a carefully scored scenic structure, are primarily important for their formal role in a "well-wrought" design.

Ultimately, it seems, all of these plays — and others, such as Tremblay's "quartet," *The Impromptu of Outrement*, and Normand Chaurette's operatic *The Queens* — involve the representation, orchestration, and manipulation of an ensemble of objectified female characters' bodies and voices within a masculinist, modernist aesthetic design that is naturalized rather than interrogated, as it is in Margaret Hollingsworth's *Poppycock* (discussed below) or staged, as it is in the Anna Project's *This Is for You, Anna* (discussed in chapter 3). And significantly, of course, the plays that we've been looking at, while providing much-needed major acting roles for women, were written — and have most often been directed — by men.

Tremblay's *Albertine in Five Times*, as translated by John Van Burek and Bill Glassco and produced at Toronto's Tarragon Theatre in 1985, is another example of a musically structured orchestration of a cast of women, in which the women's voices play off one another almost contrapuntally, occasionally merging in a line spoken in unison before diverging again into discords and resolutions that move toward a satisfying final cadence. This play, however, involves five actors playing a single character at different times in her life (with a sixth actor as her sister, who interacts with all of them). The play fractures the identification of actor with role or, more accurately, character with role and thereby has the potential to destabilize unified subjectivity and the normalized linear structure of a life narrative and thus undermine the bases of modernist unity and identity. For the most part, however, with the exception of temporarily disjunctive moments such as when Albertine at seventy accuses the others of talking funny, using words that she never used (12), the action is treated as a retrospective memory play from the point of view of the character near the end of her life: "We're not judging you," as the Albertines of fifty and seventy say to their younger selves, "we remember" (33). The potential for formal fracturing is never fully realized or is treated as a musical discord introduced in order to be resolved artificially in a closure that is purely formal and feels somewhat arbitrarily imposed.

The disruptive potential of this form, however, which might be called monodrama for several actors, is closer to being realized in one of the most dramaturgically complex plays of recent years, David Young's *Glenn*. The title refers, of course, to Glenn Gould, and the play not only draws on his life, times, and ideas but also reflects his art in its contrapuntal structuring of voices and its use, as the back-cover blurb for the published script puts it, of "Gould's early and late recordings of [Bach's] Goldberg Variations . . . as a structural template for the dramatic action." Indeed, as the liner notes to the published script tell us, "The play is divided into an opening Aria, thirty Variations and a Final Aria which, in most cases, follow the voicing, structure, and mood prescribed in Bach's score." They do so in the sense that the number of characters in each scene matches the number of voices in the variation that it represents, and the dramatic action echoes and dramatizes the melodic, harmonic, and rhythmic structuring of the music. As if this weren't complex enough, each of the play's four actors plays different aspects of Gould's "voice" and personality at different stages in his life (the Prodigy, the Performer, the Perfectionist, and the Puritan, a sort of 1990s modernist *Foure PP*), and each of these "voices" is orchestrated polyphonically to echo Gould's own mastery at letting each *musical* voice speak clearly, independently, and with a distinctive character in the performance of a contrapuntal composition.

As deeply modernist and self-obsessed an artist as Gould was, however, and as deeply formalist as is the structure of Young's play in the elaborate and complex formal unity of its self-referential design, the play, like the character on which it is based, resists modernist containment. As Geoffrey Payzant notes, "Gould was a complex person, indeed, he was a blithely multiple person," and while "There are only four characters . . . there are many voices in the play, just as there were in its namesake" (8). *Glenn*, then, in spite of its formal balances, is fundamentally dialogic in Bakhtin's sense,[9] staging the multiple and often conflicting voices and subjectivities that together constitute but never quite seem to be contained by the far from single personality of the play's Glenn. Most often, indeed, there is, as one stage direction suggests, "A sense of disharmony and conflicting purpose" between the various Glenns (16). And in the published script the resistance to characterological unity is exacerbated by the assertion in the liner notes that "at no time does the audience lose sight of the Gouldian persona behind the mask" of the various Gould "alter egos" or the other characters represented in the action (14).

If *Glenn* achieves a formal resolution in a *"glorious tintinnabulation"* of church bells (127) — which function in much the same way as the final solitary and blood-red rising moon in *Albertine in Five Times* — then that resolution is destabilized to a considerable degree by the "revolution" that the dying "Puritan" Gould feels in his head (126), blood in the brain that seems to signify more than the death of a central character. This surplus of signification is far from revolutionary, but it does disturb and destabilize an audience that has already learned from the play that the only ideal performance is one that has been "spliced" together, a compilation of fragments rather than "the result of some unbroken forward *thrust*" (85–86).

However much these plays that turn to modernist forms for their dramaturgical models may incorporate structural disruptions and internal fractures, in each play examined so far these disruptions tend to serve a primarily formal function, pushing at boundaries as the avant garde always has and experimenting in ways that serve to keep the form alive. Few of these experiments, however, perform cultural work that goes beyond the essentially conservative and affirmative role of reproducing, and perhaps rejuvenating, the currently dominant social order.

★ ★ ★

What I called "the dramaturgy of the perverse" in chapter 1, however, operates in Canada not only in reaction to the neo-Aristotelian closure of reversal and recognition, the determinations of the oedipal narrative, or the symbolic structures of the Frygian Bible but also in response to the clarity, self-containment, and self-referentiality of the modernist tradition. Several Canadian plays of the past three decades, notably plays by Margaret Hollingsworth, Michael Springate, Beverley Simons, Don Druick, Harry Standjofski, and Daniel MacIvor that I want to examine here, intertextually (or interstructurally) adopt, adapt, and pervert modernist structures of containment in ways that interrogate the ideological interests served by the retreat into "pure" form that presents itself as neutral, disinterested, and somehow above the realm of social or political interaction.

Poppycock, one of the plays in Margaret Hollingsworth's *Endangered Species: Four Plays*, makes explicit its critique of modernist self-containment and offers its own perversion of it. The play moves freely in time between 1912 and 1947, and its characters are "The Man" (played by one actor) — from whom "emerge" the "personae" of Pablo Picasso, Adolf Hitler, and Ezra Pound — and three women who "featured" in their lives: Dora Marr, Winifred Wagner, and H.D. (Hilda Doolittle). The men are virtually interchangeable: each is concerned with beauty and "absolute purity"; with names, signatures, and dates; and with "clarity" and rationality ("A tree cut down is easier to measure" [72]). And each calls the woman in his part of the play a "witch."

Hitler is "A kind uncle with a gun in his pocket" who listens to *Parsifal* and believes that "Pity means killing what is sick" (65, 69). Picasso claims for the cubists that, "Not only did we try to displace / reality, reality was no longer in the object. / Reality was in the painting" (58). He similarly believes that "Life is set up to eliminate / Those who cannot adapt" (71). Pound, who treasures "objectivity" and "straight talk," "Straight as the Greeks" (68), admires Hilda Doolittle as "a lacquer box" and *names* her

> H.D.
> Imagiste.
> I will make you a movement. I will make you.
> A legend. (61–62)

Shortly after this naming, as H.D. fellates him, Pound composes a letter predicting that

> 20th century poetry . . . will move
> against poppycock, it will be harder and
> saner, it will be near the bone, it will be
> as much like granite as it can be, the
> force will be in its adjectives impeding
> the shock and stroke of it. It will be
> austere, direct, free from emotional slither. (62)

As he and the scene reach their corresponding climaxes, and as the rhythms build around the repetition of phrases such as "harder and saner," Pound and H.D. exit to the accompaniment of Edith Piaf singing "La belle histoire d'amour" (63).

There are a number of significant and interesting parallels between Hollingsworth's treatment of the relationship of modernism to fascism and that of Michael Springate in *Dog and Crow*, which, like *Poppycock* and many modernist works, in Canada and elsewhere, features Ezra

Pound. (Walker's *Ambush at Tether's End* is typical in its deflection of modernist anxiety surrounding Pound's job as a propagandist for Mussolini when it offers a passing comic reference to the [unnamed] "fascist fellow who wrote those terrible little cantos" [149].[10]) *Dog and Crow* features a Pound who, like Hollingsworth's, likes "plain talk" and admires Mussolini as a "master architect" (19, 11). Also like Hollingsworth's, this Pound is concerned with naming (101), with thinking "objectively," with the "natural hierarchy of ability," and with "the intelligent will to order" (80). In this play, however, Pound's story is structurally parallel to that of Mussolini, who, like the Pound of *Poppycock*, conflates fellatio with clarity and death (91). The Pound plot is also structurally set in opposition to that of the communist, Grazia, who loses her eyes for the cause but, unlike Pound and his ahistorical modernism, manages to maintain her focus on "the present situation" (29). Springate's Pound is last seen in an insane asylum, where his wife, Dorothy, pleads to him, "Don't polish the fragments. / Talk" and, in anticipation of Harry Standjofski's *No Cycle* (discussed below), argues, "There are no cycles. / We can't begin again" (123, 124).

Hollingsworth's response to the fascism, sexism, and phallogocentrism that she sees inherent in the modernist movement is representative of the reaction of the dramaturgy of the perverse to modernism. It is embedded in her preference for the poppycock of her title to the clarity of imagism; in the associative structures of her plays; and in her insistence on the culpability of the artist who purports to keep art pure by keeping it separate from life. Like Springate and several other playwrights of their generation in Canada, however, Hollingsworth neither completely rejects the symbolic structures of modernism nor simply parodies them; rather, she engages in a process of creatively perverting and reshaping those structures. *Poppycock* stages rather than silently accepts the ways in which modernism positions women as the threatening or unruly Other, as it stages the castration anxieties of the modernist artist and fascist over the uncontrollable, foregrounding the perceived need for formal purity and perfection as an assertion of power, a killing of women into art. In fact, in other short plays by Hollingsworth, such as *The Apple in the Eye* and *Diving* (*Willful Acts*, 17–32, 113–18), she uses startlingly crisp, clear, and extended visual and verbal images that dominate the action to the point where the real dialogue is between action and image rather than characters. Gemma in *The Apple in the Eye*, for example, creates meaningful action out of her own projected image of an apple, action that supersedes in importance the "actual" physical situation of the reclining Gemma and her recumbent husband. The imagery is less part of the discourse of the *plays*, however, providing interpretive clues or symbolic unity for the audience, than part of the discourses of the central female characters, who create parallel associative subjectivities that seem to swallow the plays' actions and turn them inside out. Audiences are left not with hard, bright kernels of meaning but with the exposed modes and mechanisms of the production of image and interpretation.

While attempting to discover what Julia Kristeva calls the semiotic (*Desire* 133–35) — prelinguistic, preoedipal, presymbolic, and diffuse instinctual modes of associative expression[11] — Hollingsworth and her contemporaries seem to be concerned less with *jouissance* than with a more sober Canadian and somewhat paradoxical search for *security from* the threatening and oppressive constraints of the symbolic order. As Hollingsworth says of her plays in her introduction to *Endangered Species*,

> The characters are searching to introduce order into their everyday lives to help to make sense of the situations in which they find themselves. It is too frightening to abandon this search. We live in an unbalanced, unbalancing world and violence is always just around the corner. . . . How are we to make sense of it all when the very rituals we use to comfort ourselves condemn us to stay in the situations we are seeking to comprehend. . . ? (8)

Full-length plays by Simons, Druick, Standjofski, MacIvor, and Hollingsworth herself provide examples of some ways in which perverse dramaturgy has been used to try to answer her question. Each in its way "wrest[s] the purport of" those rituals by "go[ing] counter to what is reasonable or required" and by "misapply[ing]" and "misconstru[ing]" the symbolic structures on which dramatic, religious, and political authority rest.

The dramaturgies of Simons, Druick, and Standjofski have been influenced, as has much of Western modernism, by a study of "formal and ritualistic theatrical traditions" in "the orient" (Lister, "Beverley"), but these plays tap the ritual roots of theatre while simultaneously revisioning their iconographic import.[12] Simons's 1969 play *Crabdance* has been compared with both *Waiting for Godot* and *Endgame* and treated as a modernist play (Hay; Hopkins; Lister, "Crabdance"). Elizabeth Hopkins, in *The Oxford Companion to Canadian Literature*, describes the central character's struggles as ritualistic efforts "to use the buyer-seller, mother-son, wife-husband, mistress-lover roles for self discovery," efforts that "become confused circular patterns of exploitation and victimization that can be resolved only by her death." But Hopkins's description fails to account for the vitality, theatricality, and self-consciousness with which the central character, Sadie Golden, controls, performs, and perverts the rituals, including the playing out of her own death and funeral at three o'clock — each day? — and the carrying of her coffin to an upper level of the set — a "second stor(e)y" that the stage directions indicate doesn't exist. The religious (here primarily Jewish), familial, socioeconomic, sexual, and dramatic rituals that, in Hollingsworth's phrase, "we use to comfort ourselves" and that "condemn us to stay in the situations we are seeking to comprehend," together with the symbolic order that authorizes them, are self-consciously perverted, playfully misapplied, and subversively revisioned. The iconic authority of these rituals is disrupted by representing them as components of a metadrama that is self-consciously constructed by its own central character. The play itself, moreover, resists the self-containment typical of modernist drama through a pervasive metatheatricality, a self-aware overstatement of its (religious) symbolism *as* symbolism, and a resistance both to resolution and encapsulation.

Don Druick's 1988 play, *Where Is Kabuki?*, is a backstage drama at Tokyo's Kabuki-za Theatre, where "Form is form and form is Kabuki" (13, 52), which gives some idea why Japanese theatre is of interest to modernist artists from the West. The Kabuki-za is also a place where "true art is for all time" (15). Time, however, changes in the represented world of the play: the company's master playwright and the system and art that he represents are shuffled aside in the interests of box office and backers, and "traditional" culture is threatened — interestingly in a contemporary Canadian play — by the corrupting influences of "the south." Meanwhile, however, Druick's play includes in the cast list a cross-dressed Onnagata, who — as in Japanese theatrical life — maintains her stage gender throughout and engages — without remark — in an entirely conventional romantic liaison as a woman with the production's infatuated (male) backer. More importantly, however, the play, which begins as a conventional, more-or-less naturalistic Western drama about art versus economics, gradually takes on the character and quality of the old-fashioned Kabuki masterpiece the plot of which the master playwright recounts throughout. At the close, it achieves a modernist formal balance — "to finish what one starts," after all, "is the essence of tradition" (52) — but in the meantime the play has transformed itself into something at once rich and (perversely) strange.

To move from *Where Is Kabuki?* to Harry Standjofski's *No Cycle* is to cover as great a distance as that between Kabuki and Noh itself while remaining within the realm of drama influenced by Japanese forms. Standjofski's play is strange indeed by Western standards, and it goes further than any Western play with which I am familiar toward an accommodation of the deep structure of an Asian dramatic form, rather than simply its tone or trappings. Standjofski says in a note introducing the published script that "I have used the structures of a highly religious drama to talk about my time as I see it, a time of spiritual poverty — no rebirth, no cycles" (78).

The form, then, which *is* cyclical, is perverted in Standjofski's play, or rather it is used against itself, sometimes brilliantly. Not the least stroke of brilliance is the extensive use of the music of "the King," Elvis Presley, throughout the transformation of an aristocratic theatrical form that itself *trades* (like much feminist theatre today[13]) on transformation. It is the focus of the Noh on transformation — in each dramatic action of the cycle, the Sh'te, or protagonist, is transformed and, through transformation, released — that makes it different from Western theatrical traditions, which focus (as we have seen) on self-identity, recognition, and reification.

Noh is deeply conservative in its own culture, of course, parallelling Aristotelian reversal insofar as it represents its protagonist's transformation *to a former self. Structurally*, nevertheless, Noh provides a model for Western dramaturgy that is potentially liberating. Standjofski's own transformations of the Noh are significant, as he uses the traditional dramatic actions of the cycle virtually against themselves. The opening "God play," for example, entitled "Rabbit," is set at Easter and focuses on superficially playful variations on contemporary representations of rabbits — most prominent among them the Easter Bunny, which has replaced our culture's dying God. (The section's subdivisions are structured and titled after stations of the cross.) The subsequent actions run similar variations on the Noh's Warrior/History play (set on Remembrance Day and involving a dreamer and a dying woman); its Women play (set, ironically, on Father's Day and involving a lost tooth, a transformation, breast cancer, and a drowned dog); a Madwoman play (set on Valentine's Day and involving a dance between a seagull and a woman in green); and an Auspices play (set on Christmas Eve). Each section involves perversions of the expectations that it establishes, each juxtaposes Japanese spirituality with debased Christian or Western "holy days," each has to do with death, and most include unsettling fracturings of the cycle's overall enclosure. The Woman play, for example, stages the unexplained transformation of a blind woman into the (fully sighted) protagonist, Viv, it uses both French and English dialogue, and it slyly breaks the frame by making reference to orientalist appropriations of Japanese aesthetics. (Viv describes an apartment "decorated all Japanese with no chairs, just these cushions on the floor and the midget tables and the erotic drawings" [105].) The same section also plays self-conscious variations on the cycle's title, as when Viv tells her friend about her menstrual problems: "I have no cycle, eh?" (104).

In spite of the title, however, the play doesn't reject the cyclical structure of its model or of modernist self-referentiality; rather, it perverts that structure, drawing attention to its own construction in ways that I suggest are typical of the dramaturgy of the perverse. The final section pulls together dominant images from each of the preceding playlets in the cycle, in a monologue punctuated by the rest of the cast uttering *"the occasional quiet 'no'"* (109). The monologue ends with the man "stuck in a snowbank . . . a . . . drift" (ellipses in original).

> And the wheel spins.
> And I'm not moving.
> And the snow swirls up.
> And it will all go on,
> And the wheel spins.
> And I'm not moving. (111)

And the play ends with a conjunction: "And."

★　★　★

Beverley Simons (like Judith Thompson) draws on traditional and recognizable Judeo-Christian religious iconography in reproducing and "perversing" the workings of the symbolic order, while Don Druick and Harry Standjofski draw directly on the ritual traditions of the Japanese theatre. Daniel MacIvor and Margaret Hollingsworth, however, create their own secular iconographies based on the competitive rituals of contemporary society, in plays that, like those of Thompson and Simons (and, in a different way, Standjofski), revolve around overt and overstated symbolism. For Hollingsworth, this is most clearly true of the short experimental works, in which a single image or complex of images tends to dominate, but it is characteristic of almost all of her plays. She also typically flies in the face of traditional dramaturgical wisdom by avoiding theatrical focus on the "real" or objective world of action and behaviour. In her full-length play *War Babies* (*Willful Acts* 147–223), Hollingsworth uses powerful symbolic action projected by a central female character, the playwright Esme, virtually to engulf the "realistic" level of action within a radically subjective and metatheatrical "inner world"[14] in much the same way as Esme's found poem within the play engulfs its source in her husband's journalism (171–74). The subjective (and "Esme" might easily suggest "is me" to a theatre audience) perversely swallows and transforms the facts and forms that are the objects of its perception, as the constructed reality takes over from the apparently "natural."

Hollingsworth talks of the "push-pull, the liaison," of her plays ("I hate that term, 'conflict'") as being "between the character and herself. It's a push-pull between where she is and where she perceives herself to be" ("Margaret Hollingsworth" 159). In *War Babies*, it is the element of "liaison" rather than conflict, of pull rather than push, and of "where she perceives herself to be" rather than "where she is" (i.e., where others perceive her to be) that takes over the action and informs the ostensibly conventional reconciliation at the end of the play. There is not a reversal of (external) action but a shift in the subject position of the assumed *spectator*: the perceived has become the perceiver, and the audience sees from the point of view of the woman who is "normally" the object of its perception. While on one level the action proceeds in a linear fashion to tell a comic story of separation, "war," and reconciliation, on another level it posits a parallel structure and re-signs the traditional symbols of "war between the sexes," birth, and renewal.

Daniel MacIvor, particularly in what might be called his "mirror" plays, *2-2-Tango* and *Never Swim Alone*, also draws for his symbolism on competitive rituals, in his case the rituals of "relationshipping" (*2-2-Tango*) and a conflation of masculine competitive sports and corporate ambition (*Never Swim Alone*). *2-2-Tango: A Two-Man-One-Man-Show* is an elegantly theatrical (indepen)dance for two actors playing virtually identical characters named James and Jim, plus a boy with a watermelon. A gay comedy of manners for the 1990s, *2-2-Tango* uses its balanced, modernist, almost cubist structuring of surfaces to focus on psychological issues such as mirroring, desire, and distance without resorting to either psychological realism or allegory. In its intelligence and control, the play is typical of the work of MacIvor, one of the most imaginative of his generation of Toronto-based writers-performers. Its effectiveness as cultural intervention lies less with its content (the representation of gay subjectivities), however, than with its perversion of modernist form in the interests of interrogating psychological representation. The play's formal dance both stages and perverts what might be called the modernist unconscious — disruptive anxieties about the stability and permanence of the oedipal resolution.

Never Swim Alone is similar to *2-2-Tango* in its highly formal orchestration of a story of competition between two boys at a beach/men in business played out before a girl as judge. She drowned as a teen in a race to "the point" but now keeps score from a lifeguard station as the men/boys stage a highly stylized and imagistic series of competitive rituals that seem at first glance to function familiarly as modernist icons. In most traditional (Western) drama and theatre, the interest for the audience derives from the gap between the text spoken by the characters and an unspoken subtext of motivations and emotions that the audience must intuit. Every so often a work comes along that breaks this pattern by allowing the subtext to surface, usually spoken parallel to the text or illustrated by movement, mime, gesture, or facial expression, as in Necessary Angel's 1983 collective creation, *Mein*, and very occasionally, as in *War Babies*, taking over in importance or focus from the "textual" surface in such a way that the concept of representation itself is disturbed. *Never Swim Alone* and *2-2-Tango* go further than most, if differently from *War Babies*, in that in most of their scenes the actors seem virtually to *perform* the subtext, and the interest for the audience lies in trying to work out — to construct — what the text, the context, and the specifics of any "actual situation" might be. *Never Swim Alone* is held together by strict "rules," enforced by the judge through penalties, and by a rhythmic pattern of repeated rituals, riffs, and choric speeches on the way to "the [repeated] point." These rules serve, again, to highlight the question of the control of representation — not to mention interpretation (what *is* "the point"?) — and to pervert or denaturalize the symbolic order and its hegemonic control of meaning. (*Is* there a "point"?). Not surprisingly, for those keeping score of the action, the woman wins.

The dramaturgy of the perverse, then, as I have constructed it in this chapter, employs the symbolic structures of the inherited dramaturgical traditions of modernism, as the structures of the plays in chapter 1 did traditional Aristotelian, oedipal, and biblical structures, in a variety of ways. But it is, as *The Oxford English Dictionary* says, "disposed to go counter to what is reasonable or required" by them. These plays "wrest the purport of" those structures to problematize the "normal," the reasonable or required, and throw into question the ways in which these standards are silently established. The revisioning and interrogation of those structures fracture traditional concepts of focus, unity, and action and perversely twist them out of shape in order both to divide and multiply the prisms through which we see and to extend the subject positions available to Canadian theatre audiences.

In subsequent sections, I will attempt to examine some of the ways in which the new, experimental, or newly conceived dramaturgical structures of some contemporary Canadian plays attempt, not to pervert or subvert, but to move outside or beyond these inherited traditions. I hope to analyse whether and to what degree these innovative and alternative dramaturgies (themselves, of course, culturally produced as well as culturally productive) succeed in revisioning dominant narrative, dramatic, symbolic, and social orders.

PART TWO

Beyond Naturalism

Forms of Time and Process

> Ring the Bells that still can ring.
> Forget your perfect offering.
> There is a crack in everything.
> That's how the light gets in.
> — Leonard Cohen (373)

In part 1, I examined forms and structures that function to construct or disrupt unities and that work through naturalistic or modernist shapings of time and space respectively. Chapter 1 focused on dramaturgies that start from a linear and fundamentally conservative temporal shaping of dramatic action, disciplining (hi)story into chains of cause and effect over time, in which lives and histories culminate in present actions that are ultimately understandable and explained (away). Chapter 2 examined dramaturgical strategies deriving from or reacting to the modernist retreat from time and change into the pure, unchanging, and ahistorical realm of spatial form. In parts 2 and 3, I will maintain the temporal/spatial division but turn my attention to dramaturgical strategies of *multiplication*, focusing in part 2 on temporal, historical, and processual strategies of disruption and extending in part 3 modernist experimentation with space into the post-modern realm, where form is both less pure and less stable.

In part 2, then, are chapters that explore structural experiments in Canadian dramaturgy from the 1960s to the recent past that concern themselves with theatrical process (rather than product) as attempts at democratization; with explorations of history and historiography as themselves self-reflexive probings into present constructions and reconstructions of an unfixed and ever-changing past through which we (continually) remake what we "are"; and with various forms of contestation of the control of time and history and therefore of the forces that constitute "us" *as* us in the present, from the perspectives of local community, class, gender, and race.

3

The Structures of Authenticity:
Collective and Collaborative Creations

To TURN from naturalistic dramaturgical structures based on cause-and-effect development through time, on the "author-ity" of fictional narrative and of the symbolic structure shaped by the imagination of a single author, to the "authenticity" of collective and collaborative creation is in part to turn from what Alan Sinfield calls the universal/individual polarity to the historical/social one, where meaning can be contested,[1] and from the realm of general, metaphysical truth to that of particular historical facts, events, experiences, or interests. It is to turn from the heroically sweating artist, the "one" who kills into perfectly formed art (see the epigraph to chapter 2), to the multiplication of the "one" into many, the surrender of individual creative control, and the welcoming of collective sweat and other bodily and structural excesses, fissures, fluids, and imperfections.[2] Finally, it is to turn from Aristotelian and archetypally tragic or comic "action," oedipally structured with a beginning, middle, and end, explicitly derivative of a stable (preformed) subject, to "doing," which takes place as unstructured event (as phenomenon), is constitutive of individual or collective subjectivity in progress, and is the mode less of the tragic or comic than of the epic or annal.[3]

Not surprisingly, much collective creation is epi(sodi)c in structure. Theatre Passe Muraille director Paul Thompson, in famously describing the form of that company's *The Farm Show* as "more like a Canadian Sunday School or Christmas Concert where one person does a recitation, another sings a song, a third acts out a skit, etc." (Theatre Passe Muraille, *Farm Show* 7), or when he says in the opening monologue that "the show kind of bounces along one way or another and then it *stops*" (19), could be talking about the structures of many or most collective creations, which are often described by reviews as "free-form" or "revue-style" entertainments.[4] As such, this type of theatre tends to concern itself with events rather than actions and to employ an acting style concerned with "what" rather than "why," behaviour rather than motive.

Having surrendered claims to the authority of (author-ized) symbolic narrative structure and (author-itative) authorial voice, however, what claims can these plays make on their audiences' attention? As Alan Filewod notes, "some form of authentication" is required (*Collective Encounters* 10). But how is the contract between the stage and the auditorium cemented? I want to look in this chapter at four principles of authentication at work in collective and collaborative creation in Canada since the early 1970s, together with their related or emergent authenticating structures.

The first and most familiar structure, that of the documentary collective creation as represented by the work of Theatre Passe Muraille, relies on claims to fact (versus Truth), to the employment of an authenticating document or documents, and often to the "real," lived experiences of actors, the phenomenological "thingness" of things, and the stability of place over time. The truth claims of the second type of collaborative work that I will look at rely on shared experience, shared commitment, or shared process, and they are represented here by the synchronic and diachronic communities of women forged in a group of feminist collectives and women-centred plays produced by Nova Scotia's Mulgrave Road Co-op Theatre. Related to this achievement of authenticity through the mutual validation of shared experience and community is the third authenticating device that I will consider, the political one provided by shared *interest*, or social purpose, represented here by the feminist collectives that produced *Aphra* and *This Is for You, Anna*. Finally, and returning in a sense to documentary strategies of authentication but ones not usually discussed in the context of collective creation, is the appeal to both the "reality" of (physical) presence and the shared experience of biology to which much performance art turns for its truth claims. This work will be represented here by *Mary Medusa*, a performance piece created in Winnipeg in 1992–93 by Shawna Dempsey and Lorri Millan.[5]

These authenticating devices — appeals to "fact" (or document); to shared experience, process, or community; to shared political interest or commitment; and to the physical presence of the actor — are not, of course, discrete, nor are they newly observed: Robert Nunn has effectively demonstrated Theatre Passe Muraille's creation of *communitas* in *The Farm Show* (see "Meeting"); the women of Mulgrave Road

Co-op Theatre rely on the authentication of place as much as do the creators of Theatre Passe Muraille's "sociological" collectives; *Aphra* and *This Is for You, Anna* employ documentary material to great effect; and almost all collective creations to a greater or lesser extent emerge from shared political commitment of some sort. And there are other modes of authentication and validation employed in these and many other Canadian collectively or collaboratively created plays, discussed with considerable sophistication by scholars such as Diane Bessai ("Documentary Theatre," *Playwrights*), Alan Filewod ("Collective Creation," *Collective Encounters*), and Robert Nunn ("Performing Fact"). Nevertheless, I want to isolate in this chapter some of these authenticating structures and analyse their political impacts and implications within their particular cultural contexts and in some degree of isolation from one another.

Before doing so, however, I should point to the political and structural implications that these works *share* by virtue of their rejection of the inherited Aristotelian, modernist, and above all oedipal models discussed in part 1 and to their assumption — and this is the source of their *political* commitment — of what Filewod refers to as collective *responsibility* for the work ("Collective Creation" 47). And in this regard I will begin by quoting at length from Michel Foucault's preface to *Anti-Oedipus: Capitalism and Schizophrenia*, not as a purported source for the creators of the work that we'll be examining, but as a kind of structural and political touchstone against which the accomplishments of that work can be tested or measured. Foucault proposes what he calls "a certain number of essential principles" that he derives from Gilles Deleuze and Felix Guattari, read as "a manual or guide" to "This art of living counter to all forms of fascism . . ." (xiii):

- Free political action from all unitary and totalizing paranoia.
- Develop action, thought, and desires by proliferation, juxtaposition, and disjunction, and not by subdivision and pyramidal hierarchization.
- Withdraw allegiance from the old categories of the Negative (law, limit, castration, lack, lacuna), which Western thought has so long held sacred as a form of power and an access to reality. Prefer what is positive and multiple, difference over uniformity, flows over unities, mobile arrangements over systems. Believe that what is productive is not sedentary but nomadic.
- Do not think that one has to be sad in order to be militant, even though the thing one is fighting is abominable. It is the

connection of desire to reality (and not its retreat into the forms of representation) that possesses revolutionary force.

- Do not use thought to ground a political practice in Truth; nor political action to discredit, as mere speculation, a line of thought. Use political practice as an intensifier of thought, and analysis as a multiplier of the forms and domains for the intervention of political action.
- Do not demand of politics that it restore the "rights" of the individual, as philosophy has defined them. The individual is the product of power. What is needed is to "de-individualize" by means of multiplication and displacement, diverse combinations. The group must not be the organic bond uniting hierarchized individuals, but a constant generator of de-individualization.
- Do not become enamored of power. (xiii–xiv)

Mark Seem summarizes these principles in his introduction to the same book and adds another "goal" closely related to the dramaturgical structures at which I will be looking:

Once we forget about our egos a non-neurotic form of politics becomes possible, where singularity and collectivity are no longer at odds with each other, and where collective expressions of desire are possible. Such a politics does not seek to regiment individuals according to a totalitarian system of norms, but to de-normalize and de-individualize through a multiplicity of new, collective arrangements against power. Its goal is the transformation of human relationships in a struggle against power. (xxi)

It is not accidental, I think, that unlike the dramaturgical strategies analysed in part 1, in which reversal (or, resistantly, perversion) is structurally central, *transformation* is the structural commonality between all the works and methods that I will be discussing in this chapter — including, as Filewod notes, acting methods (*Collective Encounters* 39) and, as Nunn notes, the use of props, places, or bodies ("Meeting" 50, 43). And, as Helene Keyssar argues ("Drama," *Feminist Theatre*), transformative dramatic structures function to enable rather than resist fundamental social transformation.[6]

★   ★   ★

CLOCKS, COCKS, DOGS, AND CHILDREN

Reuter

AMSTERDAM, Netherlands

A SOLD-OUT city theatre stages the world premiere tonight of *Going to the Dogs*, a unique four-act play featuring the unlikely cast of six German-Shepherd dogs.

"Part of the attraction of staging the performance is the curious fact that people will actually come to the theatre to watch dogs eating, barking, urinating, fighting, sleeping and playing," said Dutch artist and broadcaster Wim Schippers, who is staging the play.

The six dogs were acquired as puppies and since April have been taking drama lessons from Amsterdam police, he said.

"The difference between people on stage and dogs, is that people act while dogs remain normal," Schippers said. "Thinking about that gives you a new perspective on the theatre."

— *Globe and Mail* 20 September 1986: A1

It is a commonplace among actors that one should never go on stage with dogs or children. The cuteness factor aside, this reluctance has to do with the fact that, together with clocks and (more problematically) nudity, dogs and children foreground representation as an issue in the theatre because the audience knows that they are "real," not acted. Clocks tick on relentlessly, reminding audience members of their dinner reservations or the costs of babysitting; dogs bark, scratch, and whimper; nudity is so relentlessly personal and perversely nonrepresentational that it always seems to be the bodies of actors, not characters, that the audience ogles; and children's eyes wander over the audience as their hands wander over their bodies, breaking the theatrical illusion in ways that, in naturalistic productions at any rate, are distracting.

But these things can also be strangely compelling. One of the most effective and successful *illusionistic* moments that I have seen in the theatre, for example, occurred during a production of Timberlake Wertenbaker's *The Grace of Mary Traverse*, directed by Martha Henry at Toronto Free Theatre in 1987. In the aftermath of a highly active representation of a violent revolution, the stage was left deserted, at which point a lone dog entered from stage right, crossed the stage slowly, sniffing at scattered debris, and completed the "scene" by exiting alone, stage left. The moment worked so well and was so convincing precisely because the dog was not "acting," there was no apparent human presence or agency, and for a moment the gap between representation and reality was bridged, the boundaries blurred.[7]

A similar effect is occasionally achieved with onstage nudity, the use of which can raise the theatrical stakes for both the newly vulnerable actors and their audiences, for whom the bodies of the actors and their characters are necessarily and disturbingly conflated. In these situations, the theatrical illusion of "real presence" is compellingly heightened, the phenomenological "actuality" (the authenticity) of dogs and bodies supersedes their semiotic significance (is not "consumed in its sense" [States 26]), and the theatre seems more fully than usual to actualize its potential to mean in ways entirely different from those of the non-performing arts.[8]

All of this raises some interesting questions for the theorist and some central issues and opportunities for a company such as Theatre Passe Muraille, whose reputation in the 1970s was built on its unique style of documentary theatre and whose financial security, in a sense, was built on an erection.

Let me explain.

The style of documentary collective creation developed by Theatre Passe Muraille and its director, Paul Thompson (a style that has proven highly influential in both writing and acting for the theatre in Canada), centred in each of the "sociological"[9] collective creations around one or more "real" objects from the community represented in the show, objects that somehow authenticated the representation, serving Theatre Passe Muraille as a kind of (temporarily) transcendental signifier.

The first of these sociological collectives, *Doukhobors* (1971), is anomalous in that it was created and performed at a geographical and cultural remove from its subject community, and as such it claimed to be only about "what we know about them [Doukhobors] as people living in Ontario" (Theatre Passe Muraille, *Doukhobors* ii).[10] As authenticating documents, however, in addition to the traditional use of photographs and projected titles inherited from historical documentary, there was what Thompson calls in the notes to the published version of the script "actual fire on stage" (i), and there was nudity. As one of those stubborn entities cited by Bert States, the phenomenological reality of which exceeds their pure signification (31), "The fire," Thompson asserts, "is important":

It's part of the purification ritual that is everywhere in the play. For the Doukhobors, fire produced a kind of purity by the process of burning away. We came back to the fire several times during the play. I don't think you can cheat with fire and get away with it.[11] Just like you can't cheat with the nudity. It's there and that's why we put it into the play. (ii)

In spite of Filewod's argument that "the cast had no personal relation to the subject" and that the show's nudity was "essentially iconographic" (*Collective Encounters* 34), then, the shared "reality" of the fire, and particularly of the nudity, grounded even this early play in a kind of phenomenological "reality." As Diane Bessai says, "in *Doukhobors*, he [Thompson] was building on the physicality of the Doukhobor spiritual experience through the capacity of the actors to project the energy of naked sweating bodies on stage" (*Playwrights* 99). And, of course, for both the actors and the Doukhobors who were the play's subject, the nakedness represented and enacted in the final scene served as shared and active protest and personal risk.[12]

Theatre Passe Muraille's subsequent sociological collectives in Ontario,[13] beginning with *The Farm Show* in 1972, eschewed the geographical remoteness of *Doukhobors* from its subject community and, in the first performances at least (*The Farm Show* in Ray Bird's barn near Clinton, *Under the Greywacke* in Cobalt [1973], and *Oil* in Petrolia [1974)], used as authenticating "objects" the place of performance and the subject community as audience. Like so many subsequent sociological collectives by the Mulgrave Road Co-op, 25th Street House, Theatre Network, and so on, these performances had little need for documentary authentication beyond the validating approval of the audiences who were their sources and subjects. It is significant, however, that with little other claim to authenticity, and unlike *The Farm Show*, *Under the Greywacke* and *Oil* did not tour.[14]

The published version of *The Farm Show* (based on the Toronto performances), Theatre Passe Muraille's best-known and archetypal sociological collective, opens with a scene in which "one of the more easy going members of the cast," on some occasions Thompson himself, stands on a map of the community that serves as the subject of the documentary and outlines for the audience the nature of the collaboration that produced the show:

> Last summer we visited a farming community near Clinton,
> Ontario. Clinton is about a hundred and twenty miles due west
> of Toronto. You go down to Kitchener and then take the number
> eight highway to Stratford, Mitchell, Seaforth, *Clinton*. Which
> would be right about *here* (*just off the front of stage left*) if it were
> on this map. . . .[15] Now beside the number eight highway is the
> community we live in. This map (*marked on naked stage*) shows
> the roads and the names of the different farmers in the area. (19)

The actor continues with the following list of "authentic pieces of
farm equipment" (Usmiani 49), "authenticating" properties that stand
in for the "reality" that the show (like the stage map) purports to
represent:

> We . . . brought back a few things from Clinton.
> This is part of a bean dryer.
> These are straw bales, not to be confused with the hay bales
> you'll hear about later.
> An old cream can. Some crates. An actual Clinton shopping cart.
> (19)

Throughout the show, these various objects, "rarely used as themselves" (Filewod, *Collective Encounters* 44), nevertheless provide what
Bessai calls "witty authenticity" (*Playwrights* 69) and Nunn calls "links
to actuality" ("Meeting" 50). They allow the scenes to *mean* and invest
actuality with a (socially) transformative potential at the level of deep
structure.[16] (As Bessai notes [*Playwrights* 97, 110], moreover, the device
was extended and formalized in the use of the farm wagon in *Them
Donnellys* [1974] and the Red River cart in *The West Show* [1975].) In
spite of Thompson's claim that "Objects become metaphors" in his
work ("Paul Thompson" 53), this is not the essentially passive stuff of
metaphor, as in conventional dramaturgies; rather, it functions as acti-
vating political parable. Moving beyond the realm of (Aristotelian)
action or (fragmentary) *doing* to the realm of (collective) *agency*, "Any
thing can become any other thing in *performance*," as Filewod puts it, as
we "witness" (or bear witness to) "the creative process of the actor
transforming fact into meaning" (*Collective Encounters* 44; emphasis
added).

    The actors in the typical Passe Muraille collective, however, trans-
form more than documentary objects into meaning: they typically

engage in an acting *process* that is itself both documentary and transformational. This acting style has been extraordinarily influential in Canada and virtually reverses the Actor's Studio Method dominant in American-style naturalism, in that its impetus is not sense memory, the discovery of motivation, or sympathetic connection with dramatic characters on a psychological level. Rather, the Passe Muraille process begins with physical and vocal mimicry in an attempt to discover from the outside, as it were, what it feels like psychologically, intellectually, and emotionally to adopt the physical and vocal postures, mannerisms, carriage, and tricks of speech of a given character — modelled, of course, on a "real" member of the subject community and recognizable to that community as audience precisely from those physical characteristics. The test of this "mirroring process" (Usmiani 47), at least initially, is not universalizing psychological truth or empathy but documentary accuracy, recognition, and assent, and in this regard it is interesting that the theatre's archives at the University of Guelph include, for example, an article from the *Advertiser-Topic* in Petrolia, Ontario, that focuses on the way in which *The Farm Show* displays in detail the differences between Lambton County and Huron County farmers ("Difference"). Similarly, a review from the *London Free Press* focuses on the actors' accurate representations of "native" Huron County characteristics, mannerisms, accents, and jargon (Malone).

Passe Muraille actors, then, function in part as "journalists" (Keys) or "anthropologists" (Endres), who in performance, as Filewod points out (*Collective Creations* 47), report the results of their own research and thereby take more direct responsibility than is usual in theatre for the documentary authenticity of the material. Much has been made of the ways and degrees to which "the meeting of actuality and theatricality" (Nunn) in this process involved "imbuing the experience with a mythic dimension" (Wallace, "Holding" 57), and in the nationalistic 1970s, of course, Thompson and the company had a considerable investment in the myth that their work provided "ordinary Canadians" with a mythology, history, and identity. But the importance of this work, ultimately, may rest less in the construction of mythologies, which tend to be totalizing, than in the modelling of transformational strategies for theatre and society. As in all representations, the value of the representation lies in its *not* reproducing point for point that which it represents, and at Theatre Passe Muraille this slippage is represented by the necessary and observable gap between the audience as subject and their representation on the stage.[17] This gap was foregrounded, of course, when the actors played tractors, farm machines, appliances, and farm animals, and it seems that the gaps themselves, not the accuracy of representation, constitute the source of both the pleasure and the politics of these (performance) texts.

In one of Theatre Passe Muraille's least highly regarded scenes — Filewod uses it as "the most extreme example" of a Passe Muraille scene that "expresses nothing more than its own cleverness" (*Collective Encounters* 30) — the company's *I Love You, Baby Blue* establishes what I take to be the authenticating documentary base of Theatre Passe Muraille's most notorious, though not most highly regarded, show, the box-office appeal of which funded the building that has given the company some financial security over the subsequent two decades. Criticism of the show on the basis of its sensationalism, however, can obscure the fact that, nearly alone among Passe Muraille productions, *I Love You, Baby Blue* accomplished the goal of attracting people who didn't normally attend theatre. For a short time, in fact, it succeeded in making theatre, in the words of the company's founder, Jim Garrard, "as popular as bowling" (qtd. in Paul Thompson, "Paul Thompson" 64), though it did so without the company's usual highly skilled group of actors/writers, who resisted the production's extensive use of nudity.

Interestingly, critical condescension also obscures the intriguing ways in which *I Love You, Baby Blue*'s use of the naked body as authen-ticating document reveals much about the pleasures and politics, strengths and weaknesses, of Theatre Passe Muraille's work. The scene to which I am referring takes place about two-thirds of the way through the show — where the "climax" might be expected to occur but demonstrably does not. It follows in the wake of a role-reversal barroom pickup scene, and it precedes a parodic lesson on "how to be a jock":

SPOT UP *as actress enters in a black body suit, white elbow gloves and top-hat. With a flourish she stands, mainstage, in front of a black back drop*

ACTRESS

To audience Ladies and Gentlemen, right here on this very stage *She covers a hole in the back drop with her hat* the most amazing phenomenon will take place. Yes! Before your very eyes, present-ing the colossal, the magnificent, the stupendous . . . Human Levitation! *Removes hat and we see a penis hanging out of the hole* Watch it rise, watch it rise. Higher and higher, no strings attached.

She demonstrates the fact Ladies and Gentlemen, we must all combine our energies here and focus, we must all think hard . . .
harder . . . Ladies! Gentlemen! *By now, the penis has either risen or
not risen. If it did, she said* . . . *"The Human Levitation!" and hung
her hat on it; if it didn't, she said, "The Human Levitation has a
headache!" and she'd cover it again with her top hat and*
BLACKOUT (55–56)

The scene, and the erection, are paradigmatic of Theatre Passe Muraille's
sociological documentary, with the role of the "real objects" from the
community being played here by the erection, achieved or not. As a
phenomenological "event" that, because it cannot be "acted," links the
body of the actor with that of the performer, the erection serves the
archetypally (masculinist) authenticating function, serving as documentary evidence of the show's subject, (unfulfilled) sexual desire,
predominantly male. At the same time, the erection serves as a kind of
ultimate signifier, standing in, as it were, for the (meta)physical force
that constitutes the community as audience for this play. What makes
this play representative rather than exceptional among Theatre Passe
Muraille's sociological collectives, apart from its exposing the company's
masculinist bias, is the degree to which it lays bare the source of its
pleasures in the lack that propels desire.

Much has been made in criticism, particularly in the work of Nunn
("Meeting"), of the ways in which "the meeting of actuality and theatricality" serves to construct what Victor Turner calls "communitas" and
Richard Schechner glosses as "that levelling of all differences in an
ecstasy that so often characterizes performing."[18] While the sense of two
communities meeting in *The Farm Show* is most often said to derive
from shared respect, as actors and farmers recognize and admire the
sheer work and craft involved in performing their respective tasks, the
"ecstasy" of *I Love You, Baby Blue* is differently and perhaps even more
centrally related to the show's subject. But the levelling of differences
to which Schechner refers is at best temporary, of course (like
an ecstatic experience), and the desire that the play explores and —
crucially — evokes for the primarily male audience that it constructs
and attracts[19] depends on the *gap* between the "thing itself" and the
signifier, the noncorrespondence, the excess of meaning — the "lack"
or "displacement" that Lacan finds at the heart of desire itself (146–78).
In a sense, unlike the metaphoric or symbolic structure of the oedipal
drama, which *replaces* "reality," the structure of *I Love You, Baby Blue*

and of other Passe Muraille collectives is essentially *metonymic*, the documentary part standing in for the absent whole of signification. It is a structure that seems, in Lacan's phrase, to "veer . . . off of significa-tion" (160), to *enact* desire by contriving to reach after a fullness of presence, and significance, that is never achieved, never satisfied: desire is eternally renewed, and closure is forever deferred.

What are the politics of such a form? Its political problems are clear, and many of them have been valuably discussed by Robin Endres and Alan Filewod (*Collective Encounters*), among others. Most of these prob-lems have to do with the illusion of freedom and democracy that can be created by the collective process itself, which, if the problems are not consciously foregrounded throughout, can mask culturally and theatrically determined inequalities, hierarchies, and relationships of power. At Theatre Passe Muraille, this lack of foregrounding resulted, for example, in the sexism and even misogyny of much of *I Love You, Baby Blue* and in the failure of plays such as *The Farm Show*, *Oil*, and *Under the Greywacke* to interrogate relations of exclusion on which the celebrated sense of community is so often and so dangerously built. The tendency of the form to offer the community an *idealized* reflec-tion of itself, moreover, is at the root of the company's popular and financial success: as I indicated above, the show at the centre of which was the disembodied erection paid for the theatre's new building. But is it politically appropriate or even acceptable to reify community values, even those of marginalized communities, by uncritically staging and celebrating them? When *I Love You, Baby Blue* stages the vicious rape of a lesbian and then represents her as having enjoyed the experience, is the authenticity of the documentary source justification for the rep-resentation, when the form itself precludes claims to objectivity and inclusiveness?

On the other hand, insofar as the sociological collective is met-onymic and episodic in structure, it is by implication — almost by definition — openly unfinished, incomplete, and (in both senses of the word) partial. In each of these plays, and in the larger influence of Theatre Passe Muraille in the establishment of localist theatres across Canada, there is a celebration of difference and diversity, an opening outward of theatrical and social possibility, a transformational *exemplum*, and the implied, if lighthearted, instruction to "go forth and multiply." And in staging, rather than masking or bridging, the gap between representation and reality, the Passe Muraille collective implicitly allows for and even invites politicized analysis.

★　★　★

AnOther Story

In an essay first published in 1978, Teresa de Lauretis called for "a *feminist theory of textual production*" that was neither a "*theory of women's writing* nor just a theory of textuality" (*Technologies* 92) but a theory of "women as subjects — not commodities but social beings producing and reproducing cultural products, transmitting and transforming cultural values" (93).[20] It is neither my purpose nor my place to propose such a theory, but it may be useful here to examine some of the ways in which women as subjects and social beings — theatre workers, community members, and audiences — have engaged in the production, transmission, and transformation of cultural values in the limited context of a small rural theatre company — the Mulgrave Road Co-op Theatre in Guysborough, Nova Scotia — inspired in part by the work of Theatre Passe Muraille. In doing so, I want to suggest that these women, both individually and as a group, have constructed what de Lauretis calls "a new practice and vision of the relation between subject and modes of textual production" (*Technologies* 92). That is, they have developed one model through which Maritime women, as theatre workers and as audiences, can take possession of their cultural (re)production, including the construction of gender.

Mulgrave Road is not a women's company (it was founded as a collective in 1977 by three men — Michael Fahey, Robbie O'Neill, and Wendell Smith — and one woman, Gay Hauser); rather, it is a touring company dedicated to the production of new work by Nova Scotians about the Maritimes, primarily northeastern Nova Scotia.[21] Nevertheless, although its organizational structure has varied over the years, the co-op was, until its move to a more traditional board structure in 1994, dedicated to operating collectively and consensually, and, as Cindy Cowan (one of its best-known playwrights) has suggested, this procedure made the company congenial to many women theatre workers in a way that regional theatres with more traditional administrative structures were not (105).[22]

Women's dramaturgy began at Mulgrave Road in 1977 with a monologue and song created and performed by Hauser in the company's first production, a collective creation called *The Mulgrave Road Show*. The actor used the now familiar image of the quilt in a song woven into the narrative form of a woman's monologue about loneliness and isolation. Hauser sat alone on stage with an old quilt in her lap, and as she told her story she punctuated it with verses of a song about a quilt "of a thousand pieces," of ". . . moments sewn in heartache / Cuttings joined in joy and pain" (Mulgrave Road Co-op Theatre 14). The song, the speech, and the image of quilting created, according to Cowan, "a powerful moment of recognition for any woman watching in the audience" (106).

This moment worked first to deconstruct the conventional and condescending distinction between arts (including theatre) and crafts (including quilting), a division that privileges the former term and relegates to secondary status much of the cultural production of women, and second to represent for Mulgrave Road the communal creativity of women in rural Nova Scotia, as the quilting metaphor has done for other communities of rural women (notably in Donna Smyth's 1982 novel *Quilt*[23]). With this monologue, in fact, Hauser initiated a pattern of cultural production that helped to shape a broad range of women's plays from Mulgrave Road in subsequent years.[24] Included in that pattern was an informal but interdependent kind of networking in which women who took part in one collective creation, scripted play, workshop, or other project[25] eventually produced or initiated the production of their own plays, often involving women from the earlier shows, workshops, or working groups. Cowan suggests, moreover, that

> what gives strength to the women in the Mulgrave Road Co-op is the attempt they have made to build upon each other's work from year to year. Picking up where the last woman left off, they have incorporated the last "message" or experience and attempted to go one step further in developing plays for women. (105)

In any case, all of the women who eventually emerged from the co-op as playwrights, including Mary Vingoe, Cindy Cowan, Carol Sinclair, Jenny Munday, and Mary Colin Chisholm, had been involved with other women in the co-op in collective creations and/or scripted plays, and this pattern has often been reflected in diachronic series of intertexts between the shows, as well as in structural reflections and parallels in what seems to be an evolving women's dramaturgy at Mulgrave Road.

Because of the unique material conditions shaping the production of theatre in Guysborough County, moreover, there is a kind of parallel synchronic process involved in any one production. There's not much else to do in Guysborough when a show is in rehearsal — the population of the town is just over 500, there is only one real restaurant (closed much of the time during the off-season — i.e., the theatre season), and the determinedly masculinist Legion Hall houses the town's only bar. The result is that the rehearsal hall itself — which, together with the usual collection of musical instruments assembled for a show, contains a small kitchen, tape decks, and other comforts — usually becomes a focal unit and social centre apart from scheduled rehearsal hours. Conversations, not surprisingly, tend to revolve around the current project. Individual shows, then, evolve through an intensely focused process of creation and rehearsal in which a group of theatre professionals engages in concentrated interactions with one another and with the community through an extended period of creative isolation and immersion. And, as Jan Kudelka said about her production of *Another Story*, "the positive thing about collective drama is that when it works in a community, you end up getting a bonding sense with that community" (qtd. in Deakin). Theatre workers in Guysborough either are part of the community in and about which they write — Gay Hauser and Cindy Cowan lived and raised their families there, and Jenny Munday remained in the town for a time after her stint as artistic director ended and later returned to work there — or are more often billeted with local residents throughout the workshop and rehearsal processes, often with the same people over several shows. This arrangement has resulted in a number of close and long-standing friendships between women of the co-op and residents of the town, friendships that become a part of the production and reproduction of theatre, and of cultural values, at Mulgrave Road and in Guysborough County. In its most immediate form, this type of contact and bonding results in characters in plays, such as Chisholm's portrait of a prominent Guysborough citizen, Co-op Theatre Society member, and friend in her play *Safe Haven*, a character performed by the playwright herself in the revival at the Blyth Festival, Ontario, in 1993. More significantly, however, as Hauser suggests, the ways in which women's plays are produced at the co-op reproduce the social interactions of the women who are the plays' subjects and audiences. Portraying these women theatrically, she claims, reinforces "bonding" *within* the company: "Rural women aren't aggressive," she continues. "What gives them strength is their friendships, their open dependence on each other, and their community. The result is if they need to mobilize to help each other they can do so quickly" (qtd. in Cowan 106–07).[26]

I have suggested that "women's plays" at Mulgrave Road incorporate an interconnected and associative range of intertexts between the plays themselves. This pattern was set by the 1980 collective creation *One on the Way*, the co-op's first "women's play," which developed from the original quilting monologue in *The Mulgrave Road Show* and from a workshop held by Hauser at Guysborough Municipal High School. Created by director Svetlana Zylin and actors Mary Vingoe, Nicola Lipman, and Hauser herself (five months pregnant at the time), the play used an evocative associative structure to deal with social issues of direct concern to rural women in 1980; it contained echoes of and references to material from the earlier collective creations, *The Mulgrave Road Show* (1977), *Let's Play Fish* (1978), and *The Coady Co-op Show* (1979); and it anticipated characters and situations later developed by for example, Cowan in *Spooks* (1984) and Kudelka and the company (including Cowan and Vingoe) in *Another Story* (1982), a collective creation about the daytime "soaps" and the women who watch them. These shows in turn inspired and were reflected in others, in an expanding intertextual (and intertextural) pattern that, among other things, insists on the *recognition* of women's work and the refusal to let it be lost (Cowan 108).

The intertextuality of these productions derives directly from their *mode* of production, it is typical of women's work at Mulgrave Road, and it forms a central part of the plays' deep structures. It also combines with the productions' immediate and recognizable references to and reflections of their specific social and cultural contexts in Guysborough County to open the shows outward to the audience as community. It attempts, that is, to create an interactive dramaturgy in which the subject is at once writer, performer, and audience and in which participation in the theatrical event functions as a constitutive act of the participant *as* subject. Achieving their sense of authenticity from a structural grounding in shared experience rather than from authenticating documents or objects, these plays seem more fully than most of Theatre Passe Muraille's sociological collectives to root themselves in the community that they share with their audiences — and more fully to function *as* collectives, even on those occasions when one woman officially fulfilled what Foucault calls the "author function" (*Foucault Reader* 101–20).

I have been concerned to this point primarily with the social production and reproduction of cultural values in women's plays at

Mulgrave Road, but what is in question, of course, is not simply the *transmission* of cultural values in the Maritimes based on community, landscape, and history but also their *transformation*, including the (re)construction of gender. These plays are socially *produced*, of course, performed *in* the world, but they are also socially *productive*, "performed *upon* the world," as Louis Montrose has put it in reference to Renaissance theatre, "by gendered individual and collective human agents" (23). Versions of society, history, and gender are instantiated, but they are also contested and, potentially, transformed.

As I indicated above, transformation has been seen by feminist theatre critic Helene Keyssar not only as a theme but also as a frequently employed structural principle in women's dramaturgy. In this formulation, transformation replaces what we saw in chapter 1 to be the essentialist, universalist, and "affirmative" (in Marcuse's sense) Aristotelian principles of reversal and recognition (of a preexisting normative subject) with an activist structural encoding of the possibility of social change. It is possible to see a development in women's dramaturgy at Mulgrave Road of transformative modes of theatrical representation that not only reject traditionally self-contained patriarchal structures of linear narrative — reversal, recognition, and closure — but also reproduce structurally and represent dramatically their own modes of production. Play after women's play at Mulgrave Road[27] experiments "interstructurally" with and around forms in which community, and the circulation of community values, serve as both subject matter and organizing principle. These plays are different from one another, and they employ different strategies for cultural intervention, but they also seem *structurally* to "quote" one another in much the same way as they contain networks of situational and linguistic intertexts.

I'd like to spend the remainder of my discussion of women's dramaturgy at Mulgrave Road looking briefly at some of the ways in which a few representative plays function. Each of these plays eschews mystification or mythologizing in favour of directly and explicitly addressing concrete historical or social situations;[28] each replaces a focus on a single central character with a structure in which the community itself functions as hero; each employs, in its own way, interwoven strands of story and lyrical expression rather than traditional linear narrative; and each explicitly or implicitly explores issues surrounding women's cultural production — or the production of women's culture.

Mary Vingoe's *Holy Ghosters, 1776* focuses on three strong women at the precise historical moment of the Jonathan Eddy rebellion and the battle that kept New Brunswick and Nova Scotia from becoming the fourteenth American colony. *Holy Ghosters, 1776* is typical of women's plays at the co-op in that it is structured around an ensemble of actors playing a community of characters rather than around the story of its best-known (male) historical figure, Richard John Uniacke (in its first production, the play was criticized for this focus by reviewers; see Senchuk). As Cindy Cowan remarks, "I suppose when you put a famous man on stage and then upstage him with three women you are inviting trouble" (108); in fact, though, the overlapping narrative structure, built around four stories at various stages of development over the course of the action, functions to create, for the audience as well as the characters, a diachronic sense of community over time that reflects the play's own intertextual and interstructural relationship to its dramatic predecessors at Mulgrave Road.[29] In spite of the almost overwhelming sense of displacement that is the experience of all the play's *characters*, Vingoe uses history, community, and landscape to create for the *audience* a somehow reassuring sense of *constant* change, finding in the shared experience of displacement an ironic but unsentimental sense of *continuity* over time. The play ends, moreover, with a powerful theatrical image of the promise of renewed community among the women as its two central female characters share a baked potato dug from earth scorched by the victorious British troops, leaving a sense of dislocation and destruction that is also, ironically, a nourishing "site" of potential change and a recognition of fragmentation and isolation as experiences that are or can be shared.[30]

Jenny Munday's *Battle Fatigue*, even more clearly than *Holy Ghosters, 1776*, sets out to recover women's history and is based on extensive personal research on the experiences of women in World War II. Like Vingoe, Munday structures the play around an ensemble of actors doubling roles and acting out different but parallel stories, and both playwrights portray the coming together of women of different backgrounds and sensibilities to frame the possibility — not always realized — of new or different *kinds* of community. Both plays, then, echo the experiences of the groups of women from different backgrounds in the communities — theatrical and other — through which they were produced. *Battle Fatigue*, moreover, makes its potential for intervention in the contemporary culture of its audiences explicit by framing its historical action within a series of present-tense scenes in which a feminist daughter stands in for the audience as she and we learn from her mother about the older woman's wartime past.

Both *Holy Ghosters, 1776* and *Battle Fatigue* also move toward a characteristic of the "new textual form" called for by de Lauretis, in which "rational historical inquiry is continually intersected by the lyrical and the personal" (*Technologies* 92). Not only do both plays intercut the documented "facts" with explorations of their subjective impacts,[31] but they also introduce lyrical passages, personal "arias" that problematize the historical and document what de Lauretis calls the "resonance of the (documented) historical event in the subjects" (92). *Holy Ghosters, 1776*, for example, features a choric character, an ageless and homeless Acadian woman, Old Aboideaux, who wanders among the marshes and whose Lear-like odes to wind and weather provide historical and poetic resonances even as the character embodies the direct and personal impacts of abstract historical events such as the expulsion of the Acadians prior to the play's action. *Battle Fatigue* less clearly and less frequently employs the lyric mode (though scene-change songs are used effectively), but the play is full of subjective expression in personal narratives about the historical past that function as personal histories or what might usefully be called "documentaries of subjectivity."

Carol Sinclair's musical play *Idyll Gossip* moves still further away from the formal realm of historical documentary and further toward both lyrical expression — through song — and the explicit exploration of rural Maritime women as producers and transformers of culture. This play also employs an ensemble of actors to portray a community as its central character; more clearly than in any of the other plays under discussion, though, it both partakes of and is about women's circulation of cultural values through the arts and women's reclaiming of agency in the construction of gender in the Maritimes. A meta-theatrical musical created by Maritime women about Maritime women creating music, *Idyll Gossip* was inspired by stories of women such as Rita MacNeil — or the women of Mulgrave Road — who struggle against the overwhelming and functionally hegemonic resistance within the conservative patriarchal culture of the rural Maritimes to women's participation in the performing arts. The play's external action is concerned with a group of rural women who gradually overcome first their own (hegemonically internalized) and then their society's reluctance to take their musical aspirations and abilities seriously; however, the sensual life and energy of the play derive from the songs that the women perform throughout, songs that assume and demonstrate the subjectivity of women as cultural workers and audience members. Ranging from satirical or parodic to deeply expressive in tone, these songs cumulatively create a powerful sense of women's subjectivity; in fact, there is a sense in which, as in the plays of Margaret Hollingsworth discussed in part 1, the subjective — traditionally regarded as inappropriate to the supposed "objectivity" "natural" to the dramatic mode — takes over from and transforms the play's external narrative, which by traditional wisdom is the *essence* of drama but which in this play is often improbable, farcical, or absurd.

These plays, then, like all of the women's plays so far produced at Mulgrave Road Co-op Theatre, function both as *products* of the cultural conditions (theatrical and otherwise) through which they have emerged and as *agents* of transformation within those cultures. But it is important not to romanticize the involvement of Mulgrave Road in the community. Although the engagements that I have described are central and essential, the degree to which the co-op is capable of effecting meaningful cultural intervention derives in part from its existence at a point of intersection *between* cultures, including its bringing to Guysborough theatre workers of different backgrounds and interests. Mulgrave Road's efficacy rests in its being at once part of, mimetic of, and external to the community in and through which it works. As such, it functions as a potentially transformative "fissure" in an often rigidly closed culture by introducing elements new to it and by providing focal points for women and others who are *members* of the community but are constructed by it as "Other" or ex-centric. The co-op itself has functioned, in part, as a continually shifting and liminal community that is both transformed by and transformative of the culture and society of Guysborough County but within parameters that, though fluid, are defined at any time by the degree to which the company's shows are products of the culture that they represent. It may not be incidental to note, for example, that Mulgrave Road has so far been able to intervene only in very limited and almost imperceptible ways in the gendered construction of class, race, ethnicity, or sexual orientation in Guysborough County, except perhaps insofar as its work has helped to make possible future interventions in these areas as the products of a shifting cultural ground.[32]

★   ★   ★

Aphra, Anna, and Mary Medusa

I can barely contain myself.
Form before content.
— Shawna Dempsey and Lorri Millan (50)

If the claims to authenticity made by Theatre Passe Muraille's early sociological collectives rest on documentary and phenomenological "reality," and those of women's dramaturgy at Mulgrave Road rest primarily on shared place, process, and community, then the three feminist collaborative projects discussed in this section draw for authentication primarily on shared political interest and to a greater or lesser extent on a validating feminist conviction that the personal is embodied, performative, and political. *Aphra*, by Maenad Productions,[33] *This Is for You, Anna*, by the Anna Project,[34] and *Mary Medusa*, by Shawna Dempsey and Lorri Millan are, in Ann Wilson's phrase, "attentive" to the social relations that inscribe their politics: each attends not only to what is "represented" but also to "representation itself" ("Politics" 174); each, as Alan Filewod says of *This Is for You, Anna*, "repudiates realist dramaturgy as the aesthetic technology of patriarchy" (Introduction xvi); and each, to a greater or lesser degree, derives its structure as much from the conventions of performance as from a prescribed (or prescripted) text. That being the case, the object of my structural analysis here is somewhat problematic: I will look at published scripts that, like those of *Doukhobors, The Farm Show, I Love You, Baby Blue, One on the Way*, and other collectives, are *records* of performances more than maps for future productions. Even more than in the case of those early collectives from Theatre Passe Muraille and Mulgrave Road Co-op Theatre, moreover, the published versions of *Aphra, This Is for You, Anna*, and particularly *Mary Medusa* (which is deliberately and experimentally published as a collection of fragments and images) are inadequate as representations of performances for which the textual — logos — was neither preliminary in sequence nor primary in importance. Nevertheless, the published scripts are what there is (left), and it is perhaps appropriate that any analysis of them foregrounds the performative nature of its own practice[35] and the process that it shares with the theatrical production of "translating" textual material into the frame of another discourse.

Aphra, first produced in Calgary in 1991, is based on the life of seventeenth-century playwright and protonovelist Aphra Behn, the first woman in England to make an independent living as a writer. It is the most conventional of the shows under discussion here, in terms of process, dramaturgy, and politics. Alone among the three, it existed as a script prior to the rehearsal process, though, as the writers say, "We wrote it collaboratively, all three of us. We spent a long time around the table deciding how we were going to do it, reading and sharing what we'd read, discussing what we'd write . . ." (Stone-Blackburn, "Maenadic" 31). The writers' process, moreover, was not purely literary, textual, or abstract. It was undertaken not only with a specific venue in mind — Calgary's tiny Pumphouse Theatre — but also, according to the creators, with an explicit objective "to explore that space" (31). The mandate of Maenad Productions, too, was less explicitly or radically feminist than those of the creators of *This Is for You, Anna* or *Mary Medusa*; as a company, in fact, Maenad Productions eschews even the word *feminist*, articulating as its goal the promotion of a "feminine vision" (Cullen, Patience, and Scollard S2). Here again, however, the mandate explicitly locates the company's work within a body-conscious realm of women's sexuality and sensuality (Stone-Blackburn, "Maenadic" 29–30) that links its work with that of the other companies under consideration and with the experimental work of feminist performance artists outside Canada, the best known of whom are Holly Hughes and Karen Finley.[36]

Nancy Copeland has argued that this mandate and process resulted in an effective dramaturgical structure or "genre" and created the space for a celebratory construction of female subjectivity. Structurally, *Aphra* is most notable for its collagelike mixing of styles and character types and its deployment of a nonlinear, retrospective chronology. The three women of the cast play a range of male and female characters, those from Behn's life mixed with the allegorical figures of Morality Man and Woman, a mummer's play-style quack doctor, and characters from Behn's own plays, scenes of which are included in the script. The actors occasionally but not consistently wear masks, sometimes employ direct address, and mix seventeenth-century prose and verse — some of it Behn's own — with twentieth-century slang ("you're altogether too lippy" [p. 58]), sometimes keeping the various conventions and time frames discrete, sometimes talking across them.

There is an awkward quality to some of this and occasionally a self-defeating earnestness that perhaps derives from a sense of historical and aesthetic distance, but the overall effect is not so much the *representation* of female subjectivity as its exuberant collective *embodiment* in a dramaturgically fragmented whole that is nevertheless more than the sum of its parts. And, if *Aphra* falls short of fulfilling the company's promise of Maenadic rites in a celebration of woman-centred sexuality, it nevertheless valorizes women's desire and points toward the similar validation of a "feminine" erotics.

This Is for You, Anna is an earlier play that first emerged from the context of Toronto's feminist Nightwood Theatre in a twenty-minute version in 1984; after workshops at the Factory Theatre in Toronto and Playwrights' Workshop Montreal, it was produced in full-length versions at various theatres, women's shelters, community centres, and alternative spaces throughout 1984–85 and first published in *Canadian Theatre Review* in 1985. The play is rightly celebrated, produced, and taught at schools and universities as one of the most powerful plays to have emerged from the collective movement as it evolved in Toronto in the 1970s and early 1980s. Part of that power derives from the raw conviction with which the play speaks, achieving the authenticity (through shared rage?) that *Aphra* seems to lack. *This Is for You, Anna* shares with performance art a foregrounded sense that, whatever is *represented*, the performers never "act," never stop playing themselves, however multiply; it shares with traditional collective creations the sense of the performers' *investment* in the material — the sense that they never cease to speak their own research, experiences, and convictions.

Like Theatre Passe Muraille's collectives, *This Is for You, Anna* began with a document, in this case a newspaper clipping about a German woman, Marianne Bachmeier, who entered a crowded courtroom in 1980 and killed Klaus Grabowski, who was on trial for molesting and murdering her daughter, Anna, saying, "I did it for you, Anna" ("Mother"). Unlike the Passe Muraille collectives, however, *This Is for You, Anna* does not exploit the documentary nature of its source material to root the action in claims to factual accuracy. On the contrary, in introducing the production as "The Story of Marianne Bachmeier," the company sets up parallels with the fairy-tale "Story of Agate" and the mythical "Story of Lucretia," which it also stages, to shift its narrative *outside* the realm of the merely factual.[37] Moreover, the play fractures any merely linear narrative account of Bachmeier's history — together with linear grammatical structures, unified subjectivity, semiotic referentiality (see Wilson, "Politics" 178), and unified or consistent generic shape or aesthetic style — to purposively and transformatively veer off into a series of complexly linked "riffs" on the subjects of violence, victimization, and the construction of (gendered) subjectivities.

The major structural features of the script as published, beyond the jazzlike sense of associative improvisation on a theme, are the imagistic contextual poles that juxtapose contemporary women's culture — here associated with mothering and milk, laundry and kitchens, talk shows and girls' stories — with such masculinist and phallic images as courtrooms, guns, and, notably, nails.

The play's mutually reinforcing disruptions of narrative and grammatical linearity, unified subjectivity, stylistic/generic consistency, and one-to-one referentiality are pervasive and connected by an equally pervasive structural motif of transformation. None of the play's many stories is told without being transformed in the telling (or without telling of transformation), as when the Lucretia myth, told in part as a bedtime story, largely in the language of contemporary "women's fiction" and accompanied by music from *Carmen*, Debussy, and *Ben Hur*, is interrupted by personal responses, fragments of dreams, lines from other women's tragedies, and objections from some of the multiple narrators, Alicia, Allegra, Amarantha, and Arabella. Similarly, the onstage transformations of actor into character after character, role after role, together with the representation of Marianne Bachmeier by each of the performers at the same time or in sequence, refuse the identification of actor with "character" on which traditional types of (responsibility-evading) empathy depend and suggest the transformative potential of the construction of character and role, in life as in theatre. The result is that the socially constructed chains that lock women into a narrow range of appropriately "feminine" roles are exposed, denaturalized, and deconstructed through transformative and performative modes of representation. "The Story of Marianne," through the use of such devices, together with the collective's refusal to let it settle into a single controlling generic shape or tone, resists the status of unitary or totalizing parable as effectively as it resists dismissal as exceptional. Like the multiplicitous symbolism of milk, nails, and other things, it suggests the liberatory potential of multiplied and transformative representation and signification.[38] The final image of Marianne 3, illuminated only by backlighting from the open refrigerator, filling a glass with milk until it spills and splatters on the stage floor, is lyrically compelling, semiotically and symbolically (versus phenomenologically[39]) in excess, and stimulatingly open ended. Provocative.

The ultimate effect of *This Is for You, Anna*, much to the surprise of audiences and reviewers who expected the expression and representation of retaliatory women's rage in a play subtitled *A Spectacle of Revenge*, was less of satisfyingly cathartic closure than of the liberatingly multiplicitous and empowering assumption of women's (and others') subjectivities — what Filewod calls "both an expression of subjectivity and a process of discovering a feminist performance vocabulary" (Introduction xvi), in life as in theatre.

The most structurally challenging and politically disruptive of the works under discussion here is *Mary Medusa*, by Shawna Dempsey and Lorri Millan, first performed (in its first version) in Winnipeg in 1992. Although their work has been performed and exhibited in theatres as well as in galleries, on film, and in various alternative spaces — Susan Bennett remarks that "they, more than any other artists I have encountered, seek out the non-traditional viewer" (41) — Dempsey and Millan describe it as "feminist, costume-based performance art" (43). As such, their work attempts to circumvent the authority of *logos*, much as the early work of Nightwood Theatre took its inspiration from the visual arts, or the creators of *Aphra* began with the exploration of a *space*, by kick-starting from physical productions — costumes — that derive from a realm traditionally gendered female and that, because of their physicality and tactility, enable a bypassing of the merely textual and cerebral. In *Mary Medusa*, these productions notably included the lacy wedding dress of the hitchhiking bride and above all the gloriously goofy but indeterminately iconic and omnipresent head of the Medusa.

Mary Medusa, which Dempsey and Millan describe as a "media and performance piece" (43), like parts of *This Is for You, Anna*, is of course also inspired by received classical legend, and like both *Anna* and *Aphra* it concerns itself with deconstructing and revisioning the subject positions available to contemporary women. With the exception of one small role — that of Athena, played by Sharon Bajer, in the Slide and Taped Audio component — "all of the characters referred to are the Medusa, performed by Shawna Dempsey" (43). This wonderfully complex confusion of character, role, essence ("*are* the Medusa"), and performance is further complicated by the fact that, structurally and generically, *Mary Medusa* combines three media pieces, five short performances, and one book, each part designed to exist autonomously as well as in combination with the others, and the whole presented as a work (always) in progress. The parts include a ten-minute videotape (with audio text and written text) called "Medusa Raw," which is framed by a fiddle rendition of "The Beauty Waltz" and images of Medusa as priest and Medusa crucified; a sequence of performances with slides, a video camera, taped audio pieces, a jewellery box, and *"a large chocolate cake"* (46); and "A Testimonial," an ancillary piece in book form that tells a contemporary Medusa story as autobiography (54–57).

The effect of the juxtaposition of genres and media, of course, is to problematize representation itself, as the open manipulation of slide and video imagery combines with the outrageousness of the performed images and actions and the cross-commentary offered by visual and audio text refuses to allow easy acceptance of *any* representation as natural, objective, or disinterested. This is particularly true of sequences in which the snaky head of "the" Medusa, the "actor" who performs all of the show's roles, appears perched atop classical columns and caryatids or floats free-standing, a pointedly disembodied "figure" on a black ground. And, as Lynda Hall argues,

> A head "floating" in the dark spaces, Dempsey evokes contempo-
> rary notions of the fluidity of identities in the process of becoming,
> and interrogates apparently transparent and evidently fixed, stable
> subject positions that reinforce heterosexual hegemony, with
> woman viewed as body and most encumbered by nature. (12)

But the major structural trope of *Mary Medusa*, in terms of charac-
ter/role/performance/subjectivity, of narrative, and of genre/form/
structure, is transformation configured as "transgression, a losing of
control" (Dempsey and Millan 44), and inscribed in the female body,
even when, as in much of *Mary Medusa*, it isn't there: after all, as
Medusa in one (dis)embodiment confides, although "a woman without
a body lacks a certain amount of sex appeal," "Being without a body is
the closest I've come to having the perfect figure. . . . [Y]ou're damned
if you do and damned if you don't. Have a body" (49). As Susan
Bennett notes about all of Dempsey and Millan's work, *Mary Medusa*

> explores and exposes those systems of exchange in which the
> female body has functioned as the currency for its Other's power
> and as the material evidence for a stability of reference to the so-
> called objective world. What Dempsey's on-stage body enacts are
> the scripts and directions that dominant cultural practice writes
> for female bodies. These scripts and directions are never, in
> Dempsey and Millan's work, performed uncritically; instead they
> are played unequivocally for their contradictions and resistances.
> (37)

In the words of Jill Dolan, writing of lesbian performer Sande Zeig, Dempsey's body "becomes a political palimpsest of experience and resistance" (*Presence* 142). And, I would suggest, of potential social transformation. This is authentication through the now "marked" body and embodied performance/experience (Phelan, *Unmarked* 3 and passim) — though indeterminately and transgressively so[40] — that is of an altogether different and more sophisticated kind than the Lacanian-phallic myth of presence represented in and by Theatre Passe Muraille's *I Love You, Baby Blue*. Here (feminist) representation is itself *configured* as transformation and transgression — including Medusa's ability to transform men into stones and the potential for "appetite" (or desire) to lead "us" to transgress:

> What if we no longer control, or worse yet, lose control our-selves? What if we "lose it" and turn our heads and each of our snakey [sic] locks against the *status quo* economics, sexual politics, and morality?
>
> Well, it could get messy. . . . (Dempsey and Millan 42)

4

The Unity in Community
(with Edward Little)

The audience gathered at the old town hall in Rockwood and walked from there along a tree-lined path by the river to the ruins of the Harris mill. Along the way, they saw historically costumed figures paddling canoes, emerging from caves, or haranguing them with grievances. Once at the mill, they found themselves part of a country fair, with music, crafts, refreshments, and a lively auction that began with farm implements but ended with the announcement that the township itself would be on the block at evening's end. The crowd then moved to an open space to watch moments in their township's history reenacted on, around, under, and above surrounding platforms. There actors mingled with, pushed through, or shouted from among the assembled crowd. The action, using styles that ranged from puppetry to polemic, focused on 1837, the Mackenzie rebellion, and the story of the so-called Rockwood Rebels. The play granted Mackenzie himself status as an exemplary citizen and thereby connected the cause of the rebellion of 1837 to the proposed "Rebellion of 1990": a community response to the pressures of suburbanization and exploitative land development.[1] For the play's last sequence, the crowd was led deeply into the mill ruins. There they mingled closely with the actors at a town-hall-style debate about development, conservation, and the future of the township. The evening ended with a song.

The Spirit of Shivaree, written for and about the community of Eramosa by Dale Colleen Hamilton, a fifth-generation citizen of the southern Ontario township, was performed by the community itself in the summer of 1990 at the site of the historic Harris Woollen Mill on the banks of the Eramosa River, and it represents a different kind of collective/collaborative structure and process than those of the plays examined so far, along with a different approach to theatrical and historical time. It was greeted by the regional press as Canada's first community play. That the show's producers had advertised it more specifically as the first community play in Canada using the Colway Theatre Trust process, a model developed in Britain in the late 1970s and early 1980s,[2] made as little difference to reporters and entertainment editors as did the long history in Canada of community-oriented theatre. That history extends from civic and historical pageantry in the early twentieth century through the workers' theatre movement of the 1930s to the collaborative and collective creations of "localist" theatre companies such as Passe Muraille, 25th Street, NDWT, Mulgrave Road, and the Mummers Troupe and artists such as James Reaney, Rick Salutin, and David Fennario in the 1970s and 1980s.[3] It is ironic but not insignificant that, in a theatrical terrain in which a sense of place, local history, and community solidarity are deeply rooted values, the first use of an imported model of this type of theatre, with its accompanying suggestion of authentication through external validation (including the participation in script-development workshops of "outside" professionals such as Fennario and Salutin), should be celebrated as a landmark of and focus for local pride.

Local pride is one thing that the community play is designed to foster, and it is accomplished through what Julian Hilton calls "rites of intensification" (60) — the celebration, representation, and reification of a community that demonstrates its worth both as the creator/producer of the play and as the object of dramatic representation. Community, however, often defines itself by what it excludes, and the celebration and reification of this process can also lead to an unhealthy kind of xenophobia and an entrenched conservatism. Hilton points to other aspects of community theatre, then, that he calls "rites of passage" (60), which have less to do with affirmation of the community as it is currently constituted or understood than with social change, cultural intervention, or community advocacy in the face of a threatening or dominant Other. In Canada, this Other often means a large metropolitan centre, as it did in the Eramosa project, in which "traditional rural values" were pitted against the stereotypical unscrupulousness of developers and bankers from Toronto. It is along the continuum from an essentially conservative cultural affirmation (the solidification of community identity and values) to cultural intervention (the activist initiation of social change) that the community play locates itself as a site of negotiation in the ongoing construction of community defined as a process.[4]

★   ★   ★

The construction of community, or community understood as a process rather than as a stable entity, is implicated in what social theorist Derek Phillips describes as the difference between "territorial" communities, which are defined primarily by geopolitical boundaries, and "relational" communities, which are defined by the nature and quality of interrelationships between a membership with shared interests (12). Relational communities exist, in varying degrees, as, within, and across territorial ones. The tension between coexisting territorial and relational communities is an important factor in understanding the community play as a site of negotiation between cultural affirmation (rites of intensification) and social intervention (rites of passage). If territorial communities tend to carry with them the received values of shared history inscribed in the definition of place over time, then relational communities (while often also sharing histories and values) are more likely to be concerned with issues of common interest such as shared activity, recognition, empowerment, and social change.

Distinctions between territorial and relational notions of community have other implications for the community play as well. Power in our society is often territorially defined (through land ownership, municipal and regional governments, and so on); however, apart from moving out or in, membership in territorial communities is nonvoluntary. As Phillips points out, both membership and values in territorial communities are often "inherited" in the sense that many members become implicated in the traditions and practices of their communities "*before* they are able to explicitly recognize and reflect on what they have in common" (14). Yet, compared with more voluntary forms of association, the implicit hegemony of this unquestioned and unquestionable "inheritance" must also be considered against the fact that territorial communities inevitably include a much more heterogeneous membership than is usually the case for communities based on common interests. Relational communities, at least those that are not racially, ethnically, or otherwise prescribed, are more likely to be determined by voluntary participation in the *process* of community and its actively and intentionally evolving identity.

Community participation, together with the primacy of process over product, is what best distinguishes the community play from other kinds of theatrical activity that take community as their subject, and for this reason we have decided to begin our discussion in this chapter with an analysis of the nature of that participation and that process rather than with the more usual critical account of the script or performance text as product. For it is community process that provides the deep structure of the Colway-style community play and fundamentally shapes the script, the performance text, the experience of the audience, and the play's meaning.

In Colway-style community plays, eliciting participation is a principal element in the two-year process of creation. These plays are generally rural in setting and subject, and they routinely involve a "core" group of professionals, usually from outside the community (director, designer, playwright, production manager, etc.), a cast of one to two hundred community members, plus hundreds more in various aspects of organization, administration, research, script development, and production. Colway sees its work as creating theatre not only *for* but also, more importantly, *with* a community. Footage from the video *Dignity and Grace: The Story of the Eramosa Community Play* The Spirit of Shivaree[5] (see Fox and Hamilton) reveals considerable concern at a meeting of the professional "core" about "letting go" and the "humbling" process of letting the community "take ownership." The rewards of the process, unlike those of more traditional theatre, are less likely to be aesthetic or artistic than social or cultural, and they are consistently articulated by the participants in the rhetoric of mutual support, solidarity, and renewal of community.

The emphasis on broadly based community involvement in (almost) all aspects of process and performance — Colway teams use the term "inclusivity" — distinguishes what we are calling "the community play," as practised by Colway, Reaney (in *King Whistle*), or their pageantic predecessors, from the larger body of what we have termed "community-oriented" theatre.[6] Most often in community-oriented forms a comparatively small group of theatre artists or workers creates a theatrical representation of and for the larger, "host" community, holding, as it were, a mirror up to the community as a rallying point for community concern. In the Mummers Troupe's production of *Gros Mourn*, for example, the company visited a Newfoundland community in crisis over the appropriation of its land for the creation of a national park. The company engaged in an intensive creation/rehearsal process within the community and quickly mounted an interventionist production that served to focus and express the protests of the residents of Sally's Cove (see Chris Brookes 78–96). In *Gros Mourn* and similar productions predicated on relational notions of community beyond geopolitical boundaries, cultural intervention often extends overtly to encompass community empowerment within larger social, political, and legislative structures. The Mummers Troupe in Sally's Cove; Black Rock Theatre in working-class, English-speaking Montreal; Theatre Passe Muraille in Clinton, Ontario; Cahoots Theatre Projects in the "multicultural" community of Toronto; or Buddies in Bad Times in the gay and lesbian community of that city — all share an insistence that the hitherto marginalized community represented in the play gain voice and agency within the larger social structure. The theatre, to use Tony Howard's term, functions as a "mouthpiece" (43). In this regard, all community theatre workers, both as "communities" of performers and as representatives of a host community, may be seen as functioning along lines described by Raymond Williams, for whom communities and other forms of association are "the necessary mediating element between individuals and large Society" (*Long Revolution* 95). In this formulation, theatre companies, which are in but not entirely of the community, serve as the shifting fissures or "faultlines" around which change can be negotiated (see Sinfield, *Faultlines*). To a lesser extent, the professional core plays this role in the Colway-style community play.

While community-oriented theatre in general tends to be situated on a shifting border between localist and nationalist concerns, then, the community play's emphasis on celebration and broad community involvement makes it the most localist of the community-oriented forms. Although the community play may become regionally or even nationally interventionist,[7] it is primarily concerned with relational notions of community insofar as they exist within the project's territorially defined boundaries. From the perspective of the community play, Williams's "larger Society," at least initially, does not extend beyond the territorially defined community. The community play as a "form of association," through its relatively vast size, protracted two-year process, and emphasis on empowerment through participation, situates its *participants* as the mediators in a process of publicly defining the community to be celebrated and, perhaps, changed.[8] The potential insularity of this focus on community is reflected in the words of John Oram, director of the Colway Theatre Trust and *The Spirit of Shivaree*, who says in the *Dignity and Grace* documentary that the community play process "feels a bit like a war, drawing people together. In a war you know who your enemies are. In the community play you know who your friends are" (Fox and Hamilton).

Initially, the principal elements that the community play uses to draw people together are the "inherited" notions of shared territory, history, and values. Once involved, the "community" of participants, both in their role as mediators and through participation in the various structures and processes of the play, present for their larger society not only a play that demonstrates behaviour and ideals constructed as exemplary but also an exemplary community structure. As Hamilton herself expresses it in *Dignity and Grace*, and as the "Landscape Architect" puts it in the final scene of the play, "Eramosa Township could be a model" (78).

To this end, in both process and product, the community play adheres to what Phillips describes as the "communitarian ideal" (10). According to him, this concept of community depends on four central characteristics: "a common geographical territory or locale, a common history and shared values, widespread political participation [through collective activity], and a high degree of moral solidarity" (14). The first two characteristics, because of their relationship to "inherited" elements of community, can be considered to be "conceptual" and to be implicated primarily in the *form* and *content* of the community play as product. However, the specific nature of these geographical and historical elements is also subject to a *process* of selection and negotiation. These conceptual elements play a foundational role as an initial rallying point for community consensus and participation, and they are a particular concern of the small group involved early in the process. And, as Colway leaders tend to point out, community support is facilitated by the early involvement of "shakers and movers." They tend to be established and influential community leaders with some history of community representation.

Territory, history, established residency, and representation (in the electoral sense) tend to present an image of community in preconceived conceptual terms. The community play process, however, by emphasizing the second two characteristics noted by Phillips (shared activity and moral solidarity), moderates the tendency of territory and history to control the definition of the "shared values" that the play celebrates. These last two characteristics, which can be seen to be primarily processual, are most directly implicated in the community play's creative and communal *process*.

On the culturally affirmative hand, solidarity, creativity, collective cultural expression, and creative play *are* constructed and celebrated by Colway as exemplary behaviour in the model community. In addition, the focus on "what best serves the play" (Oram) fosters the two elements that Phillips sees as constitutive of "solidarity": a sense of social interdependence, and a sense of belonging. On the other hand, such solidarity (to the extent that it focuses on relational aspects of community) also provides the possibility for reconfiguration within the community across class and other lines. It does so through the encouragement of collective activity in the development of networks, communication, and cultural skills; through the experience of working toward common goals in groupings that may transgress the community's implicit social boundaries; and through the celebration of both personal creativity within a cultural process and pride in shared accomplishments.

In addition, the community play offers its participants various opportunities for contributing to its creative and decision-making process through public meetings, community events, theatre skills workshops, and formal policies such as "inclusivity" and "democratization." Inclusivity insists that no one who wishes to participate is to be excluded. Democratization is implemented through a central steering committee and various subcommittees. The steering committee, principally composed of "shakers and movers," is charged with policy making. It is the core of community representation, and it largely controls the conceptual notions of community to be represented. In the interests of community empowerment and autonomy, Colway recommends that no member of the professional core sit on this committee (though in the case of *The Spirit of Shivaree*, in which the playwright was a member of the community, she did serve on the steering committee). Each of the numerous subcommittees is headed by a member of the steering committee, and subcommittee members are in turn encouraged to solicit additional support and membership. Subcommittees deal with results-producing functions such as historical research, fundraising, promotion, and the solicitation and coordination of volunteers. A primary goal of the committee structure is to spread the organizational and practical load of the project quickly, while encouraging the broadest possible range of community participation. The number and size of the subcommittees are limited only by the community's willingness to participate. In this regard, a primary strategy of the Colway process is to solicit support from existing community groups, clubs, and organizations, which then encourage participation from their memberships.[9]

But if the community play's process lays the foundation for building "the unity in community," as well as for reconfiguring the boundaries within that community, then its protracted duration and hierarchical control of conceptual elements also provide ample time for conservative forces — the status quo of community power, privilege, and stability — to organize, exercise traditional leadership skills, and assert hegemony. The possibility of cultural intervention in the community play rests in large part, then, with its processual potential for reconstruction and reconsideration of what community means. But its capacity to contain that intervention comfortably, to hold it in check, rests in large part with the degree to which the community play as a theatrical product, through its focus on landscape and history, has tended to define community in terms of the historical continuity deriving from the stabilizing influence of place over time. A community play uses documented and conjectural history to tell and retell stories to and about its territorial community, and in the Colway model this territorial focus is considered an essential element in community building. On a practical level, focusing on and celebrating "the land" and associated values foreground "community spirit" and thus work to elicit participation and help ensure that the play's representation of the community is noncontroversial. On a fundamentally conservative pedagogical level, in telling its story a community play is involved in both remembering and constructing a collective past that, by emphasizing continuity, builds and reinforces what Benedict Anderson calls an "imagined community" or, in communitarian terms, a "community of memory."[10]

A community of memory engenders solidarity and the continuance of "inherited" values by "retelling its story, its constitutive narrative, and in so doing . . . offers examples of the men and women who have embodied and exemplified the meaning of the community" (Bellah et al. 153). In the case of Rockwood and Eramosa township, the essential and essentially conservative values to be shared — "family and land and heritage" — were depicted as spanning centuries and therefore as being common to exemplary pioneers and contemporary residents alike (Hamilton 83). Through consensus over land stewardship, preservation of farmland, and a willingness to fight for issues of control, the land was reified as a principal mediating element between old and new settler and between heterogeneous community groups. As the character Mackenzie puts it, "It's nice to know that some things never change" (76).

The Rockwood project was first conceived as a response to issues of land control, and it is not incidental that the script of *The Spirit of*

Shivaree is dedicated not only "to those past and present who call Eramosa home" but also "to the land." Nor is it surprising that many of the most resonant moments in the community plays that have been mounted in Canada have been about this conjunction of landscape and history, in which landscape somehow contains (in both senses of the word) history, including future histories. When news of the Mackenzie rebellion came to the world of *The Spirit of Shivaree* by way of sentinels posted at the tops of the limestone cliffs that border the river and the playing space, it created a stir among the characters and a chill among members of an audience for whom the historical "feel" of the occasion was immediate and poignant. Even more poignant, and more potentially constraining as the dead hand of the past, was the ghostly presence of ancestral characters — pioneer rebels and their families, including Mackenzie — looming in the windows of the mill ruins, presiding over the proceedings as the voices of history that have, in Bellah et al.'s terms, "embodied and exemplified the meaning of the community."

This documentary-style "authentication" and reification of received and reproduced (as opposed to re-created or revisionist) history and its emotional affirmation of the continuity of territorial community over time is reinforced in the play's tendency to ritualize history. *The Spirit of Shivaree* and the other community plays produced in Canada have engaged their audiences as participants in historical pageants, processions, and parades that have preceded and punctuated them. Each of these plays has employed evocative historical icons that again tend to function as conservative, affirmative, and stabilizing forces in the production of value and meaning. These iconic moments are often accompanied by lyrical ballads, marches, anthems, and choruses that reinforce a communal and unifying sense of shared past and present purpose, evoking, at the same time, a familiar resonance of civic boosterism and local pride.

The use of landscape as the unchanging repository of history and value is also inscribed in the historical bodies of actors who, in the case of the Rockwood play, were cast to play their own ancestors. When Richard Lay played his great-great-grandfather, William Lyon Mackenzie,[11] particularly in scenes set in the present, in which he presided over the interpretation of his past and its meaning for the township's future, the privileging of bloodlines revealed an essentialist notion of identity and a fetishizing of ancestral descent that were essentially conservative, whatever the intentions of the show's creators.

At one point in the performance, moreover, Mackenzie clearly elided past and present for both the audience and the ancestrally cast actors when he claimed that "I would never have made it to the border alive without the aid and assistance of country people such as *are* gathered *here tonight*" (emphasis added).[12] This erasure of historical difference, combined with the fact that the play-making process is consensual, noncontentious, and therefore generalizing, again meant that the interventionist potential of the process tended to be subsumed in the role of community empowerment (see Little and Sim 58).

The interventionist potential of the historical narrative of *The Spirit of Shivaree* — a story of armed rebellion — and of the fact that the play's central heroes — the "Rockwood Rebels" and Mackenzie himself — were advocates of violent revolution, then, was safely contained for the audience by the reassuring icons of continuity embodied in the use of familiar landscapes, faces, and names. And of course neither Mackenzie nor any other of the play's rebels carried a gun.

★   ★   ★

The play's use of landscape, history, and dramatic form were not exclusively conservative, however, and, though its interventionist potential was held in check to some extent, the play can nevertheless be seen, even as a theatrical product, to have served in several ways as a site of negotiation for social change. Even its employment of historical narrative is less clearly or simply affirmative than may at first appear. The history on which the play most frequently draws is less the traditional, official, or national history of the acts of great men than an explicitly revisionist and localist social history, often popular history, in which Mackenzie, for example, can cite what "the history books don't tell you" (Hamilton 56). Town and county histories, the records of community groups, local newspapers, Lion's clubs and women's auxiliaries, even residents' attics, were scoured as repositories of local history. *The Spirit of Shivaree*, in fact, stages a debate at the outset of the action in which versions and ownership of history are contested. A scene in which a lecture on history by Sir Francis Bond Head, governor of Upper Canada, speaking from what would be called in a medieval mystery cycle a *locus*, or scene-specific symbolic platform above the crowd, is interrupted by a woman who argues, speaking in French from the *platea*, or public playing area that she shares with the audience as populace, that "God doesn't only speak English and . . . history didn't begin when the white men came."[13] In response to her claim that Bond Head "got the story wrong," the governor replies that he is "talking about history, not stories," to which she replies that "stories are histories and histories are stories" before she is silenced by an armed guard in an overt exercise of historical power (9). This sequence explicitly demonstrates not only that "history" as story is ideologically constructed and coded but also that to control history is to exercise power. The scene also works to demystify that power and render it contestable.

The site at which power is *made* contestable is the community play itself. The play's carnivalesque eclecticism of genres, styles, and voices demystifies any representational realism and gives the audience a democratic role in reconstructing the history of its own community, as opposed to a stake in the reproduction of a dominant myth of "identity" (and in the suspension of its own disbelief).[14] As celebratory pageant rubs shoulders with documentary agit-prop, and as declamatory rhetoric mixes with sentimental melodrama and scenes of sit-com silliness, the audience is encouraged actively to engage in its own purposeful history making and to negotiate its past and future histories in a market-place of open debate and exchange.

History, however, is not the only fissure opened for contestation by the community play in general or *The Spirit of Shivaree* in particular. Community plays tend to attract as participants a preponderance of women, and since traditional histories typically relegate women to oblivion, or at best to supporting roles, playwrights and directors must of necessity, if not by design, create opportunities for women to participate through one or more of the examination and excavation of women's roles in history; the invention of unrecorded roles for women in the plays; and the cross-casting of women in men's roles. Each option has its own interventionist potential in a patriarchal culture, and each was exercised in *The Spirit of Shivaree*. Dale Hamilton was conscious in writing the script of the job of recovering women's lives and histories. As she says in *Dignity and Grace*, "that was a very deliberate act on my part, to remind people that there were women there. And when the men were off meeting or being thrown in jail, they [the women] were holding . . . things together" (Fox and Hamilton). This process of recovery, in fact, extended to the invention of a nonhistorical character, "Ensa Cameron," who, like Hamilton herself in 1990, provides an activist voice for change in the represented community of 1837. During the scene depicting the township meeting of the "Rockwood Rebels," the men resolve to "go directly to the Centre Inn Tavern and therewithin commence to mind our own business" (Hamilton 36). Ensa is the only woman to attend the "political meeting." It is she who objects to the resolution and proposes action, and it is she who hides the fleeing Mackenzie under her skirts when he apocryphally passes through Rockwood en route to Navy Island. Ensa, then, plays a powerful woman's role in the play and represents an explicit example of revisionist history.

Equally effective in the revisioning of women's roles in society was the casting of women to play male roles in the play, perhaps most notably the roles of the British soldiers who patrolled the *platea*, intimidated the audience, and arrested the rebels. As actor and production coordinator Janet MacLeod said in the video documentary of the project, "for women to become the vehicles of power like that . . . was quite a new experience" (Fox and Hamilton).

The experience of empowerment for the actors, of course, was central to the play as process, but the casting of women as soldiers was part of another potential intervention effected by *The Spirit of Shivaree*. Among its most effective and disruptive devices, in fact, was the blurring of the lines between character and actor and between actor and spectator. This blurring was effected in part by the use of cross-casting, masks, and emblematic costuming, in part by the mixing of contemporary and period costuming and clothing, and in part by the use of the *platea*, the temporally and spatially shifting public arena at the centre of the playing area where "the people," past and present, actors, characters, and spectators, contested and negotiated histories, values, and visions of the future. At one point, the action is interrupted by an actor/character who claims, "I don't want to be in this play anymore. I don't like the part they gave me" (Hamilton 64). Later, in a complex conflation of both historical time and theatrical role, a certain "Bill Mackenzie," in the "ah, fertilizer business," recognizably "played by" the historical character, William Lyon Mackenzie, in turn played by his great-great-grandson, says, "I suggest that *you* hold a public meeting, right here, as soon as this play is over, and that *we* face these issues head on" (emphasis added). When the imagined *"crowd"* agrees, the character comments to the "real" *audience*, "Me again. You didn't think I'd miss a good uprising, did you?" (66).

Among the most interesting and effective moments in the play is a series of "contemporary vignettes," as they are called in the script. They are presented as public testimonials spoken from a variety of community perspectives by a seventh-generation man, a farm mother, a subdivision mother, a newcomer, a commuter, and so on, while "the characters were taking off costumes, applying modern makeup, accessories, etc." (60).[15]

This use of the play as a site for public and popular debate was made explicit when the action and the audience moved to the interior of the mill for the final, town-hall sequence, which rounded out the framework initiated by the fair, auction, and marketplace of the opening sequences and returned the play to the people. If one of the virtues of the community play process was, as John Oram says in *Dignity and Grace*, that it "resulted in cast members talking about the issues involved" (Fox and Hamilton), then the performance, serving as a kind of carnivalesque marketplace of contesting versions of what the play's closing song celebrates as "home," provoked the same debate within the larger community.

The fair with which *The Spirit of Shivaree* opened is a standard feature of the Colway-style play, but in this case it provided something more, as a framework, than the usual opportunity for broad participation, some fundraising, and a smooth transition into the play proper. Culminating as it did in a theatricalized auction, the opening sequence framed the entire play within the context of community celebration as commercial exchange. Initially, items such as a communally produced quilt (now itself a historical artifact) were auctioned off, but capital investment (represented by the developer, "Newman," with his dark glasses and cellular phone) soon replaced "fair" dealing: "Merle and Gordon Cameron," local residents, were outrageously outbid for a much-needed pickle jar by Newman, who planned to use it as a decorative umbrella stand. The marketplace had highjacked the fair.

If *The Spirit of Shivaree* presented itself, then, as a carnivalesque and celebratory mingling of people, styles, and genres (as a fair), then it did so in full consciousness that carnivalesque play occurs within a public place, *platea*, or "market square" that exists within and is dependent upon lines of economic force that are external to it. In this case, these lines included "fair market value" for pickle jars, antiques, and agricultural land that farmers can no longer afford. In fact, the fair is highjacked, as local fairs always are, by a marketplace over which the community has little control. As Peter Stallybrass and Allon White note,

> The tangibility of its boundaries implies a local closure and stability, even a unique sense of belonging, which obscure its structural

dependence upon a "beyond" through which this "familiar" and "local" feeling is itself produced. . . . It is a place where limit, centre and boundary are confirmed and yet also put in jeopardy. (28)

They go on to say that "It is a gravely over-simplifying abstraction . . . to conceptualize the fair purely as the site of communal celebration," and they point, finally, to "the deep conceptual confusion entailed by the fair's inmixing of work and pleasure, trade and play," as a source of anxiety for "the bourgeois classes" and implicitly as a potential source of social change (30).

Among the definitions of "shivaree" (or "charivari") in *The Oxford English Dictionary* is "a babel of noise," and *The Spirit of Shivaree* can be seen as such a babel. As both process and product, it can be seen to serve as a carnivalesque marketplace at which community celebration becomes a bargaining site for the negotiation of values. These fluid and contesting values in the community play are represented by its rites of intensification, on the one hand, and its (internally generated and externally imposed) rites of passage, on the other; by notions of community that are territorially and/or relationally defined; and by tension between cultural *affirmation* and continuity based on conservative notions of history and landscape and cultural *intervention* based on a politics of social change. Perhaps "a babel of noise" is a less accurate description of the community play, however, than a babel of voices, *sharing* a territory and engaged in the ongoing process of imagining and *building* there a relational community of common interest.

5

Replaying History

History is always in practice a reading of the past. We make a narrative out of the available "documents", the written texts (and maps and buildings and suits of armour) we interpret in order to produce a knowledge of a world which is no longer present. And yet it is always from the present that we produce this knowledge: from the present in the sense that it is only from what is still extant, still available, that we make it; and from the present in the sense that we make it out of an understanding formed by the present. We bring what we know now to bear on what remains from the past to produce an intelligible history.

— Catherine Belsey (1)

Today we are already elsewhere.

— Michel de Certeau, *Writing* (33)

HISTORIOGRAPHERS and literary theorists in recent decades have concerned themselves with the writing of history less as the uncovering of an objective body of material actually existing in the past than as the construction of a narrative that exists as a function of the society that produces it.[1] Current models of historiography recognize that the past, insofar as it is external and objective, can only exist as fragments, "facts," and documents that are, in their own cultural terms, impenetrable. They recognize, that is, that "truth" inheres not in the facticity or actuality of events but in the ways in which "we" understand them and construct their histories. This is not to deny that facts exist outside narratives but to emphasize the difficulty of interpreting and acting on them once they pass into discourse. Historical representations, including theatrical ones, nevertheless frame social memory, shaping and reshaping a culture's sense of its past and altering ongoing individual and collective social memory. At its best, contemporary history writing recognizes that every "received" historical fact has been shaped and reshaped from conflicting imaginations, mental projections, and mappings that bear particular cultural, ideological, and political inscriptions. Such writing acknowledges and incorporates into its analysis an understanding of history as necessarily conditioned by an accumulation of the ideologies, assumptions, and (conscious or unconscious) interests of recording and interpreting consciousnesses from both the present and the intervening past. Historiography, then, becomes the ongoing process of *re*making history, of "making it new," as fiction or as myth, and therefore of shaping a culture's pasts, present, *and future.*

While historiographers have concentrated on the instability of history, literary and cultural theorists and writers of fiction have been exploring the instability of literary and other *texts.* Contemporary literary theorists have discussed the cultural specificity of interpretive acts, the role of the reader in the creation of texts, asserting that the meaning of a text locates itself in the act of reading (in an ever-shifting present) rather than in the text as objective and stable artifact. Meanwhile, writers of historical fiction have foregrounded within their works the acts of writing and reading, using metafictional self-consciousness to highlight the reader's active role in the interpretive re-creation of history.

For many Canadian writers of "historiographic metafiction" (see Hutcheon, "Canadian Historiographic Metafiction"), theories about the instability of history and of text have been particularly appealing and liberating, and their critics have responded to the new self-consciousness with equally self-conscious sympathy. Interestingly, however, while Canadian playwrights and theatre collectives have for many years been making use of self-reflexive, metadramatic forms in ways that highlight the instability of both history and dramatic texts, most Canadian drama and theatre critics, intent on purely thematic issues and on the supposed *construction* of national myths through drama (see Carson, "Canadian"; and Rubin), have been slow to respond to deconstructionist Canadian plays on historical subjects as historiographic metadrama.

But theatre practitioners have always been aware of the instability of the theatrical event where the re-creation *is* the (performance) text, of the need to "make it new" with and for each new audience each night, and of the fact that each member of each audience constructs a different text. For theatre workers, then, the new historiography, and the new self-consciousness about history as construction, are not so new. Ever since Shakespeare and his contemporaries invented the chronicle history play in the late sixteenth century (out of the ashes of the medieval mystery cycles), the re-creation of history on the stage has frequently represented the past metatheatrically through dramaturgical structures that function dialogically as negotiations between present enactments and the documentary "facts," acts, and artifacts on which they are based. These plays, moreover, have often included explorations of the concept of the historical persona as one whose historical "acts" and whose "role" in history gain their significance from their audiences and from their self-conscious theatricality rather than from essentialist or individualist notions of human character. Shakespeare explores in his history plays such paratheatrical things as ritual, role playing, the performative nature of speech, and the relationship between the historical act and theatrical enactment by focusing in metatheatrical ways on the tension between the "role" and the "person" who performs it (see Calderwood; Righter; and Van Laan). In our own century, too, political theatre companies and collectives since Brecht and Piscator have employed presentational, audience-centred forms of documentary drama to deconstruct traditional "authoritative" views of history and to replace them with self-consciously revisionist, populist, or oppositional re-presentations of history (often "from below") as (social) performance and process.

Canadian plays on historical subjects have come under the direct influence of the Elizabethan-style presentational staging of Shakespeare by way of the Stratford Festival stage; by way of the essentially presentational style of radio drama and documentary on the CBC, for many years Canada's de facto national theatre (Miller, "Radio's Children"); and by way of the European tradition of presentational political theatre as transmitted through Joan Littlewood and Roger Planchon to the Canadian pioneers George Luscombe and Paul Thompson (see Arnott; Usmiani 18, 45; and Vogt). Finally, in a country in which the mainstream of theatre was dominated for many decades by imported plays and foreign directors, Canadian drama has been shaped by the fact that it has tended to occupy alternative spaces and to play an alternative role culturally: for reasons of size and budget, its treatment of historical subjects has required nonillusionistic devices such as doubling, modern dress, and rudimentary, metonymic props; moreover, its tendency under the circumstances has naturally been toward both politically alternative deconstructions of dominant national myths and metatheatrical questionings of dominant dramatic forms that it views as oppressive or colonialist in impact.

It is not surprising, then, that so many Canadian plays on historical subjects have eschewed any attempt to canonize official history or to establish a stable national mythology; they prefer, instead, to make use of the metatheatrical possibilities of nonillusionistic, presentational theatre to re-present the making and remaking of history as a necessarily ongoing process. In Canada as elsewhere, however, metatheatre is not always or automatically political; in fact, the formal tendency of self-reflexive art and theatre to turn inward, away from the social and toward an infinitely regressive *mise-en-abyme*, potentially places such structures in a politically suspect alliance with the worst excesses of formalist modernisms. *Historiographic* metatheatre, however, while it shares the dangers of theatrical self-indulgence and political or theatrical elitism flirted with by theatrically ludic *jeux d'esprit* such as Christopher Durang's *The Actor's Nightmare* or Daniel MacIvor's *This Is a Play*, is frequently rooted in a historiographic tradition that is necessarily connected with "actual people" in actual historical, social, and cultural contexts.

As a test case of the political efficacy of historiographic metadrama as a form, it may be worth looking briefly at the Donnelly plays of James Reaney, a student of Northrop Frye who has most frequently been analysed as a mythopoeic poet/dramatist and cultural regionalist/ nationalist. Unlike the playwrights discussed in the remainder of this chapter, who employ metatheatrical techniques for expressly political purposes, Reaney, who is political only in the sense that he is a committed regionalist, sees the process of the theatrical creation and re-creation of history and myth as necessary and valuable in its own right, though like them he uses metatheatre to deconstruct any attempt at a stable or objectifiable historiography. For Reaney, however, it is the need for a constant and ongoing reimagining of history by each new audience as a communal invention of self in the shared process of creation that calls for metatheatrical self-consciousness, and for him ritual and game playing are the central activities of a theatre in which engagement with process is paramount. Consequently, while Reaney attempts, like the other playwrights under discussion here, to reestablish contact between drama and its ritual roots, he does so by analogy with *sacred* ritual — in *The Donnellys*, the Roman Catholic liturgy is invoked — rather than with the populist rituals of sports or the popular entertainment forms invoked by writers such as Rick Salutin and Michael Hollingsworth. But for Reaney, as for the others, there is a self-conscious need to invoke and employ ritual forms in which the actors act for, on behalf of, and in concert with an audience as a community (see Knowles, *"Homo Ludens"*).

Reaney is conscious of the theatricality of history, and like many Canadian playwrights he invokes Shakespeare while metadramatically deconstructing that theatricality. As he says in an interview with Jeffrey Goffin, "when you see a portrait of a General at a battle, they're very heroic looking, even god-like. They're not realistic. They quite often dress up. Like kings dressed up for battle — like Henry the Fifth" (13). As most critics of his work have pointed out, Reaney explodes such theatrical myths; part of the function of the famous "medicine show" play-within-the-play in *Sticks and Stones* (1973), the first play in the Donnelly trilogy, is to subvert the received myth of the Donnellys, replacing it with his own "corrective" version in which his *own* created character, the "real" James Donnelly, stands outside time to mock the medicine-show parody of Thomas P. Kelly's popular history, *The Black Donnellys*. One critic praises the theatrical impact of Reaney's juxtaposition of the "real" with the "false" Donnelly but nevertheless labels the device "spurious":

> For by presenting the traditional view of the Donnellys in caricature, the dramatist discredits earlier versions of the story and implies that what he presents is truth. In the theatre, however, the nature of "truth" is shadowy. It is less relevant to ask which of the two interpretations of the violent conflict between the Donnellys and their neighbours is accurate than to speculate about why Reaney thinks his own version of the story is more "real" than the one he denigrates. (Carson 223)

But surely the shadowy nature of "truth" in the theatre is part of Reaney's metatheatrical point, here and elsewhere, when he reminds us that "I'm not in Hell for I'm in a play" (*Donnellys* 24), or when he compares the brevity of life to that of "actors' words" (42).

Few critics of Reaney, in fact, have acknowledged that the questioning of theatrical verity within the context of a play implicitly calls into question *any* claim to absolute truth on the stage, including its own; indeed, most critics have concerned themselves with Reaney as a *builder* of myths who, in the words of one, "demythologizes in order to mythologize anew" (Bessai, "Documentary into Drama" 201). But it is equally possible to argue that it is the *process* of mythologizing and remythologizing that is important in Reaney's work, together with the degree to which that process requires audience or community assent, lifting traditional suspension of disbelief to the level of imaginative participation in the creative process. Early in his career as a playwright, in his children's play about putting on a play, *Listen to the Wind*, Reaney explodes the concept of theatre as a place where an illusion of reality is created explicitly in order to "draw the audience into the creative process," forcing it "to provide lighting and production and sets and even ending" (Bessai, "Documentary into Drama" 188). In *The Donnellys*, mounted using a modified, author-centred version of collective creation, Reaney engages the audience in the play of history *as* play and in the act of piecing together fragments and documents from the past as a creative "exercise," valuable in itself and never complete or conclusive. Gerald Parker places Reaney's work in the context of Paul Klee's insight that the artist comes "more and more to see that the essential image of creation is genesis." "The important thing about genesis," Parker comments, "is that it, as a process, is never finished. The artist 'hazards the bold thought that the process of creation can scarcely be over and done with as yet, and so he extends the universal creative process both backward and forward, thus conferring duration upon genesis'" (Parker, "History" 151, quoting Klee 87). Reaney's interest in historical subject matter, then, has to do with continuing the "universal" process of creation by transforming history dramatically into "pure story," extending that process by involving the audience in it. Reaney has drawn attention to the entanglement of "pure story" with "all the history we have to deal with" in the making of *The Donnellys*, remarking that the plays result from the combination of "our STORY STYLE and the past swamp of fact" (qtd. in Parker, "History" 152). He uses a theatrical style that asks the audience on one level to engage its imagination with the transformation of simple stage props — sticks, stones, ladders, and the like, into fiddles, swords, roads, and fences — and on another level to contribute similarly to the piecing together of meaningful "history" from the raw materials of historical fragments and documents. The method suggests that the plays' metatheatrical self-consciousness, in which characters stand outside the plays to comment on their own roles, is designed to contribute to the elevation of audience engagement above empathy with character and plot to the level of imaginative engagement with the artist and with the creative act of inventing the past.

The process with which the audience engages its imagination, of course, is explicitly that of becoming. Reaney's concern with how "the Donnellys *decided* to be Donnellys" (*Donnellys* 11; emphasis added), with christenings and confirmations as theatrical rituals, and with how one chooses and earns one's name, subjectivity, and role is reflected in the metatheatrical ritual structure of a trilogy that is ultimately about the audience as a community in the process of continually reinventing its history, its name(s), and its sense of self. As Mary Jane Miller has observed,

> the trilogy itself is just as much about how the Donnellys came to be that particular family, narrated and re-educated by initiates, as any Kwakiutl or Haida dance-drama which shows how Hamatsa Raven accepted the initiate into the high ranks of the Cannibal Hamatsa society. The right to the song or story is earned and the right to sing and dance it is a proud possession which must be validated by the consent of the whole community. ("Use" 35)

Like Shakespeare in his second Henriad, however, where the stability of song, story, and community — that is, of history — cannot be assured after the murder of Richard II (see Calderwood 10–29), Reaney attempts through theatrical ritual to *restore* and *re-create* in a post-lapsarian world the sacramental bond between word and thing, sign and referent, history and story. In both Shakespeare and Reaney, this bond is presumed to have existed before the fall of language but can now exist only temporarily and only in the realm of the imagination, where it must be continually re-created and, in Miller's terms, revalidated. As Peggy Phelan phrases it,

> Language always expresses a longing to return to someplace where language is not needed. Lacanian psychoanalysis and the story of the Garden of Eden are alike in that the Imaginary Paradise they each posit as "origin" lacks linguistic *and* visual distinctions between who one is and what one sees. After what the Bible calls the Fall and Lacan calls the Mirror Stage, the eyes of everyone open, difference is discovered, and the fighting (for) words begin(s). ("Reciting" 29)

For Reaney, the act of communal re-creation of self, finally, *is* the play, and its function is the profound yet essentially simple one of insisting that we accept that our perception of reality and of self within the social formation, like our understanding of history, is a construction. In spite of the universalizing tendencies of Reaney's mythopeoic, Frygian conception of "pure story," then, and in spite of what often seems to be a Jungian belief in a collective imagination or unconscious, there is a politically liberating strand to his dramaturgy that derives in part from his committed localism. And, as he argues (avoiding, however, the issues of who "we" is and of who *controls* the stories), "Maybe if we get used to seeing our society as being based on story, we'll wake up and realize that we can get a better story . . ." (qtd. in Dragland, "Afterword" 222). The function of metadrama in *The Donnellys*, then, is primarily to engage the audience in the process of imagining history not only to "make it new" but also continually to *realize* it, and in the process continually to reinvent and realize our selves — including our specific and historicized social formation.

The remainder of this chapter will look at three groups of Canadian historiographic metadramas that have employed the techniques of metatheatre in related but distinct ways that foreground issues of class, race, and gender, respectively, in replays and reenactments of history that work to revise the contemporary social formation by explicitly — and often through their dramaturgical structures — raising questions about the ownership of history and the constituency represented by the communal "we."

★   ★   ★

CLASS ACTS

Rick Salutin is a self-professed cultural nationalist, and, although he has not been active in theatre in recent years, he is one of Canada's few avowedly socialist playwrights. As such, he is essentially concerned with historiography and theatre as social processes rather than as products:

> I know cultural nationalism often seems like a kind of archeological activity, unearthing, trying to discover[,] . . . but I think it should be a product of the future rather than the past. You're trying to create something, and you just grab anything you can do it with for the sake of building something for the future. . . .

As long as it doesn't get metaphysicalised, so that you're trying to discover your soul, as if it really exists back there, and all you have to do is scrape away the layers. . . . ("Rick Salutin" 192)

His history plays, then, make no attempt to transport their audiences back in time through an "authentic" reconstruction of an authoritative myth of the past. Rather, Salutin produces his scripts through a collective process that subverts the very concept of historical or dramatic "authority," and he avoids illusionist naturalism and period costumes in favour of a presentational metatheatricality that similarly subverts traditional Aristotelian concepts of empathy and catharsis in the theatre.

In creating *1837: The Farmers' Revolt*, Salutin worked in Toronto with Theatre Passe Muraille in 1972–74 to research, produce, and write (in that order) a play about what official history calls the Mackenzie rebellion in Upper Canada.[2] (Salutin's conscious change from "the Mackenzie rebellion" to *"The Farmers' Revolt"* is significant and is itself political.[3]) The collective method was, as his published rehearsal diary makes clear, a self-conscious rejection of the hierarchical structure of the traditional theatre, a version of theatrical revolt that deliberately parallelled the play's historical subject. Similarly, the presentational style of the production, which engaged the audience imaginatively in the process of "creating" history through play, was designed to highlight the parallels between the events of 1837 and what Salutin calls a widespread "determination to throw off colonial submissiveness in all areas" of cultural and economic life in Canada in 1973. As he says in his preface to the play, "*1837* was a theatrical expression of that [determination], making it [the production] more of a political event, and not just, or even primarily, a theatrical one" (202).

Like the Passe Muraille collective creations discussed in chapter 3, *1837* was researched and created by actors functioning experientially *as actors*: Salutin's diary entry for 15 December 1972 records the actors' discovery, walking through the Old Toronto sites where the events on which the play was based took place, that "December was a hell of a time to make a revolution here" (189). But more significantly, they discovered the revolutionary impulse itself through the connections between their own lot as "the real proletariat of the theatre" (187) in a colonized culture and the lot of the farmers in 1837. Their method is echoed within the play through the use of metadrama: in an early scene, the farmers help one of their number to tell the story of his confrontation with the authorities in Toronto by "acting out" the story, assuming roles and "discovering" what happened and what it felt like. Placed in his situation, as the actors of *1837* placed themselves in the situations of the farmers, they find the story, or make it, in response to the storyteller's question "What would you do?" (13). As William Westfall, the reviewer for *Canadian Historical Review,* pointed out about the method, "drama was the vehicle to carry the group from their own frustration with the present back to a new past. Drama led to history, history did not lead to drama" (72).

The play was mounted using only five actors, who doubled all the roles and who constructed with Salutin and director Paul Thompson a series of vignettes based on historical documents. These vignettes were, in effect, historical performances that drew attention to their own theatricality, deconstructing the myth of 1837 as presented by established history and establishment historians. As Robert Nunn says, the play "treats its historical figures quite legitimately as actors on the stage of history, who invested their gestures with a larger-than-life histrionic quality acting both as agents and actors in the assumption that their deeds would shape the destiny of a nation"; as Nunn goes on to say, it then "dismantles" their stage ("Performing Fact" 57). But scene after scene of *1837* also presents history as people's theatre and people's theatre as political agitation. In a ventriloquism scene, for example, a colonial "dummy" on the lap of the imperialist ventriloquist, "John Bull," finally finds his own voice, in which he urges his audience, onstage and off, to rebel against colonial oppression (231–33).[4] In another scene, a provocatively paternalistic speech by Lieutenant Governor Sir Francis Bond Head is transformed and trivialized by being delivered verbatim from its documentary source by a larger-than-life theatrical "Head" pieced together by the bodies and limbs of four actors (224–25). Not incidentally, and unlike the opaque narratives of traditional Canadian history, the metadramatic devices, here and elsewhere in the play, *insist* on the instability of the documentary source. As metatheatre, then, the play deconstructs the histrionic gestures of the colonial leaders while celebrating a people's theatre that serves, as Nunn says, "not . . . as a reflection of what might have been done then but as a model of what needs to be done now, and in fact is being done in every moment of the performance of *1837*" ("Performing Fact" 59). Far from providing a cathartic release of potentially revolutionary impulses, the play attempts to serve as what Brazilian writer-director Augusto Boal calls in his work a "rehearsal of revolution" to come (141). *1837* ends with an exchange between the defeated rebels Lount and Matthews on the gallows: when Matthews laments that, "Sam, we lost," Lount, as the voice of the play, replies "No! We haven't won yet" (64), and the play opens outward from theatrical to political action.

The shift from theatre, myth, and history to direct political action is the central structural principle of Salutin's 1977 play, *Les Canadiens*, which exploits the theatricality of hockey, the popular ritual of *Hockey Night in Canada*, and the myth of the Montreal Canadiens to examine the nature and role of national myths of identity. The play's first half sets the history of Quebec, told as a series of defeats in the theatre of *war* and in the arena of *politics*, against the story of *Les Canadiens*, represented as a series of triumphant victories in the *popular* theatre of the *hockey* arena, complete with announcer, scoreboard, and organist. Salutin here disposes quickly of the histrionics of the leading actors in traditional Canadian histories: General Wolfe, for example, is represented as self-consciously composing, to the accompaniment of a recitation of Gray's "Elegy," a tableau of his own death in battle as Benjamin West's painting, ubiquitous in Canada, of *The Death of General Wolfe*; however, the bulk of the first act concerns itself with what the playwright has come to view as a more dangerous use of popular theatre and popular mythology. Acknowledging and even celebrating the need for myths and heroes in the construction of a national sense of identity, Salutin ultimately *exposes* the cathartic capacity of myth, art, history, and sport to sap the popular will to effect political action.

The self-conscious theatricality of the play's stage metaphors — the gun with which Wolfe is shot at the play's opening, for example, is represented onstage by a hockey stick that is passed down the years through the play's first act as the "torch" of Québécois resistance — insists on the audience's recognition of theatre and history *as* representations, effective as models but debilitating as substitutes for action within the political arena itself. The second act focuses on the evening of 15 November 1976, when the on-ice battle between the Canadiens and the St. Louis Blues at the appropriately named "Forum" is ignored by a crowd that responds ecstatically to scoreboard reports from the Paul Sauvé "Arena" of election results leading to the first electoral victory of Quebec's nationalist Parti Québécois. The hockey stick is no longer gun or torch, hockey reverts to being "just a game," and the Canadiens, relinquishing their role as standard bearers of the Quebec spirit, are demythologized to become "just a hockey team" (197). Whatever the future of the Parti Québécois, the play suggests that neither a hockey team nor a political party can ever serve again as escapist symbol or myth in lieu of action. (While the post-mortem mythologizing of René Lévesque suggested that Salutin may have been somewhat sanguine, it is nevertheless clear that, by the middle of the 1990s and in the minds of most Quebeckers, the Parti Québécois had lost its mythological aura. It remains "just a[nother] political party.")

In the end, like *1837*, *Les Canadiens* resists formal closure and opens out into the world, the social formation, and the future. As Mary Jane Miller describes it,

> In a wonderfully appropriate open ending we see a play within a play within a play, a fragment of a game of shinny, narrated as if on television by a bunch of kids who suddenly collide with the play's reality, an actual instantly recognisable hockey star. In this scene, the past, the present, and the future meet. . . . ("Two Versions" 68)

Les Canadiens, then, metatheatrically analyses the roles of myth, history, and popular theatre, deconstructing cathartic empathy with legendary heroes as with characters in realist dramaturgies, as "bread and circuses" come to be replaced by political action in the social realm.

Michael Hollingsworth's epic series of Canadian history plays, *The History of the Village of the Small Huts*, produced by Toronto's Video-cabaret International, shares many dramaturgical characteristics and political positionings with Salutin's work, particularly with *1837*, but it employs them and filters them through quite a different set of generic and structural frames. Like *1837*, the plays in the *Small Huts* series feature history's working-class populace as well as its (usually debunked) "heroes," and the eight plays that constitute the series insist on historically and culturally contextualizing the events depicted rather than universalizing them by focusing on issues of individual motivation and psychology.[5] Thus, as Michael McKinnie argues in his analysis of part 7 of *The History*, *The Life and Times of Mackenzie King*, Hollingsworth's cycle continually "marks" historical time by contextualizing fragments — historical radio broadcasts, archival film clips, "quotations" from period films, and so on — that situate the action in history and in the social realm. "[T]he audience is able to recognize the historical period through these constructions," McKinnie argues, "while at the same time recognizing the quoting fragments *as* fragments, rather than as metaphors standing in for the whole truth" ("King-Maker" 182).

Like Salutin's play, too, Hollingsworth's cycle draws on and metatheatrically stages forms of popular theatre, though in the case of

Hollingsworth and Videocabaret these forms derive primarily from television and popular film, adapted and politicized in part through their transfer to the stage.[6] Thus, for example, the ways in which film and, particularly, television fragment the *mise en scène* and the bodies of the actors through close-ups and montage are translated through an inventive "black-box" technique developed by designer Jim Plaxton, in which the audience sees the stage and the actors through a back-lit scrim in tightly focused pools or slashes of light, allowing characters and scenes to be juxtaposed in ways that parallel a filmic edit and eschewing proscenium depth perspective in ways that parallel the shallow depth of field of videotape. The effect is to allow foregrounded scenes, characters, and bodily parts to appear as if in close-up while upstage scenes appear smaller, as if "shot" from a greater distance, but taking up an equivalent percentage of the surface "screen." The effect differs from its televisual or filmic counterpart, however, in that it denaturalizes the convention, metatheatrically drawing attention to itself in a way perhaps more closely parallel to the extravagantly performative "close-up" representation of Sir Francis Bond('s) Head in *1837*, described above, or to the unapologetic intercutting of surfaces common in music video. As McKinnie points out, "Jim Plaxton's black boxes draw attention to the packaging of history and Shadowland's outrageous costuming reinforces the idea that the Village series is about performance — not simply performing history as theatre, but pointing out the performance that is history" ("King-Maker" 166).

More significantly, however (as McKinnie also points out), the effect is to shift our figurative sensibilities from the metaphoric to the metonymic, encouraging us to imagine not a parallel, internally coherent, and already completed fictive universe (or signifying system) that stands in for or replaces the real but a larger picture of which we are conscious of seeing only fragments and which we are invited to "read" actively, critically, and (co)constructively. As Peggy Phelan says, "Metaphor works to secure a vertical hierarchy of value and is reproductive; it works by erasing dissimilarity and negating difference; it turns two into one"; but, as she also points out, "Metonymy is additive and associative; it works to secure a horizontal axis of contiguity and displacement" (*Unmarked* 150).

This metonymic fragmentation as employed by Hollingsworth is reinforced through other televisual and populist techniques, such as the nonliterary, scattershot approach to dialogue in a script that seems to the *reader* more like a film or television screenplay — a sitcom, almost certainly — than like "dramatic literature." In a typical scene, quoted from part 2 of the series, *The British*, two officers, Captain Dalyell and Major Henry Gladwyn, find themselves listening to the offstage screams of the Pontiac massacre at Detroit:

DALYELL: Good God, listen to that.
GLADWYN: Poor devils, poor devils.
DALYELL: What are they doing to make a man scream like that?
GLADWYN: Poor devils, poor devils.
DALYELL: There are only two kinds in this world, the poor and the lucky.
GLADWYN: Oh the poor devils, poor devils.
DALYELL: Once, seven years ago, I had the great misfortune to be in Calcutta. But I was one of the lucky ones. The Thuggee put me in the Black Hole, but others were not so lucky. I saw the Thuggee hammer twenty nails into the head of my best friend. He screamed like that man is right now.
GLADWYN: Poor devils, poor devils. (Hollingsworth, *History* 77)

Here again the script resists the traditional "fleshing out" of motivations and psychological explanations for its audience, as it resists the heroizing or demonizing individualism of naturalistic/biographical models of the history of great men (sic). As McKinnie says of *The Life and Times of Mackenzie King*, the play

is as much about the times of Mackenzie King as it is his life, taking an almost sociological view of Canada between 1918 and 1937. King is not permitted to define himself as being in command of his world, to amplify his own influence, because he exists within a social and historical context. The play demonstrates how material conditions shape King's actions, and illustrates some of the consequences of those actions. . . . Thus the basic structure of *Life and Times* is fragmentary; twenty years of Canadian history are performed by 57 characters (some fictional and some not) through 122 scenes. Finding a "central story" in the play is difficult, for it conflates the structure of historical chronology — which demands some adherence to the linear progression of time — with that of the television newscast. ("King-Maker" 170–71)

Hollingsworth's *History*, then, functions in ways similar to the popular tabloid arts of fragmentation, popularization, overstatement, and bizarre juxtaposition that popular-culture analyst John Fiske argues, perhaps too sanguinely, are empowering for socially disenfranchised audiences (123–27). Thus, the plays' costumes and props, designed by Toronto's Shadowland, perhaps best known for its contributions to larger-than-life and populist social events such as Toronto's Caribana Festival parade, feature oversized, overstuffed, and overstated metonymic fragments rather than fully conjured, realistic character dressings or scene settings, and the jump-cuts between Elizabethan-style parallel plots offer such simple but bizarre, politically telling, and resolutely *socializing* juxtapositions as the following sequence of seven short scenes, quoted in full from *The Life and Times of Mackenzie King*. The characters are Mackenzie's political opponent, Prime Minister R.B. Bennett; the family and pet dog, Blackie, of an invented working-class character in the Depression, Joe Slomovsky; and King himself, together with his famous dog, Pat (the dogs are played by hand puppets), with which he consulted and communed both before and after Pat's death:

Scene Seventeen

(. . . *[T]he lights fade in. Joe, Judy, and their daughter enter. The sound of a dog barking.*)
JOE: Shut up, shut up. Shut up or I'll wring your nuts. He's eating us out of house and home and he never shuts up. Don't look at me like that. There's no work.
JUDY: And there's no food.
(*The sound of a dog barking.*)
DAUGHTER: And Blackie's hungry too.
JOE: Yes.
DAUGHTER: Oh Blackie.
(*Daughter exits. The sound of a dog barking. Joe and Judy look at each other. The lights fade.*)

Scene Eighteen

(*In another playing area the lights fade in. Bennett enters.*)
BENNETT: How do you get a belly like this, you ask? I eat six meals a day. You don't get a belly like this eating three. For breakfast I have eleven eggs and two pounds of bacon, and a loaf of bread. That gets me started. Oh bacon, bacon. Bacon, God I

love it. Love it, love it, love it, love it, love it. I can't imagine a world without bacon.
(*The lights fade.*)

Scene Nineteen

(*In another playing area the lights fade in. Judy and daughter enter. Joe enters holding a bag wrapped in butcher paper.*)
DAUGHTER: Blackie, Blackie, where are you? Where is he?
JUDY: Muffin.
DAUGHTER: What?
JUDY: I have some terrible news. Blackie ran away.
DAUGHTER: Oh no.
JUDY: I took Blackie out on a leash for a walk. And he saw some dogs running in a pack and he ran after them barking all the way. I wasn't strong enough to hold him, wasn't strong enough. He ran away. Don't cry. He's with the other dogs now. He'll be happy. We'll get another one one day.
DAUGHTER: It's not the same.
(*The lights fade.*)

Scene Twenty

(*In another playing area the lights fade in. King and Pat enter. King holds a frying pan.*)
KING: Oh Pat, you're king here. And you are going to eat like a king. Look Pat, look. Your favourite. Steak and pork chops. The steak is medium rare and the pork chops are well done. Eat it all, Pat, eat it all.
(*The lights fade.*)

Scene Twenty-one

(*In another playing area the lights fade in. Joe, Judy, and their daughter are eating.*)
JOE: Jesus that's good. Meat, meat, oh meat.
JUDY: Yes.
JOE: Jesus that's good. Meat, meat, oh meat.
JUDY: Yes.
JOE: Jesus that's good. Meat, meat, oh meat.
JUDY: Yes.
JOE: How is it, Muffin?
DAUGHTER: Oh it's good, it's good, it's good.
(*They eat. The lights fade.*)

Scene Twenty-two
(*In another playing area the lights fade in. Bennett is reading letters from distraught citizens.*)
BENNETT: If you want to know who is responsible for all the debt look at yourself in the mirror when you are shaving. There are people who say let's spend more money, well and good, but where's the money coming from? Where is the spirit of our pioneers who tilled the soil and worked in your forests? Did they go to the government whenever they wanted anything? They did not ask government to be a wet nurse to every derelict.
(*In another playing area the lights fade in.*)
KING: He is a dog of a man. A brute. A dog!
(*The lights fade.*)

Scene Twenty-three
(*In another playing area the lights fade in. Joe and Judy enter.*)
JOE: Might have no choice. Might have to go on the dole. We got to eat.
(*Daughter enters.*)
JUDY: Muffin, what's the matter?
DAUGHTER: My friend Shirley talked to her friend Joanie whose father owns the butcher shop and she said Daddy walked into the butcher shop with Blackie and walked out with a big bag and no Blackie. Is that true?
JUDY: Muffin.
DAUGHTER: You ate Blackie, you ate Blackie, you ate Blackie. You ate Blackie, you ate Blackie, you ate Blackie. You ate —
JOE: You had some too.
(*The daughter grimaces. The lights fade.*) (307–08)

Hollingsworth and Videocabaret, then, on the broad (in both senses) canvas of *The History of the Village of the Small Huts*, are revisioning Canada's entire history through a populist and resistant socialist lens, having created a dramaturgical and theatrical structure that is popular, metonymic, actively "writerly" (Barthes, *S/Z*), and determinedly open ended.[7]

★ ★ ★

Playing Indian

While Rick Salutin and Michael Hollingsworth have used populist historiographic metatheatre primarily to highlight the theatricality of history in probing questions of class, Sharon Pollock, Rex Deverell, Monique Mojica, and Daniel David Moses construct in very different ways metatheatrical dramas of historical revisionism that concern themselves with issues of race and representation, particularly the representation of Canada's Métis and Native peoples.

In contrast with Reaney, Salutin, and Hollingsworth, Pollock tends to make use of period costumes and settings in her history plays, and she does not employ a collective or collaborative process. She does, however, consistently employ metadramatic framing devices to foreground the role of the audience in the "realization" of Canada's past. In the preface to the published script of *The Komagata Maru Incident*, Pollock asserts that, as a nation, "until we recognize our past, we cannot change our future" (vi), and throughout her career as a playwright, from her early plays of social activism to her explorations in the 1980s of a more personal past, she has developed an increasingly complex dramatic mode of "re-cognition" through a style of theatre that presents itself — most explicitly in *Blood Relations*, discussed in the third section of this chapter — as "acting out."

Her earliest plays to deal with issues of race do so primarily by pointing out injustices historically performed and historiographically erased by Canada's currently dominant cultures. As such, they tend to focus on the white men who perpetrate the injustices rather than on the "Indians" (Natives in *Walsh*, prospective Sikh immigrants in *The Komagata Maru Incident*). In *Walsh* (1973), Pollock deals with the relationship between Major James Walsh, North West Mounted Police, and Sitting Bull, living in exile in Canada after the Custer massacre at Little Big Horn. The play opens with a brief vignette through which Pollock forestalls empathy and identification with the potentially charismatic Walsh by showing him in his later years as a broken and bitter man. This metatheatrical induction scene ends with Walsh's unsympathetic hitting and shoving to the floor of a prospector collecting money for a boy whose father has frozen to death. The action anticipates (or, in the play's historically chronological time scheme, echoes) Walsh's precisely parallel humiliation of Sitting Bull, played by the same actor as the prospector, at the climax of the main body of the play. The effect of the device is to present the play as a demonstration, acted out in the manner of an Elizabethan history play (appropriately, the play was produced at the Stratford Festival in 1974), of Walsh's failure to reconcile his individual humanity, including his friendship with Sitting Bull, with his historical role as he dons his costume, the tunic of a major in the NWMP.[8]

Walsh tries throughout the play to differentiate between "Major Walsh," in uniform, the representative of "the Queen and the Canadian government" (54), and "White Forehead," Sitting Bull's friend. The effectual split between man and role disarms and emasculates Sitting Bull: "In the past," he says, "I have risen, tomahawk in hand. I have done all the hurt to the whites that I could. . . . Now you are here. My arms hang to the ground as if dead" (54). But Walsh's failure to reconcile himself with his role ultimately destroys not only Sitting Bull but also Walsh himself, who pleads movingly to a superior officer for the integration of the two aspects of himself:

> What do you think happens when I take off this tunic? At night, in my quarters, what do you think happens to me . . . ? Do you think McCutcheon hangs me up from some god damn wooden peg with all my strings dangling? Is that what you think happens? Do you think I'm a puppet? Manipulate me right and anything is possible. I'm a person, I exist. I think and feel! And I will not allow you to do this to me. (86)

But ultimately the man who proudly boasts "when have my actions betrayed my words?" (51) is reduced to speaking the evasive language of the bureaucrat: "I shall give your proposition every consideration" (106). The man who is able to say, "White Forehead does not say this, Major Walsh says this" (49), is reduced to doing up his costume/tunic and assuming his role as a way of protecting himself before his final interview with his former friend (98). The method and the metaphor are familiar from Shakespeare's explorations of the "player king" in his history plays and tragedies (see Righter 102–24). At the end of the play, after Walsh has tacitly consented to the extradition of Sitting Bull to the United States, we see the major "quite willing," as Robert Nunn notes, "to substitute the myth of the savage Indian for the reality he knew first hand, to substitute 'style' and 'image' for substance: he illustrates his plan to stage a mock attack, Indian style, on Eastern dignitaries" ("Sharon Pollock's Plays" 75). When the news arrives that Sitting Bull has, inevitably, been murdered on his arrival in the United

States, Walsh's final action in the play is to remove his gun and tunic and with them the role that has been his life. As Nunn says, then, "*Walsh* set[s] the myth of 'Openin' the West' side by side with its dreadful acting out" (75), and the method is typical of Pollock.

In 1976, Pollock again experimented with the metatheatrical representation of an inglorious, racist incident from Canada's past, in which pleasant myths of Canadian generosity and freedom from prejudice are deconstructed by direct confrontation with a less pleasant enactment of history. In this case, the play deals with an incident in 1914 in which Canadian Immigration Department officials refused to admit into the country a boatload of Sikhs from India even though, as British subjects, they were legally entitled to entry. Pollock's dramaturgical strategy in *The Komagata Maru Incident* is to present the play's acting out of its audience's "repressed" past as parallel to the story of Inspector Hopkinson, who, "acting" on behalf of the department, brutally represses his own part-Indian past by "acting out" the racist attitudes of his white Canadian compatriots and superiors. But the central subject of the play is its predominantly white audience, for whose benefit both Hopkinson and the theatre company "act." This is made clear by the metatheatrical presentation of the play as a carnival side show by "T.S.," a ubiquitous master of ceremonies who, as Pollock indicates suggestively in the cast list, "plays many roles." At one point, he insists that the audience confront racist attitudes within Canada by acknowledging its own complacent use of such attitudes:

> Ladies and gentlemen! It walks! It talks! It reproduces! It provides cheap labour for your factories, and a market for your goods! All this, plus a handy scapegoat! Who's responsible for unemployment! The coloured immigrant! Who brings about a drop in take-home pay? The coloured immigrant! Who is it creates slum housing, racial tension, high interest rates, and violence in our streets? The coloured immigrant! Can we afford to be without it? I say "No!" It makes good sense to keep a few around — when the dogs begin to bay, throw them a coloured immigrant! It may sound simple, but it works. Remember though — the operative word's "a few." (36–37)

Elsewhere we are confronted with our ability to detach ourselves from action that "doesn't concern us" but for which we are necessarily passive accomplices: "Ladies and gentlemen, can you truly afford to bypass this splendid spectacle? Run, my good friends, you mustn't walk, you must run! Cotton candy, taffy apples, popcorn and balloons! All this and a possible plus, the opportunity to view your very own navy in action with no threat to you!" (62). As Nunn comments,

> As an audience we are alienated from an automatic acceptance of the predominance of "the White Race" [in the audience and] in our country: it didn't just happen; choices were made and continue to be made to maintain it. The play forces us to either criticize or justify the state of affairs: we cannot take it for granted. ("Performing Fact" 56)

The final effect, then, far from being cathartic, is to insist that we realize our history as part of our present by engaging our imaginations with its acting out and by acknowledging our responsibility for what has been performed *for* us.

Pollock's 1991 radio play, *The Making of Warriors*, is not metatheatre, strictly speaking, but it rounds out her work dealing with race, particularly Native issues, and it does metadramatically foreground the radio format and evince a self-conscious awareness of issues of the appropriation of voice and the ownership of historical narratives that is not apparent in her earlier historical plays. Pollock experiments effectively and intriguingly in *The Making of Warriors* with a kind of contrapuntal form in an attempt to explore the links between slavery, feminism, and Native rights, as a fifty-four-year-old middle-class white woman — an author surrogate, as Pollock acknowledges in the introduction to the published script (101) — attempts to historicize the present and the personal by filtering history through reminiscence, story, dramatization, and the presentation of documentary evidence as radio news. As she says, addressing the issue of appropriation,

> I think that I can write a story [dealing with Native history] so long as I find a way within the structure of the story to acknowledge my angle of observation. I'm the result of my middle-class, white upbringing in a conservative part of the country, in a racist country, in a colonized country, next to the largest, most powerful country in the world. I am aware of that and I try to educate myself and sensitize myself to how that has formed me. . . . (100)

What *The Making of Warriors* does, then, is to take advantage of the radio format and program style — what Pollock calls its "mingling of subjective and objective perspectives" (101) — to write, as the play's three women say, "an exploration of/a story about/a personal reminiscence" (105) that combines the dramatized life of a nineteenth-century American anti-slavery protofeminist with news-style reports of events leading to the FBI's murder of the Canadian-born Native activist Anna Mae Pictou Aquash on 24 February 1976. In a third structural strand, the author-surrogate obsessively recalls not having witnessed this murder when she drove through the reserve where Aquash was killed and passed a group of white men standing with "something on the shoulder of the road. . . . A red . . . ski jacket perhaps" (113): "I slowed down. I didn't stop. Why should I stop? I was just . . . passing through. On my way. Somewhere" (106; three-point ellipses in original). The ultimate effect of this structural counterpointing of styles and perspectives, like the play's deployment of historical narratives, is to urge its audience toward political action — to resist merely "passing through." The play's title, moreover, ultimately comes to signify its intended impact — the construction of a resistant audience as warriors.

Rex Deverell's 1985 play *Beyond Batoche* is also structured around the playwright's self-conscious awareness of the problematics surrounding the writing and possible appropriation of "alternative" histories by playwrights from the dominant culture. *Beyond Batoche*, more overtly metatheatrical than *The Making of Warriors*, is also self-reflexive in a more direct sense: it dramatizes the playwright's attempt to find ways of creating for CBC Radio, with Wayne Schmalz, a documentary radio play about Batoche and the Riel resistance, *The Riel Commission*, in the same year as Deverell composed *Beyond Batoche*.[9] The radio play shares with *The Making of Warriors* an attempt to frame its documentary material by a distancing formal procedure, in this case an "inquiry," as the play's subtitle calls it, "into the survival of a people." Like *The Making of Warriors*, too, *The Riel Commission* explicitly and metatheatrically draws on the conventions of radio — in this case, the type of radio documentary for which the CBC is best known.

Donald Sutherland plays the commissioner who hosts the proceedings in *The Riel Commission*, a royal commission that hears "real" submissions read from historical documents and taped from contemporary sources, notably a public forum held in Regina in 1985. Wayne Schmalz somewhat disingenuously calls the result "the unmediated expression of many points of view" (Introduction viii), but in fact the play contains and shapes the materials — mediates their reception — through lines written for the commissioner by Schmalz and Deverell and of course through the process of selecting and shaping the sources. Interestingly, the proceedings are introduced by Sutherland speaking as himself, telling of how he was approached to play the role and of his long-standing passionate interest in Riel — adding, moreover, that "there's a lot of guilt in my passion" (Deverell and Schmalz 64).

It is this passionate and interested guilt — together with Schmalz's account of being approached following a press conference with Sutherland by a young Native woman who "came up and asked me if I was serious about what I had said, that it was time for natives to do their own stories" (viii)[10] — that seems to be at issue in *Beyond Batoche*. The play stages, crucially, a conflict between a white liberal script-writer, Matt, unconscious of the nature of his "investment"[11] in the story of Riel (whom he wants to make over in his own image [94]), and the young Métis schoolteacher, Yvonne, recruited by his wife to serve as a consultant on the television film on which Matt and his colleagues are working. Acknowledging that "We forgot that the Métis people weren't obliterated at Batoche . . . that there's an ongoing reality here," Matt convinces his producer and the (white) actor whom they have contracted to play Riel that "We should have a kind of partner from the Métis community working with us day by day as we develop the screenplay" (103; ellipsis in original). When Yvonne suggests that they "go to some of the people[,] . . . talk to some of the people on the street[,] . . . see what the system does for a people" rather than maintain historical distance (110), she argues for a dramaturgy that accomplishes what *The Riel Commission* attempts and that Deverell wants his plays to accomplish: "I want them [the audience] to come away from my plays feeling that they can do something, that they don't have to be passive or manipulated by the system. They are worthwhile and can influence social contexts. They have the power, or can find the power, to make changes" (qtd. in Scholar 331). And Deverell tries to do this in *Beyond Batoche* when he has Matt quit the project, realizing that it is not Louis Riel but John A. Macdonald with whom he has the closest ties, and leave its direction and ownership in the hands of Yvonne. In a scene that seems to recognize the limits of the "What would you do?" empathetic technique of history writing in *1837*, Matt gets into character as Macdonald and discovers the darker side of the faith in "essential humanity" — his belief that "what is in other human beings is also in myself" (127) — a faith that has always enabled him to write. Attempting to create a credible Macdonald in a moment for which he has no historical documentation, Matt asks himself, as the tavern dwellers of *1837* did before him, "what would you say?" and launches into an improvisation that climaxes in a vision of a united Canada that he shares with "the father of his country":

> I saw it. And it came to be . . . but not by itself. *Viciously.* I dragged it . . . I dragged it . . . I tore it . . . away from mere potential . . . mere possibility . . . mere wishful thinking . . . and made it a reality. I did what I had to do. And not all of it was good, or upright, or straightforward. And people died in the building of it. And people died in the finishing of it. But I did it! And no one will separate us again. No one will drive a wedge between us. Certainly no ignorant, savage, half-breed from the Northwest. Riel shall hang. Riel shall hang though every dog in Quebec bark in his favor. (131–32; ellipses in original)

At this point, a stage direction indicates that *"Matt has worked himself up into a surprisingly emotional drunken pitch in this speech. The effect should be that he is left staring into his own soul and what he sees there is racism"* (132).

After Matt leaves the project, his colleagues produce with Yvonne something that seems to resemble *The Riel Commission* under Métis supervision, and it is represented as being a positive result for all concerned.[12] The metadramatic structure of *Beyond Batoche*, however, which circles back to a chastened Matt/Deverell sitting down to write the opening lines of the play that we have just watched, ensures that the play itself fails structurally to address the problems that it raises. What Scholar calls the "loop," in which "Deverell attempts to capture, or re-define, the mystery of art" (338), allows the play to lapse into metadramatic solipsism about the problems of art and artists, to tell the story of the writer — Deverell — who has made his mistakes but now knows better. In this way, the focus shifts away from the very contemporary social function to which Deverell and his writer-surrogate seem to aspire — the interrogation of a social system that continues to sanction injustices to Métis and Natives — and toward the dominant culture's ultimately self-justifying, self-congratulatory, or authorizing solutions to its own problems of art, guilt, representation, and appropriation of voice.

Historical revisionism has not been undertaken by the dominant culture alone, however, and it is perhaps not surprising that plays by a woman of mixed race such as Monique Mojica, discussed below, should be quite different from anything that Deverell or his Métis character Yvonne is likely to conceive. It is important to recognize that the (slowly) increasing success by the early 1990s of Native activism in fighting for self-government, which of course involves the interrogation of European modes of social organization and the creation of new Native social, legal, political, and cultural formations, has its parallel in the Native interrogation of European ways of structuring in narrative (including historical narrative) and in the creative arts, including drama and theatre, together with the creation of new historical and artistic forms emerging from historical and contemporary Native life, culture, and experience.[13]

Almighty Voice and His Wife (1991), by Delaware poet and playwright Daniel David Moses, stages a Native reclamation and reappropriation of the story of Almighty Voice, which has been the subject of several stories, poems, and plays by white writers, including the play *Almighty Voice* by Len Peterson (1974), in which the character is represented as a tragic hero. In his version, Moses constructs a disjunctive two-part drama, the first half of which is a relatively realistic, if lyrical, dramatization of the relationship between Almighty Voice and his wife, White Girl, moving through the now legendary stories — and that's part of the point — of Almighty Voice's killing of the cow, his killing of the mounties, and, finally, their killing of him. Subtitled "Running with the Moon," the act is divided into nine scenes, framed by the changes of the moon, including its emblematic colour changes ranging from blood red (*"the moon bleeds"* [12]), to "HONEY MOON" ([40], a love scene), and finally to white (52). This lunar structure is suggestive of the natural world, of course, but also, crucially, of "metamorphosis," "transformation," and "possibility," which Moses has indicated are central to his way of thinking — and which are reflected in his extensive use of shape-shifting puns and allusions ("Daniel" 156).

The second act abruptly transforms the play itself into the realm of musical comedy-cum-satirical-vaudevillian medicine show, as the ghost of Almighty Voice — "Almighty Ghost" (56), in historically ironic *"white face"*(53) — together with an "Interlocutor" (also in white face) stage the appropriation of his-story by a series of "other" voices, in a metadrama entitled "The Red and White Victoria Regina Spirit Revival Show." The act is staged for an audience constructed as white,[14] and it is filled with searingly angry and ironic refrains: "We have the bucks and you do not / Is it a wonder that you get shot?"

(77). It is also in the second act where, ironically, the oral quality of the performative history of *Almighty Voice* is emphasized — a quality that Moses has said moves him deeply ("Daniel" 158) and that serves in this play a deeply disruptive, destabilizing, and deconstructive function. The act, and the performance within that it represents, are structured as a review, subtitled "GHOST DANCE," which passes from "OVERTURE" through "BARITONE SOLO," "THE STUMP" (a kind of interlude), "THE WALKAROUND," "TENOR SOLO," "THE PLAYLET," "DUET," and "STANDUP" to a "FINALE." In the finale, Moses stages what might best be seen as an appropriation of Aristotelian recognition in which the Interlocutor is recognized by Almighty Voice as *"Ni-wikimakan"* — "my wife" (96). Throughout the act, the Interlocutor has served as the white "master" (55) — internalized hegemonically by the appropriately named "White Girl," of whom the ghost remarks, "This is what they've done to you" (66) — for whose benefit "Indianness" is *performed*:

> These fine, kind folks want to know the truth, the amazing details and circumstances behind your savagely beautiful appearance. They also want to be entertained and enlightened and maybe a tiny bit thrilled, just a goose of frightened. They want to laugh and cry. They want to know the facts. And it's up to you and me to try and lie that convincingly. (57)[15]

In the final scene, White Girl removes both the costume and the mask (the white face) of the Interlocutor in a gesture of hope for future histories, somewhat abruptly and perhaps sentimentally represented, as in Tomson Highway's better-known play *Dry Lips Oughta Move to Kapuskasing*, by *"a baby-sized bundle"* (97) that she lifts to the audience *"as the spotlight drifts away to become a full moon in the night"* (96–97).[16] In spite of the sense of imposed closure provided in this finale, however, *Almighty Voice and His Wife* effectively clears the ground of an accumulation of historical misrepresentations and appropriations of Native life and history, destabilizes *any* claim to "authoritative" representations of the past, and provides tentative models for a reclamatory and transformational dramaturgy of Native historiography.

Monique Mojica's *Princess Pocahontas and the Blue Spots* and her radio play *Birdwoman and the Suffragettes*, published with it in 1991, invoke historical modes, memories, and structures of meaning that, as in *Almighty Voice and His Wife*, are neither documentary nor deictically mimetic and that push further than does Moses the deconstructive and, less problematically than in Moses, *re*constructive use of transformational forms and of oral and performative conceptions of history and myth. These plays use a carnivalesque cacophony of stylistic and generic materials first to foreground metatheatrically the deconstruction of the Western (and here explicitly patriarchal) historical record as documentary and stabilizing inscription, and second to foreground the construction of histories conceived as performative and transformative cultural memory.[17]

Birdwoman and the Suffragettes, produced by CBC Radio for *Vanishing Point*'s 1991 series "Adventure Stories for Big Girls," attempts to reclaim for Native women the story of "Sacajawea," "the trusty little Indian guide" (67) on the Lewis and Clarke expedition in 1804–06, from the dubious honours bestowed on her by a cabal of caricatured suffragettes in the play's 1905 (and 1991) present tense. Mojica reassembles fragments from the historical record, eschewing the chronological ordering of events and avoiding the presentation of a simply corrective account — a group of Native "grannies" in 1926 retell the story with no more final authority, and no more disinterestedness, than do the play's suffragettes in 1905 — to concern herself at least in part with a history of (interested) historical *representations* of Sacajawea and an interrogation of the uses of history itself. Finally, history conceived as inscription and preservation, employed to honour, encage, and in a sense keep the dead dead,[18] is set in contrast to history as orality, as memory, employed in the service of enfranchisement and of keeping the ancestors alive and "present." The suffragettes, in search of the "eternal womanly" (83), honour and appropriate the story of a Native sister, naming her Sacajawea and listing monuments, parks, and museums named after her: we learn early on that Sacajawea was the name given by whites to the woman first known as Phoenaif ("Grasswoman") and later Tsakakawea ("Birdwoman") (69). Meanwhile the subject of their history, who calls herself variously "Tsakakawea-Birdwoman/Porivo-Chief Woman/Shoshone Woman," feels trapped. "If you remember me," the character intones as she struggles to break free from the bronze confines of a statue raised to commemorate her ("captured again"),

> remember a child fighting to stay alive
> remember a slave girl gambled away
> remember a mother protecting her child
> remember a wife defying the whip

remember an old one who loved her people
remember I died at home on my land

Now, the Birdwoman's name —
    Tsakakawea
is caged in statues, paintings,
    lakes and rivers
        mountains, peaks and ridges
        poems made of fog and lies
and, . . . and a flying machine
"The Spirit of Sacajawea" — Oh!
    (low laughter)
    cannot contain the spirit
so, high above the clouds,
Hawk's screech.
the Birdwoman beats her wings,
    sounds her voice
    soars,
    and is free. (84; emphasis added)

What *Birdwoman and the Suffragettes* stages, then, or more accurately, as radio drama (and therefore continuously with an oral tradition), gives deliberately destabilizing *voice* to, is an encounter between history as *writing* (which de Certeau characterizes as a conquering of both distance and time that functions to construct, colonize, and control various kinds of otherness) and the *voice* of history (as Sacajawea "sounds her voice"), an orality that, as in *Almighty Voice and His Wife*, serves as a destabilizing assertion of alterity.[19]

The destabilizing function of orality in *Birdwoman and the Suffragettes* is served primarily by the metatheatricality of *performance* in *Princess Pocahontas and the Blue Spots* (1988–90), in which the fluidity of spatial, temporal, and even genealogical borders (Mojica herself is part Kuna-Rappahannok, part American Jew born in New York City and living in Canada) is figured forth structurally in an enacted, performative cultural history of Native women in the Americas (including the de-monized mothers of Métis nations) from contact to Anna Mae Aquash. As such, the play resists the construction of categories characterized by de Certeau as definitive of European history writing.[20] Mojica's stage play moves freely across the categories of history, fiction, and myth; across material and political boundaries inscribed and mapped onto

Western representations of Turtle Island (North America); across the temporal markers of historical periodization; across linguistic barriers; across the typographical distinctions between prose and verse; and across the borders between performance genres such as music, dance, drama, performance art, and stand-up comedy, between comedy and tragedy, and between "high" and "popular" cultural forms. In fact, the play might seem to combine the shape-shifting qualities of the Trickster figure ubiquitous in various Native cosmologies with what de Certeau, in *The Practice of Everyday Life*, discusses as *"la perruque"* (24–28) and as the "tactics" practised by marginalized groups who must shift their ground in resistance to the "strategies" deployed out of the institutionalized and entrenched positionings of the hegemonic culture (35–39). In performance, moreover, the borders between the play's characters/subjectivities are not always easy to discern. Some of the speech headings in the published script, in fact, come as a surprise to a reader who has seen the show, since in performance Mojica herself seems to encompass, if not contain, all the roles that she performs, which are not clearly distinguished or demarcated and by which in part she has been historically and culturally shaped in precisely the way in which she is theatrically constructed by them as a performer in the play.

Princess Pocahontas and the Blue Spots is not easy to follow on the page, and this is a function not only of its deconstruction of stereotypes of Native women, its fracturing of characterological and other boundaries, or its historical revisionism. Structurally, the play is both challengingly disjunctive and ultimately visionary. Its organizing structure is explicitly based on "transformations" rather than scenes, invoking change rather than linear growth or development, inciting Native women — conceived multiplicitously as "Word Warriors" — to "pick up their medicine" and "fashion" their "own gods" from their "entrails" (59), and providing models of how to do so.

In her introduction to the published script, the playwright/performer asserts that "the theme of the set, costumes and props is . . . transformation" (17), and she provides a "Note on structure, transformations and transfigurations" in which she describes her post-production discovery of the play's dramatic structure while preparing the play for publication. She points to its thirteen scenes as "transformations" based — like the first act of *Almighty Voice and His Wife* — on the cycles of the moon and to its "4 sections where there is a transfiguration of three women or entities who are one. . . . 13 moons, 4 directions; it is not a linear structure but it is the form and the basis from which these stories must be told" (16). The play-ending "call to arms," sung in Spanish and English and danced to an Andean rhythm, emerges from a visionary structure that models change and demonstrates the strength of a Native nation residing in "the hearts of its women" (60): powerful, fluid, and transformational.

★   ★   ★

FEMALE IMPERSONATIONS

In spite of her parodic representation of suffragettes in *Birdwoman and the Suffragettes*, a representation that is itself a contribution to feminist debates in the 1980s and early 1990s about white feminist hegemony, and in spite of her critique of the contemporary feminist movement in *Princess Pocahontas and the Blue Spots*, the plays of Monique Mojica may be seen to enact the intersection of Native with feminist historical revisionism. Certainly, the dramaturgical strategies that Mojica employs interrogate historical formations that are patriarchal as well as European, and they share many dramaturgical features with plays by non-Native women going back to the early 1980s and beyond.

Sharon Pollock's 1980 play *Blood Relations* may be seen as her first overtly feminist work.[21] Unlike her later monodrama, *Getting It Straight* (discussed in chapter 7), *Blood Relations* is much less radically revisionist, or structurally disjunctive, than Mojica's plays, but it nevertheless makes a considerably more complex use of its metadramatic framework than did the earlier *Walsh* and *The Komagata Maru Incident*, extending and inscribing structurally their exploration and deployment of empathetic "acting out."

Blood Relations, in which Pollock turns to the more private and indeterminate history of Lizzie Borden for her subject matter, is perhaps a history play only in that it is set in the past and Canadian only in that the playwright is Canadian and the story inhabits the Canadian imagination. The play nevertheless represents a significant extension of the approach that Pollock developed in her earlier plays on Canadian history. The play's present tense is 1902, ten years after Lizzie was acquitted on charges of murdering her father and stepmother. Plagued with questions from her friend, an actress from Boston, about whether she was indeed the murderer, Lizzie has the friend "act out" events leading up to the murders, and it is this enactment that forms the body of the play. As the actress pieces together her play within the play, rejecting the roles imposed on her by a patriarchal society that insists on telling her how to "act" like a lady, she imaginatively constructs a past and a play (in much the way that Salutin's actors in *1837* constructed *their* history) that allow her to experience the cathartic release of identification with a double murder that, insofar as she empathizes with the murderer, has been enacted *for* her. But after she has taken the audience with her toward a murder to which she and they give imaginative consent, she raises the axe over "her" sleeping father, and the lights go out. When they come back up, the actress turns to Lizzie, who, playing the role of the maid, Bridget, has been an onstage audience throughout, and says, "Lizzie, you did." Lizzie responds, "I didn't," and, in the play's final line, which arguably includes the audience in its reference, adds, "*You* did" (70; emphasis added), insisting that the actress and the audience take responsibility for the action to which they have consented, the past that they have imagined and thereby created.[22] The impact, moreover, is underscored by a parallel action that occurs in the brief moment between the blackout and these final lines. When the lights come up, and before the actress addresses Lizzie, Lizzie's sister Emma asks, once more, "Lizzie, did you?" Lizzie replies, echoing, in the image of the historical actor as puppet, Major Walsh of Pollock's first history play,

> Did you never stop and think that if I did, then you were guilty too? . . . It was you who brought me up, like a mother to me. Almost like a mother. Did you ever stop and think that I was like a puppet, your puppet? My head your hand, yes, your hand working my mouth, me saying all the things you felt like saying, me doing all the things you felt like doing, me spewing forth, me hitting out. . . . (69–70)

Ultimately, then, for this play, the "facts" — that Emma "wasn't even here that day" (70) or even whether Lizzie "did" or not — are less important than the imaginative truth, the past that we must allow ourselves to imagine and therefore to bring into being as part of our present. We are, for Pollock, both nationally and individually (as her highly personal exploration of her own and her family's past in her 1984 play *Doc* suggests), responsible for what we are and for what we have been; in historiographic terms, that is, we are responsible for what we *have become*. In the construction of this and Pollock's other history plays, it is incumbent upon us to rethink our comfortable myths of identity if we are to recognize ourselves and take responsibility for our future histories. Pollock's metatheatrical re-creations of the past, then, in *Blood Relations* as well as in her earlier plays, serve as a kind of social psychotherapy, as an "acting out" that insists we write our own "true" stories, act out our own plays, and refuse to evade responsibility by defining ourselves, in feminist terminology that applies equally well to Canadian post-colonial nationhood, as "the Other in somebody else's perceptions" (Nunn, "Sharon Pollock's Plays" 79).

Beth Herst's 1992 play *A Woman's Comedy*, like *Aphra*, discussed in chapter 3, takes the life of seventeenth-century playwright Aphra Behn as its subject. Behn, of course, a contemporary of Betterton, Dryden, Otway, and others, was a popular Restoration playwright and a popular subject for salubrious slander as a woman who wrote for a living — indeed, the first of "her kind" in England, at a time when earning a living for a woman, in whatever way, was considered the near equivalent of prostitution. *A Woman's Comedy* is an astonishingly accomplished first play, a "restoration" of the story of Behn, written with understated precision, economy, and grace. It probes the sexual and psychological intrigues that surrounded Behn, in a moving metatheatrical exploration of gender and genre, theatrical convention, and the social construction of identity that expertly blends the historical with the contemporary.[23] *A Woman's Comedy* is not, however, so openly or riotously metatheatrical as *Aphra*, *Almighty Voice and His Wife*, *Princess Pocahontas and the Blue Spots*, or Sally Clark's *Jehanne of the Witches* (discussed below). In fact, it is the naturalness with which metatheatricality occurs, scarcely disturbing the surface of the dialogue, that is surprising in this play, as Herst manages effectively to imitate the witty, slightly risqué repartee of Behn's own plays. Indeed, much of *A Woman's Comedy*'s self-reflexivity is a function of its meticulously crafted use of shifting linguistic styles and its fluid employment of changes of scene and time. In scenes that flow seamlessly from one location and time to the next, usually carried over by a character who appears in both, Herst also shifts seamlessly between a convincingly stylized Restoration dialogue for public scenes and a more naturalistic and intimate, but equally carefully crafted, dialogue for private scenes, particularly those between Aphra and her actress friend, Betty, dialogue that would not entirely be out of place in either a Restoration or a modern play. The effect, as Ann Wilson points out in her introduction to the published script, is to create a resonance between past and present "intersections of social, sexual and financial economies" (148).

In the play's second scene, a sexual negotiation between Lord Greville and Betty, when Greville's repartee is persistently praised by his accomplice, the "fop" Archer, Betty interjects:

BETTY: I see, my lord, you carry your own chorus with you.
GREVILLE: Being an indifferent performer, I would not take the stage alone.
BETTY: False modesty, sir. You are no amateur. 'Tis well known you've trodden the boards before.
GREVILLE: An interlude or two, I confess. Brief entertainments, nothing more.
BETTY: Have you no new plot in hand?
GREVILLE: There is a scene I would play out, but it wants private acting.
BETTY: I never play, save to the full applause of the whole house.
GREVILLE: I have no doubt. Do you never give command performances?
BETTY: That would depend on the terms of engagement.
GREVILLE: Name them, madam. For I am eager to raise the scene, and would begin the action straight. (168)

And so it goes, with the negotiations played out around puns involving sexual and theatrical performance in the best Restoration style.

Theatrical genre, however, is also at issue here, and questions of social and theatrical form are paramount in a play that is itself structured with considerable craft. Throughout the action, which focuses on Behn's unconventional relationship with her pedophiliac lover, Jack Hoyle, the son of an infamous regicide, on her declining health, and on her writing to pay the bills by satisfying what is presented as the decadent tastes of her audiences, Behn attempts to have a serious work produced, one that, however, like life (which "rarely observes the decorums of art"), "violates all the rules of form": "Your heroine misused, betrayed, attacked on every side. Left alone at the last, neither widow, maid, nor wife. And yet she lives on, past the final act. The Town will not countenance such a moral" (221). But as Hoyle tells Aphra earlier, in refusing to choose between comedy and tragedy as a script for their relationship ("The one must always finish in marriage," he argues, "the other in death"), "You break forms at your peril, and run the risk of being damned for the attempt" (170). Before she dies, indeed, Aphra burns her heretical (and of course apocryphal) script.

In the final scene, Herst stages what Michel de Certeau might call historiography's return of the repressed or what "historiography does not want to know" (*Writing* 343). She does so, as Daniel David Moses does in *Almighty Voice and His Wife*, through the use of a revisionist ghost — a ghost *writer* who returns in the final scene, is concerned with history's "shadows" and "ghosts," and knows that "they never got the story straight" (236). Herst's history is concerned, however, less with de Certeau's first, straight-talking pole of history as narrative, "the story which is recounted," than with his second, "what is produced." Herst is concerned, that is, with opening "within the text of [her] culture the rift of something that happened elsewhere and otherwise." She wants to "effect displacements, add other parts, set up intervals and comparisons, . . . discern the trace of something other in these signs" (de Certeau, *Writing* 288). *A Woman's Comedy* does so with power, intelligence, and grace, and it does so sufficiently successfully, given the masculinist bias of theatrical production that still prevails in Canada, that Herst's work has rarely been revived since the Tarragon Theatre premiere of the play in 1992. As revisionist women's history, called comedy in its title but nevertheless ending in death, her work breaks forms and continues to do so for Herst, as it did for Behn, at her peril.

I noted earlier Ann Wilson's comments on the resonances between past and present in Herst's play. One of the most resonant reverberations, which has to do with both history and form, is concerned, with ironic metatheatricality, with the reception of *A Woman's Comedy* itself and Herst's response to that reception. In "*A Woman's Comedy*: Male Plots or Female Experience?" Herst takes up objections to the play by one male reviewer, who argued that her play had missed the point: "the point of Aphra Behn's story," he argued, "was her wit, not her ability to suffer" (qtd. in Herst 77). In an articulate and provocative response worthy of the Behn of history and of her own play, and full of echoes of Behn's predicament, Herst defends her version of an Aphra who "was not the glittering, invulnerable heroine of a Restoration comedy, all wit, elegance, and repartee. Her history was more ragged, less shapely than that." "[W]ondering about the ways in which men and women conceive and tell life stories," Herst argues, echoing her own play, that "in her life Aphra Behn rejected the plot her society prescribed, the woman's plot of economic dependance, legal non-status, anonymity, silence. She wrote a new story for herself by writing" (77).

> [M]y recent experience has brought home to me, in the most emphatic way possible, that there can be a profound difference between the stories men and women live, imagine, tell and hear, stories about themselves, and about each other. . . . Ultimately, there can never be a single story, a right story, to be told or heard about any life, male or female. (78)

While *A Woman's Comedy* is a metatheatrical restoration and revisioning of the history of a neglected Restoration playwright that plays out in its represented action and actual reception the undervaluing of feminist experimentation with form and genre, Sally Clark's *Jehanne of the Witches* metatheatrically revisits the too-well-known history of Joan of Arc and, in Barbara Godard's phrase, "dismantles the representation of tragedy as the tragedy of representation" (30).[24] Both plays are metatheatrical rehearsals of the historical record as it relates to maligned women of the distant past, but *Jehanne of the Witches* concerns itself most directly with the social construction of gender, the suppression of women's mythology as witchcraft, and the construction and retrenchment of patriarchy in the fifteenth century. It is an extraordinarily complex play, framing the story of Joan of Arc within the context of a performance supervised and directed by Gilles de Rais — history's Bluebeard — in which Jehanne is played by a young boy whose performance, it is hinted, may culminate in his "real" death at the stake *as* Jehanne but who in Clark's play, of course, is played by a woman. This casting, together with the revelation to the audience only at the end of act 1 that what it has been watching is a performance, serves to make the character of Jehanne more apparent and "real" than that of the boy who plays her, particularly when both are played in Clark's play by a woman. Gender — and history — could hardly be more thoroughly problematized (unless one takes into account the fact that in the play's first production the role of Gilles de Rais was played by Sky Gilbert, Toronto's best-known transvestite actor). Jehanne, in fact, played in the frame scenes of Gilles's reenactment by the boy François, is told by her mother that she/he can't be a man because "you have breasts" (120); in a frame scene, however, François denies his resemblance to Jehanne on the basis that his/her breasts are "fake" (120); yet, of course, the François/Jehanne whom the audience sees tapping his/her fake breasts is played by a woman whose breastplate covers "the real thing." The breaking of the illusion — together with the audience-stage contract of suspension of disbelief — so late in the play, and the continued and unsettling shifts in the second act between frame and story, of course, radically unsettle the representation and throw into question the very nature of historical enactment. The nature of the play's resistances — Jehanne's resistance to being a woman and *Jehanne*'s resistance to tragic form, in particular — constitute resistance to the inevitability within patriarchal structures and discourses of the victimization of women in the sacrificial contracts — to which women, like the François/Jehanne of Clark's play, have not consented — that make representation possible.

But the real magic in a play that attempts to reinstate magic in the face of repressive and manipulable misogynist "fact" is the playwright's managing to assert the truth of "the Old [matriarchal] Religion" (110) and of her women's version of history while simultaneously asserting the constructed nature of any claim to truth. Clark accomplishes this largely through the combination of a kind of free-floating intertextuality and a generic shape-shifting, both of which destabilize traditionally gendered representation and reappropriate misogynist forms (such as tragedy) that rest on the sacrifice of women in order to expose them and together with them what Godard calls "the universality of the order of phallic law" (25).

The shift from "the Old Religion" to Christianity, then, is represented in the play as a generic, structural shift toward a linear, patriarchal, and sacrificial vision and away from a women-centred, transformational faith in which "the power is to serve" (101) — a faith that "forbade the shedding of blood" (130) and that centred on the cycles of the moon. "She," after all (the moon), is of "much more use to us than God is" (27). While Isabelle, Jehanne's mother and a follower of the old faith, tells her that "It is in the nature of power to have cycles. You can't use power without replenishing yourself" (120), the new faith requires sacrifice. There are intimations throughout that the sacrificial victim is to be Jehanne herself, and these hints are confirmed when Gilles explains that, in the new dispensation, "The power, to be any use at all, had to be consummated" (105). "Blood," he explains, "was needed for the sacrifice."

> It's the blood sacrament. Christ and his disciples. We have to move with the times. We can't deny that the Christian Church is in control. And they got their power from the sacrament. Jehanne

said that I was perverting the Old Religion. That I was turning it into sorcery. But even with the power of her voices, she couldn't deny that she was the Divine Sacrifice. (130–31)

Gilles's play, then, staged years after Jehanne's burning, is a ritual effort to invent tragedy and to conjure up the spirit of Jehanne by replaying her sacrifice (and carrying it out on the body of François). What Clark's play does structurally is to deconstruct Gilles's appropriative attempts to "merge the two religions," "to be a witch and a Christian" (110), and to forge a new power from that merger. "My Christian mystery play," Gilles says, "is also an ancient invocation" (128). But his drama is metatheatrically disrupted by François, who resists the (masculinist) plot that requires his/her sacrifice and whose actorly identification with his character — "I can feel her, sire" (124) — intrudes on the drama on a number of occasions, to the consternation of the other actors. François tells Gilles, for example, that Jehanne did not consent to be sacrificed. "That last scene's wrong," he says of a sequence in which Jehanne is depicted as resisting the pleas of her mother and Saint Margaret to return home, become a woman, and bear children, "Jehanne wanted to go back to Domremy" (124).

That the "boy" who argues this is presented in Clark's play by a woman constitutes what Godard calls "a double substitution and superposition which *stages* the female body playing out its sacrificial role": "Tragedy is staged and unmasked as masculine ritual." "[N]o longer embedded in a narrative life story," Godard argues, "life story is contained within the frame of ritual, expos[ing] the gendered differential in this signifying practice. The absent, mutilated female struggles to reemerge from the boy's body in which she has been confined by the theatrical institution" (28; emphasis added).[25]

"Jehanne" appears to Gilles twice near the play's end, not conjured up by his rituals but, the first time, because "I felt like it" (128), to tell him that

the King of Heaven does not look like that! He's not a wise old man, sitting on a cloud. My voices — Saint Catherine, Saint Margaret — women's voices. Even the Archangel Michael was a woman. That's why I could never describe my voices. No one would follow me if I told them they were women. You've made your own world here, Gilles. It's of, for, and about men. Even I am a man in your creation. . . . Women have only one use in your world. Kindling for your fires. You betrayed me, Gilles. You betrayed me to your male God. (127)

Jehanne appears the second time in the flesh, as a mature woman — "not your boy, anymore" (134) — who was not in fact sacrificed but who returns for "justice" and to witness *his* confession and consignment to the flames.

But the play doesn't end there. If it did, it would be a tragedy — the tragedy of Gilles de Rais.[26] The play ends not with any conclusive or clarifying invocation of closure but with a curious and problematic monologue by a new character, Marie de Rais, Gilles's daughter, played by the actress playing Jehanne/François and therefore legible as a third reappearance/resurrection of Jehanne. Instructed by a voice to go to the pyre where her father was burned to erect a fountain to Saint Marie, the Milk Goddess, she finds that everyone at the fountain prays to her father, and she delivers a monologue that surely throws into serious question the whole issue of (mis)representation, historical or otherwise, and the ways in which stories, statues, fountains, and plays are used:

> All the barren women in the village pray to Saint Gilles to be made fertile. Pregnant women ask Saint Gilles for plentiful milk for their babies. They say my father is returning the lives he took. The people of Nantes love my father. Every year, in honour of his death, they come to his shrine and they beat their children. (141)

The monologue and the play end, however, with an assertion of rituals and representations grounded in fertility and birth rather than in violence and cruelty and with a replacement of masculinist forms of dramatic narrative by women-centred stories of nourishment and continuity:

> I stopped hearing the Voice shortly after I built the fountain. It makes me very sad. I miss my Voice. I realize my talking of milk and child-birth is a bit of a letdown from what you're used to. No battles. No blood. Just the simple continuance of the human race. (141)

PART THREE

Beyond Modernism

SHAPES OF SPACE AND PLACE

What part 2 has been in relation to my first chapter's discussion of naturalistic dramaturgies, part 3 aims to be in relation to the analysis in chapter 2 of modernist dramaturgies. That is, whereas part 2 focused on responses to and multiplications of dramaturgies based on the development of character and action through *time*, part 3 deals with developments and multiplications that grow out of modernist dramaturgies that retreat from the temporal, historical, and social realms into those of (pure, formalist) *space*. While part 2 focused, then, on temporal structures of multiplication concerned with process, what follows in chapters 6 and 7 concerns itself with spatial structures of multiplication that operate in theatrical environments and discursive spaces respectively. To a greater or lesser extent, both spaces are treated here as *social* sites of negotiation and contestation, in which "position" has both spatial and political resonances and the politics of social placement come directly into play.

Both chapters assume that space — theatrical, environmental, or discursive — is anything but stable, static, self-enclosed, or purely formalist. Indeed, whether it is the essentially elitist or conservative politics of R. Murray Schafer or the explicitly left-wing positionings of Guillermo Verdecchia that are being played out, space in these chapters is seen as at least potentially transformative and always differentially constructed and perceived according to particular social, cultural, discursive, and physical positionings in which controls of focus, authority, and authenticity are decentred and rendered problematic. This section owes a great deal to Michel de Certeau's distinctions, in *The Practice of Everyday Life*, between "place(s)," the established positions from which the currently dominant *strategically* defend their authority, resisting the temporal dimensions of chance and change, and "space," the undefined geographies through which the disempowered *tactically* shift ground, seize the moment, respond improvisationally to whatever they are presented with, and resist the solidification of time into an unchanging and stable spatial realm of universal structures and values.

As is the case throughout this book, but perhaps more dramatically here than elsewhere, the styles of writing in the chapters in this section are consciously inconsistent, chapter 6 sprawling over a broad range of theatrical environments and chapter 7, a collaborative effort with Dr. Jennifer Harvie, adopting the form of a dialogue supplemented by extensive notes in order to imitate and play out the positional problematics of the relationships between the monologic, the dialogic, monologue, and dialogue.

6

Environmental Theatre

The bifurcation of space must be ended. The final exchange
between performers and audience is the exchange of space.
— Richard Schechner, *Environmental Theater* (xxvi)

IN CANADA, what collective creation has been to naturalistic drama,
environmental theatre is to the modernist tradition: if, in its pushing
and questioning of process and its insistence on particular kinds of
authenticity, much Canadian collective creation can be seen as post-
naturalist, then much Canadian environmental theatre can be seen as
post-modernist.[1] Not surprisingly, the history and range of environmental theatre in Canada are as proportionately small, relative to the rich
tradition of collective and collaborative work, as the body of modernist
writing for the Canadian theatre is small in relation to the dominance
of naturalistic forms on Canadian stages.

There has nevertheless been a significant body of work produced
environmentally in Canada since the late 1960s and early 1970s, work
that treats the politics of theatrical space in ways that are analogous, in
the context of modernist forms of focus, optics, and power, to the ways
in which collective and collaborative work, in the contexts of rehearsal
techniques, theatrical organization, and the construction of characterization and narrative, treats the politics of process. In terms of dramaturgical structure, what collective and collaborative work performs in
the temporal dimension environmental theatre effects spatially.

Richard Schechner, who coined the phrase "environmental theatre"
and first theorized it in the late 1960s and early 1970s, traces its contemporary roots in the West to modernist developments in music and
the visual arts, notably through composer John Cage, Dada, and a
number of avant-garde visual artists, mostly American.[2] Schechner,

together with Michael Kirby, also draws heavily in his accounts of environmental theatre, particularly his own work, on Oriental, African, and other "primitive" forms of ritual and performance in much the same way that modernist artists in other forms ransacked rhythms, images, and techniques from cultures that they constructed as Other. In spite of its attempts to multiply focus and democratize theatrical space, environmental theatre as it developed and was theorized in the United States in the 1960s was post-modern primarily in the historical sense that it grew out of a modernist aesthetic, and it shared with the modernist project, as outlined in chapter 2, a tendency to cannibalize other forms and traditions, to objectify women (who tend to appear in the literature as "girls" and on the stage as subservient and "usually at some stage of undress" [Sandford xxii]), and to focus on ahistorical, formalist, and self-referential patterns and structures in which the individual human subject is either mechanized or treated as the individual/ universalist object of asocial varieties of mid-century American psychotherapy (see Schechner, *Environmental Theater* 193–226). The first strand of Canadian environmental theatre discussed in this chapter, represented by the work of R. Murray Schafer and Hillar Liitoja, grows directly out of these 1960s experiments in the United States and shares many of their most characteristic features.

But environmental theatre in Canada has also, in a different and distinct manifestation, been post-modern in an explicitly political way that has more to do with Linda Hutcheon's articulation of "the politics of postmodernism" than with the depoliticized excesses of post-modernism as it has come to be understood through writers/ prophets such as Baudrillard, Lyotard, and many American theorists. Ever since Schechner coined the term, environmental theatre, at least in the stated intentions of its creators and theorists, has articulated — if not always achieved — an explicitly political agenda problematically disposed toward its modernist predecessors. This is particularly true in its politicization of space and democratization of focus, its insistence on the engagement or implication of audiences within the dramatic frame (or its explosion of that frame outward), and its deployment of socially transformative modes such as ritual, shamanism, or magic.[3] In his reintroduction to the 1994 edition of *Environmental Theater*, Schechner argues that,

> In a word, environments ecological or theatrical can be imagined
> not only as spaces but as active players in complex systems of

transformation. Neither ecological nor performance environments are passive. They are interactants in events organically taking place throughout vivified spaces. A performance environment is a "position" in the political sense, a "body of knowledge" in the scholarly sense, a "real place" in the theatrical sense. Thus, to stage a performance "environmentally" means more than simply to move it off of the proscenium or out of the arena. An environmental performance is one in which *all the elements or parts* making up the performance are recognized as alive. To "be alive" is to change, develop, transform; to have needs and desires; even, potentially, to acquire, express, and use consciousness. (x)

It is its post-Brechtian concern with consciousness, its implications for the construction of social space within and beyond the theatre, and its more or less explicit concern with the operations of power in society that have made environmental theatre congenial to many contemporary Canadian theatre workers, including those, such as Richard Rose and John Krizanc, discussed in the second half of this chapter, who have for the most part abandoned such things as audience participation and audience-performer contact (see Nelson 92–93).

★   ★   ★

March 1993. Once the audience had assembled in the rectangular and empty industrial space on George Street in Toronto's east end, occupied at the time by Buddies in Bad Times Theatre, the small platform stage at one end of the room picked itself up and began to move with apparent hesitation into the centre of the room. It paused there for a moment before continuing on to the wall at the opposite end of the space, forcing spectators to scramble out of the way. The stage rested for a moment before once again lifting its skirts and continuing its perambulations about the room, so that in the end not a single spectator was left stationary. Once everyone had been forced to move at least once, the stage settled for the moment in the centre of the room, and eight cast members — six of them naked and smeared with mud — emerged from a trapdoor in its centre and began to dance around the platform, enticing, cajoling, and otherwise confronting the audience. Eventually, the platform broke up into constituent parts, and the entire space was shared among actors, spectators, shifting platforms, lighting effects, and sound sources. As reviewer H.J. Kirchhoff said, "you keep moving," but "when you move . . . you find yourself in a spotlight, with naked people next to you or in front of you, doing things engaging, vulgar, and/or amusing. You move, and find yourself involved with something else." I had my portrait done, in crayon, by a naked woman seated next to me. Later I found myself face-to-groin with a cast member urinating into a glass. "[Y]ou keep moving."[4]

As this description of Pow Pow Unbound's 1993 production of *Stage* suggests, the roots of at least some environmental theatre in Canada remain firmly in the participatory/confrontational 1960s tradition as represented by Richard Schechner and The Performance Group's infamous *Dionysus in 69*. And those roots are firmly within the tradition of the modernist avant-garde.

It is not incidental that the two most dedicated practitioners of (and polemicists for) environmental theatre in Canada, R. Murray Schafer and Hillar Liitoja, were trained as musicians and began their careers with a fascination for the work of the archetypal modernist poet (and fascist propagandist) Ezra Pound. Although his early interests were, not insignificantly, in painting and sports (Colgrass 33), Schafer is first and best known as a composer 'and educator, having won the first international Glenn Gould prize for outstanding contribution to music, having published widely on music education and soundscape theories (including the widely read and much translated *The Tuning of the World*), and having had his music performed internationally. Schafer's first work was *Ezra Pound and Music*, the compilation and editing of Pound's writings on music after Schafer met the American imagist poet in Venice in the late 1950s and debated with him "about poetry and music and, very likely, politics," according to Robert Everett-Green ("Polemics"). In an article based on an interview with Schafer in Toronto in 1991, Everett-Green also quotes the composer's opinions on (European) quality and (Canadian) vulgarity, multiculturalism, assimilation, and nationalism,[5] opinions that would not sound out of character coming from the post-war Pound, whom Everett-Green describes as Schafer's "one time poetic mentor" ("Polemics").

Perhaps more to the point, Schafer's artistic influences and interests are entirely compatible with those of Pound, together with other modernists with whom Schafer has been linked or has linked himself, such as Berg, Schoenberg, Webern, and Stravinsky; Joyce, Lawrence,

Eliot, Cocteau, and d'Annunzio; Kandinsky, Klee, Buckminster Fuller, the Bauhaus, the Dadaists, the Italian Futurists, and the Russian constructivists; as well as theatrical practitioners and theorists such as Reinhardt, Meyerhold, Vahktangov, Artaud, and, both notably and frequently, in the wide-ranging interdisciplinary aspirations of Schafer's "theatre of confluence," Wagner.[6] Several of these artists, not incidentally, have been linked in their philosophies, or their subsequent deployment by others, with the European extreme right. I have no wish to suggest that Schafer's political opinions are in any way allied with neoconservative extremism. It is, however, worth considering his major work, *Patria* (which Schafer translates as "homeland" but which might more accurately, and more disturbingly, in light of his brand of nationalism, be read as "fatherland"[7]), in the context of his explicitly elitist, antirepublican, and antidemocratic political views, which are embedded to some extent in the deep structure of his work.

In his book *"Patria" and the Theatre of Confluence* and elsewhere, Schafer frequently inveighs against a contemporary society in which "Heroic myths are not popular . . . because there is no room in them for mediocrity." He laments the ways in which "republicanism [has] dwarfed everyone" (197), and he suggests that "an unwritten article in the republic's constitution is the right to remain ignorant" (198). He laments, then, a time in which "the victims" — by which he means the uneducated, the physically, mentally, or emotionally handicapped, and immigrants[8] — "are treated as invalids, requiring crutches and social workers rather than the inspiration of heroes" (198).

The "artist," however, clearly is "not a social worker" for Schafer, who frequently and at some length articulates his feeling of alienation from an unappreciative and mundane (Canadian) society and who prefers to align himself with what he sees as an artistic and intellectual elite for whom hermetic and other mystical texts remain meaningful, as they have been for the "highest" civilizations:

> Such texts do not originate in low civilizations. They occur in the highest. A few individuals — at first a very few — sidestep society to regard it in a totally different manner, from a transmundane perspective, accessible perhaps only to the physically inactive. Such were the gnostic philosophers; such were the alchemists to whom they are related. And by a comparative gradient so far unexplored, we see resemblances between these individuals, hermetically sealed off from the masses, and certain modern artists:

Joyce, Kafka, Beckett. We see it also in the arrogance of d'Annunzio, the spinsterish voice of Eliot, the fustian politics of Pound, everywhere where figures of maximal intelligence have been isolated or have sought isolation from the public arenas of social life. (141)

Not surprisingly, then, Schafer's work for the theatre for the most part eschews any form of participation that empowers the audience or involves it in the process of creation, "lest theatre should fall victim to collective or herdesque whine" ("Theatre of Confluence" 38). Schafer is interested, finally, not in participation but in presentation, not in process but in product — "the fact of art," as he says, or "arti-fact" (46). He thus argues that "There is no reason why an audience, prepared to be an audience, should expect to be anything but an audience":

> The assumption that the audience knows best what it wants is questionable. The blurring of the distinctions between the giving and receiving of art can be tragic. In the West everywhere one notices this frightful descent into homogeneity, blurring distinctions, obliterating the idiosyncratic, dragging the leaders down and the led up onto some middle ground of fulcrumed banality. Both communism and democracy are systems dedicated to smoothing out differences between men [sic]. Of course you *can* make a congenital dunce into a prime minister but this is no guarantee of improvement in the state. Those who are prepared to pass the responsibilities of the artist to the audience will merely be rewarded in the same way as the liberals who first prepared the revolution of democracy: their heads were the first to fall when mass-man [sic] took over. (37)

Schafer's "theatre of confluence," moreover, is explicitly articulated throughout *"Patria" and the Theatre of Confluence* as being multi-disciplinary, not out of any interest in the pluralistic problematizing of each artistic discourse or in any multifaceted or democratizing multi-plication of perspectives. On the contrary, it is defined and defended as an art form "conceived on all levels simultaneously [and] elaborated coevally" ("Theatre of Confluence" 46), "a kind of theatre in which all the arts may meet, court and make love" in the service of achieving a transcendental unity (31) — a "counterpoint between the senses" (34) — that is greater than that available to any one art form on its own.

Schafer's work, then, distances itself from some of the most character-istic — and politically interventionist — features of the environmental theatre movement in the United States in the 1960s. Nevertheless, his musical and sound compositions — particularly his theoretical work, *The Tuning of the World* — seem to be comparable to, or compatible with, those of one of the 1960s gurus of environmental theatre, John Cage. Schafer is also like Cage, Schechner, and others in paying tribute to, drawing on, and arguably appropriating non-Western languages and forms of ritual and expression — as well as the rituals, legends, and languages of North American Native peoples, Greek mythology, and the Catholic Mass — in a kind of condescendingly Rousseauesque primitivism and faith in what he calls "the recovery of the sacred" ("Theatre of Confluence II" 7–10).[9] Interestingly, many of Darko Suvin's critiques of the "liberal sentimentality" of what Suvin calls the "Rousseauist approach" of the 1960s Happenings movement apply closely to Schafer's work (287). Suvin points out that political, eco-nomic, and ideological analysis in Happenings was eschewed in favour of a naïve and ahistorical faith that "a return to supposed fundamentals outside civilization will illume present-day life" (287). In Schafer, as in Happenings, this substitution of "pseudo-biological values" for historical ones arguably results in "a Eucharist without a Real Presence, a dumb Symposium" (287).[10]

As in many modernist works, and as in the "interculturalist" work of theatre practitioners and theorists such as Peter Brook, Ariane Mnouchkine, and Eugenio Barba, the deployment of Native, Egyptian, Japanese, Greek, or other forms tends in Schafer's work to be done somewhat indiscriminately, flattening cultural differences in a search for "the unity of all things material, spiritual, natural, and divine" (Schafer, "Theatre of Confluence II" 5), a search that is completely congruent with his expressed distaste for multiculturalism and other pluralistic policies and practices (Everett-Green, "Polemics"). As for Brook, Barba, and the visual artists of the modernist period who turned to African and "Japoniste" raw materials for inspiration, the forms, traditions, and artifacts of other cultures tend in Schafer's work to be ransacked for those elements that conform to Western literary, mythical, or psychological archetypes and appropriated in the service of an essentially colonizing artistic vision. Interestingly, Schafer's inter-est in non-Western modes of expression is primarily an interest in form. "[O]ne does not interpret rituals so much by their contents," Schafer argues, "as by their forms: the special spaces and times they occupy, the ritual objects they employ, the roles of the participants, the decorum and ceremony" ("Theatre of Confluence II" 15). And the forms, he suggests, are both "deliberately structured" ("Princess" 24) and reflect universal archetypes that are "more or less unchanging" (qtd. in Everett-Green, "Polemics").

Schafer's theatrical work, apart from the early opera *Loving* (1965), consists of the *Patria* cycle, a monumental work, begun in the late 1960s and still, after a prologue, six completed parts (with four more in various stages of development), and an epilogue, very much in progress.[11] Throughout the work, archetypal, mythical, and mystical sources are tapped and harnessed to Schafer's essentially mythopoeic/dialectical vision of the achievement of unity. Structurally, however, the *Patria* cycle as a whole is determinedly unfinished and open ended — "a kind of picaresque," as Schafer describes it — and at the same time curiously closed (qtd. in Everett-Green, "Polemics"). He notes, for example, that

> At the end of *The Princess and the Stars*, which is the prologue, the sun descends and says to Wolf, "Go and look for your princess. It will take you through many lifetimes, and many forms." But the archetypes are more or less unchanging. There's an accumulation of experience which makes the characters more complete, but which doesn't necessarily amount to psychological growth. (qtd. in Everett-Green, "Polemics")

As this passage suggests, there are potentially an infinite number of performances, "episodes," works, or events that can be produced within and under the auspices of the *Patria* cycle, in which Schafer displays a genius for recycling his earlier work. The cycle's component parts, moreover, are designed to stand on their own, have never been performed together, have only been performed out of sequence, and indeed relate to one another only in terms of deep structure and a fund of generalized, overarching mythical source materials. However, the fact that there is an existing prologue and a planned epilogue, together with an insistent assertion of universal and unchanging archetypes, suggests that any openness to the structure is more apparent than real. And, as Schafer indicates in *"Patria" and the Theatre of Confluence*, the epilogue to the series, invoking an all-encompassing closure, brings it "full cycle, concluding at the lake from which it first began" (214).

Where the cycle begins is with its so-called prologue, *The Princess and the Stars* (1981), which is staged at dawn on the shore of a lake in the autumn and which establishes the (invented) "legend" on which the whole cycle is based. It tells the story of the Princess, daughter of the Sun-God, who falls to Earth listening to the cry of the (male) Wolf, the double of the Moon. Once there, she is accidentally wounded by the Wolf and captured beneath the lake by the Three-Horned Enemy. The Wolf then sets out in search of the Princess to seek forgiveness and compassion, through which he will find and redeem both himself and the "patria" and inherit the Moon. In Schafer's account, the rest of the cycle follows directly from this scenario:

> The unifying motive of the *Patria* works is Wolf's journeys through the many labyrinths of life in search of the spiritual power which can both release and transfigure him. He will travel under many names and assume many guises: impersonating a human as the displaced immigrant D.P.; as the Greek hero Theseus; as the dead Pharaoh seeking to be raised to heaven by the sun; or as the King in the "chymical marriage" or heiros-gamos of the alchemists. At times he may assume a great pre-eminence; at other times he may be chased away as a fool, a criminal, or a "beast." As the labyrinthine nature of his wanderings intensifies, the Princess becomes personified for him in the figure of Ariadne, who helped Theseus escape the Cretan labyrinth in the well-known Greek myth. The thread-gift provided by Ariadne in the *Patria* series is the thread of music. Ariadne's gift is her haunting voice; this is what sustains and transforms Theseus-Wolf during his journeying.
>
> Each of the *Patria* pieces is designed to exist on its own and many explore different theatrical settings and techniques, though all follow the theme of Wolf's search for his spirit in the guise of the Princess as it was introduced in *The Princess of the Stars*. ("Princess" 22)

The structure of the cycle as a whole, and of each of the constituent parts through which this narrative is played out, is a combination of, first, Hegelian dialectic, in which equal opposites contest with one another but in which, ultimately, their conflict brings about a synthesis that represents for Schafer the mystic unity of all creation, and, second, a mythopoeic pattern of renewal that is rooted in theories based on structuralist anthropology as articulated in Frazer's *The Golden Bough* and in the work of literary theorists such as Frye and Barber (see chapter 2). Thus, the *Patria* cycle is cyclic, beginning with initiation and moving quickly to separation or fall (in the seasonal or biblical sense), as represented in the prologue, *The Princess of the Stars*. It then moves through various kinds of descent into mazes, labyrinths, or necropolises, configured as quest journeys "for unity and the home-land" (*Patria* 11). Eventually, it moves out of these dark, nighttime, or wintertime experiences of deprivation, trial, barrenness, or confronta-tion to various kinds of rebirth and apotheosis configured as reunion, sunrise, the arrival of spring, or the ascent into heaven. The final, joyous reconciliation is completed in what Schafer calls the epilogue (*And Wolf Shall Inherit the Moon*), which is not yet completed but is outlined in some detail in *"Patria" and the Theatre of Confluence*. Individual parts of the cycle play variations on this overall shape, as the focus shifts from the early parts of the narrative (in *Patria 1: The Char-acteristics Man, Patria 2: Requiem for the Party Girl*, and *Patria 3: The Greatest Show*), through the "half-way point" (*Patria* 154) in *Patria 4: The Alchemical Theatre of Hermes Trismegistus*,[12] in which separation is recapitulated and union foreshadowed in the alchemical conjuction of Sol and Luna (*Patria* 154), to the final movements toward group (*Patria 5: The Crown of Ariadne* and *Patria 6: Ra*[13]) and individual (*Patria 7: Asteria*[14]) emergence from the labyrinth at dawn, to various kinds of harmony and unity (*Patria 8–10*, projected), culminating in the reunion and apotheosis of the Princess and the Wolf in the epilogue (*And Wolf Shall Inherit the Moon*).

Like the universalist and transcultural appropriation and deploy-ment of the (conflated) languages, legends, and myths of other cultures in the *Patria* cycle, Schafer's use of this familiar mythical narrative structure (which is, of course, fundamentally Western and most clearly embodied in Greek mythology and the Christian Bible) can be seen in its political and social effects to be ultimately conservative and culturally affirmative, not only in its invocation of closure but also in its reinscription of traditional gender roles. According to Schafer, the Princess and the Wolf, or Ariadne and Theseus, are animus and anima symbols, the poles of the cycle's dialectic that are "ultimately destined to blend together in perfect wholeness" and are treated throughout the cycle "as equal partners" (*Patria* 161). They might also be seen, however, as the embodiments of essentialist male and female principles (sometimes also called by Schafer "Dionysian and Appollonian"[15]) that conflate sex and gender, reinscribe restrictive gender roles, and reinforce as universal gendered behaviours that are anything but equal. "The female" in the *Patria* plays — as embodied variously in the Princess, Ariadne, and others — exists primarily as an inactive muse, guide, helper, or embodiment of spirit for the central, active, and clearly more important male — embodied by Wolf, Theseus, D.P., and others. The "universal" mythic quest, then, is represented by "Wolf's search for his spirit in the guise of the Princess" (*Patria* 82), who exerts no agency and occupies no independent subject position. As Schafer says of *Patria 2: Requiem for the Party Girl*, in which Ariadne is imprisoned in a mental institution, "Ariadne, like Uroboros, the self-devouring snake, is caught in an unsettled circularity where she will remain until Wolf, through redemptive love, can restore her to her native element in the heavens" (*Patria* 82).[16]

In narrative terms, then, the *Patria* cycle can be seen to employ and embody a deep structure that is deeply conservative, elitist, antidemocratic, colonialist, culturally appropriative, and antifeminist. What's more, while Schafer can write intoxicatingly about the magnificent and mystical moments and transmogrifications in the cycle, the actual staging of those moments, as he and his creative team move from the conception to the act, can too often be awkward, embarrassing, or even risible. Too often, in Urjo Kareda's phrase, "the drama . . . is at once both snobbishly obscure and condescendingly obvious" ("R. Murray Schafer").

But it is too easy to dismiss Schafer because of his apparent arrogance and frequent failures. In spite of his political positions and his deployment of culturally affirmative forms of narrative, moreover, the effects of his work in performance can in practice (or reception) be far from closed, monolithic, or repressive. Not surprisingly, this is partly because Schafer, a self-styled maverick who enjoys making unfashionably reactionary public statements, is simultaneously unwilling to align himself openly with "political ideologies" of any kind (which in effect means resisting consistent or identifiable political positions) and deeply critical of current social "realities." The early parts of the *Patria* cycle are, in fact, conceived in part as plays of social protest. In "The Theatre of Confluence," written during the planning stages of the cycle, Schafer evinces an interest in Brecht (45) and indicates his intention to create "pocket opera": "I wanted an aggressive, present-tense opera. Swift, direct, agitational. Not a palliative. Not ceremonial drugging. Not prettifying" (47). He is, moreover, consistently critical of the cultural status quo, often on the ground of its colonialism. The orchestra, for example, he condemns as "a very colonial exhibition. Almost all the instruments are made from materials from plundered territories: ebony, ivory, granadilla. They're all things that have come from cultures and peoples that have been subdued" (qtd. in Everett-Green, "Polemics"). In *"Patria" and the Theatre of Confluence*, moreover, he describes *Patria 1*, which deals with the societal rejection and eventual suicide of a recent immigrant to Canada, as "a work of social protest" and instructs the director to make the work "as political as desired" (66). *Patria 2* he describes as having been based on what he felt were the "deplorable" conditions at Riverview Mental Hospital in Essondale, British Columbia (76).

More significantly, on the structural level, Schafer's interest in mystical, mythical, and alchemical transformations serves fundamentally to shape his artistic vision and inevitably opens the way for transformation of the social formation. Schafer clearly and explicitly believes that "This must be the first purpose of art. To effect a change in our existential condition. This is the first purpose. To change us" ("Theatre of Confluence II" 5).

It is Schafer's interest in change, or transformation (to the degree that his director, in a publicity flyer, can refer to *Patria 4 as* "a nightly transformation"), that leads to his reliance on ritual forms and on the figuring forth for his audience of change as both a personal and a social possibility. Admittedly, his articulation of this principle is most often couched in individualist, mystical, or "existentialist" rhetoric, as when Schafer insists that, if the rituals of *Patria 6: Ra* are not performed properly and with complete faith in their efficacy, "the sun may not rise" (*Patria* 181), or when he approvingly quotes Mircea Eliade's *Rites and Symbols of Initiation*: "In philosophical terms, initiation is equivalent to a basic change in existential condition; the novice emerges from his ordeal endowed with a totally different being from that which he possessed before his initiation; he has become *another*" (178). "When properly performed and experienced," Schafer argues elsewhere, rituals "can facilitate existential changes or become a palingenesis of spiritual renewal" ("Theatre of Confluence II" 15).

But his rituals can also potentially go beyond individual renewal (of what is, implicitly, already there) to figure forth social change and the emergence of new orders. Existential changes and spiritual renewal, of course, happen within the individual rather than the social realm, but Schafer seems, again, to share with his neo-Romantic but socially radical 1960s forebears, such as Jean-Jacques Lebel, the belief that "if there's still a chance of changing life it resides in the transformation of the human being" (Lebel 268). The ritual structures of the *Patria* series, I would argue, whether or not this is the intent of Schafer and his creative team, can be seen to function structurally to implant change as a *social* as well as an existential possibility and therefore, potentially at least, to work against the complacency of audiences in the face of a repressive social order. As Schafer argues, the purpose of all rituals is "to prepare one for the change" (*Patria* 177). And the most potent disruptions of what seems clearly to be a culturally affirmative *narrative* structure of the *Patria* works, and therefore of their socially reproductive potential, derive from their deployment of space, their focus on liminal moments and locations, and the ways in which this deployment and focus affect audiences' experiences.

When Schafer addresses the question of form in his essay "The Theatre of Confluence," he talks first about space and spatial relationships, noting that "the moment an architect encloses space in the form of a building he makes a social comment about the people who are to inhabit that space" (39). Later, in *"Patria" and the Theatre of Confluence*, he goes further: "The moment you organize space you dictate the social actions permitted in that space" (60). Schafer's interest in environmental theatre, then, has directly to do with creating possibilities for social actions that are constrained by traditional theatrical environments: "one has three options with regard to the conventional theatre: to be sentimental about it, to be exploitative, or to leave it behind" (*Patria* 60). While in *Patria 1* Schafer opts for exploitation, as the cycle proceeds he increasingly moves out of traditional theatrical environments, designing a kind of observation gallery for *Patria 2* at the Stratford Festival's Third Stage[17] and then moving toward remote nontheatrical spaces ranging from lake- or oceanside settings (at the shifting boundary between water and land) to (carnivalesque) fairgrounds, train stations (as points of departure and arrival), and parks (as meeting places between city and country, art and nature). Eschewing traditional audience-stage configurations, theatrical settings, and standard curtain times, these settings are notable primarily for their liminality: each functions as a site of transition between realms, taking place at dusk, midnight, or dawn on shorelines, fairgrounds, and train stations — ironically, in the case of *Patria 4*, at Toronto's Union Station. And in deploying these settings, of course, Schafer is seeking what he calls "nodal points" (*Patria* 177), what Sarah Hood calls "the moments of transformation at the heart of life." That many of these settings are outdoor, natural environments is also no accident, since "What distinguishes [a natural environment] from the traditional theatrical setting is that it is a living environment and therefore utterly changeable at any moment" (Schafer, "Princess" 23). And the move to a changeable environment is a move outside the mechanisms of normal social (and theatrical) control:

> When musicians play across a lake at a distance of half a kilometer or more, how are they conducted or supervised? Of what value then are conductors and managers? . . . Can we arrange a contract to remove the hazard of rain? And what about the managerial staff? We need boatmen not caretakers, trailblazers not electricians, naturalists not publicists. (28)

From his earliest statements about "The Theatre of Confluence," preceding the creation of any part of the *Patria* series itself, Schafer has expressed an interest in "transformable environments," in part because such environments "would bring about a theatrical *form* which was more fluid" but also because they would provide "a *form* of possibilities" (42; emphasis added), at least some of which are social.

The reconfiguration of space in the *Patria* series, finally, is more than simply a question of a movement outdoors. Schafer has said that "the metaphor for the whole series has been the labyrinth" (*Patria* 11), and, as he points out in his proposals for *Patria 7: Asteria*, "the intricate structure [of the labyrinth] is not merely the scenery to the drama: it *is* the drama" (*Patria* 195). The translation of the labyrinth from verbal metaphor to physical realization, where it can become part of the audience's *experience* of the show rather than simply its understanding, is partially realized in *Patria 3: The Greatest Show* and *Patria 6: Ra* and is planned for more thoroughgoing realization on the level of individual audience participation in *Patria 7*.

Patria 3 may serve briefly as an example of the tensions between democratic and resistant multiplicity and the elitist, universalist, or culturally affirmative aspects of the work as a whole, particularly as performed in its constituent parts.[18] *The Greatest Show* is set in a fairground where, for the audience members, as reviewer Pamela Young notes, "the fair itself becomes a kind of labyrinth" in which they become "trapped."[19] The setting, consisting of various carnivalesque attractions and monstrosities at tents and booths scattered throughout the fairground, is intriguingly reminiscent of Ben Jonson's *Bartholomew Fair*, as Schafer himself notes (*Patria* 125), in which the same tensions occur between the desire for authorial control of meaning, interpretation, and text and the anarchic, Rabelaisian, populist energies of Bakhtinian carnival, as writers with expressed contempt for "the masses" nevertheless create genial, unsettling, but audience-empowering fairs/shows.[20]

Schafer summarizes the action of *The Greatest Show*:

> Wolf and Ariadne appear as spectators but the Showman, Sam Galuppi, compels them to volunteer for two magic acts in which Ariadne is chopped into pieces and Wolf is made to disappear. While the police stalk the grounds hunting for Wolf (who is suspected of some unspecified crime) pieces of Ariadne's anatomy begin to appear in some of the side shows. From a burlesque beginning, the show becomes more macabre until the magicians, attempting to reconstitute the hero and heroine, bungle the job and produce Three-Horned Enemy, who destroys the entire fairgrounds. (*Patria* 210–11)

The mythological underpinnings of the story, the gendering of the hero and heroine, and the linearity of the plot are clear from this account and familiar from the rest of the cycle, though also apparent is the failure of the action to come to a satisfying conclusion, at least as experienced by audiences in the isolated performance of this portion of the cycle.

The show's elitist and universalist tendencies, together with its disturbing orientalism and misogyny, are evident even in the published script,[21] in which a combination of orientalist exoticism and enacted violence against women, both presented more or less as entertainment, is readily apparent. Even in the script, however, some sense of the apparent and potentially empowering anarchy of the event in performance is legible, as when Schafer comments in the introduction, placing the work in the context of the entire cycle, that "the plot of *Patria 3* crumbles, or at least is reduced to small-scale counterplotting and frog-croaking[,] . . . and the main themes are all splodged [sic] like a bad paint job" (2). Indeed, it is difficult at times to know when or whether a particular side-show event contributes to or deflects attention from the "main action." The script also includes stylistic impurities and heterogeneities, together with irreverently self-parodic sections, as when "Professor Earnest Beauty" lectures on the mythological themes of the *Patria* series, "with special reference to the Beauty and the Beast and Theseus and Ariadne myths" (Category I, 1) at a venue called "the

University Theatre," where Schafer himself is later called to give "a short introductory talk to *Patria 3: The Greatest Show*" (Introduction 40), for which he "wears a Tibetan jacket and looks like the aging doyen of some East-West cult of marginal credibility" (Category I, 27). Finally, the script acknowledges its own fragmentary nature as the score for an event that "NO ONE WILL GRASP . . . AT A SINGLE VISIT" (Category A, 3). But, as Schafer asks in the introduction, "So what if instead of a five-act fauteuil monstrosity we produce a confection of 100 atrocities; amusing, ironical, linked only in the head of the wandering visitor?" (3)

But it is not necessarily linking that goes on in the mind of the wandering visitor, or the linking may not be in the construction of a unified or coherent whole. One of the best accounts of the experience of the play, as opposed to its plot, themes, or setting, is provided by the associate director of the Peterborough productions in 1987 and 1988, who focuses on "the autocritical theatricality" of the show and on the ways in which "The security of your ontological status as 'audience' is . . . disrupted" (Neill 221, 217): "The questions echo in our minds. Where are the Ideals? The Nobility? The Divinity? There is no Wizard Oil to cure the world's woes, and Zip the Idiot might well be running the show. The darkness extends beyond the theatre, and the monsters still smile" (221). Reviews of the production tended to focus less on the mythmaking, the role of this work in the larger cycle, or the ultimate containment of the show's anarchic energy than on the discontinuity and randomness of the experience of the show in performance. As Everett-Green described it in the *Globe and Mail*,

> The spectators literally roam around inside the work, happening upon bits of it in random order. Some acts can only be seen after winning at a carnival game, others by being in a certain spot at the appropriate time.
> The pieces of the puzzle do not link together as narrative, but as doodles in different styles on similar themes. Their random progress steadily widens the reference of Schafer's symbols, and makes the contrast of his themes — creation and dismemberment, heroism and betrayal — more violent. ("Peek")

Martha Tancock, reviewing the production for the Peterborough *Examiner*, was more direct and perhaps less positive about the experience. Describing the show as "fuel for the irrational," "a clever conundrum whose impact is both stimulating and unsettling," she thought that, "buffeted between warring forces, the audience is played for a fool. . . . This show is a Pandora's box of distractions and deceptions that tease and taunt but never really satisfy."

However much it is later contained, then, the physicalization of the labyrinth in *The Greatest Show* (its shift from the realm of allegory to that of audience experience), particularly on the level of individual audience participation, can be a powerful experience of fragmentation, dispersal, chaos, or perhaps even freedom that is unforgettable — and arguably has more lasting impact than the openly orchestrated closure effected in most of the parts and in the cycle as a whole.

★   ★   ★

If the deep structures of R. Murray Schafer's *Patria* cycle and the cultural work that they perform are replete with contradictions between the populist and the elitist, the mystical/prophetic voice and the irreverent voice of social satire, the totalizing vision and the fragmenting spatial practice, then the environmental theatre of Hillar Liitoja and his Toronto company, DNA Theatre, is perhaps even more fraught with contradiction. Like Schafer's, Liitoja's roots are in music, including piano studies in Toronto with Anton Kuerti and in Paris with Pierre Sancan; in the American and European avant garde, including an early fascination with the work of Richard Schechner, André Gregory, Tadeuz Kantor, Jan Fabre, and particularly Richard Foreman, with whom Liitoja served an apprenticeship in the early 1980s; and in the poetry and poetics of Ezra Pound, which are the subject of no fewer than his first nine theatrical productions.[22] Like Schafer, too, Liitoja works not from scripts but from "scores," time charts that plot his works' characteristically fragmented individual performances and actions, light and sound cues, in what is ultimately, as Nigel Hunt says, a "musical structure" in which "the director becomes an editor or conductor" keeping the disparate segments in sync (46).[23] Finally, Liitoja shares with Schafer an attitude to audience that is fundamentally dismissive — "I don't concern myself with the audience. I concern myself with the vision" (Gilbert et al. 26) — and an attitude to process that is individualist rather than collaborative: "I'm not interested in actors. I'm interested in performers. An actor portrays a character, plays a role; whereas a performer does what I tell them [sic] to do" (22). Indeed, he sounds much like Schafer as an antidemocratic modernist individualist,[24] rejecting the idea of theatre as a cooperative form and claiming to

> have no fear whatsoever of presenting my vision, undiluted. I want all the power of all the decisions. I do not want to break, even remotely, the boundaries between a set designer, a lighting designer, and a musical arranger. I want to do it all myself.
>
> The best work I've ever seen has always been exclusively the product of one man's [sic] vision. (20)

While actors talk of input into the process — actor Andrew Scorer claims that "there's actually more creative input from the actors than is usual in a play" (qtd. in Hunt 46) — and Liitoja himself admits that he solicits and sometimes incorporates their ideas, he also "makes the final decision as to what goes in, what goes out, where whatever goes, and how many times it's repeated" (Gilbert et al. 20). As Sky Gilbert, another regular Liitoja performer, puts it, "paradoxically, one feels very much a part of the process and at the same time at the mercy of a rather sado-masochistic hallucinatory imagination" (27).

What this process results in structurally, however, is a shaping of the theatrical experience for audiences that is anything but contained, closed, or comfortable and that is in its effects, on occasion at least, much more socially interventionist than Liitoja routinely admits.[25] The productions are structured spatially and temporally through analogies with music, poetry, and the visual arts rather than with dramatic, mimetic, or narrative literature, they begin before the audience arrives, and audience members are encouraged to wander through the playing area, changing seats and restructuring perspectives at will. Paul Leonard, analysing "the scenography of Hillar Liitoja," has drawn attention to the ways in which the "environment — both visual and aural" — is "material" in DNA's work, something through which audiences move, structuring the apparently random events as "private experience" (31). He argues that, since "there will remain numerous flourishes that are invisible except to one or two audience members," "the aural and visual environment helps to foster a monadic world in which communication is not a social act but a private experience" (31). Nevertheless, this fragmentation can also be seen as empowerment, a democratization of experience that eschews control of focus and gives choice back to audiences whose experiences are at least to some extent self constructed. DNA shows involve the simultaneous presentation of various actions that can't be "taken in" totally, "a random presentation of fragments of various levels of speech and images," as Paul Lefebvre puts it, "indisputable, real fragments, that destroy the very idea of realism, replacing it magnificently with that of reality" (qtd. in Hunt 49). Liitoja sees this as a challenge to audiences: "I love to see the audience figuring things out — in vain! I love these people being stimulated, their minds trying to figure out what's going on with their senses. . . . We're stuck in outmoded ways of perception; it's nice to have things jolted and reevaluated" (qtd. in Hunt 49; ellipsis in original). And Sky Gilbert concurs, arguing that the "often abrasive aesthetics" of Liitoja's work issue in a "frontal assault on our society's way of thinking in which reason is valued over instinct, and narrative over rhythm" (qtd. in Hunt 49).

Although Hunt sees the effects of this assault as "ultimately. . . non-intellectual" (49), and Leonard as "purely sensory, . . . devoid of intellectual content" (31), the cultural work that it performs may operate more to frustrate traditional ways of understanding than simply to shift audiences into an asocial (private) or anti-intellectual realm of "physical or emotional reaction" (Leonard 31) — one that merely reinforces individualism or societally dominant binaries between public and private, intellectual and emotional, realms. It may be closer, that is, to Brecht than it seems, and in fact much of the action of most of Liitoja's productions depends on, or can be actively disrupted or diverted by, audience response. As Liitoja said in an interview with journalist Kate Taylor, "there's an unbelievable rigidity, control, and precision . . . that can be totally shattered by an audience member doing a simple thing" ("To Make").

For most audience members, then, the effects of the shows are anything but comfortingly cathartic: "Let the audience alone to deal with their own trauma!" Liitoja argues. "Why do you want to counsel and comfort them afterwards?" (Gilbert et al. 27). As Robert Wallace suggests,

> DNA's refusal to effect "closure" in its work, like its rejection of linear narrative and its reliance on repetition and interruption, frustrates the audience's expectations of the theatre and challenges their assumptions about the world in which the theatre exists. The audience becomes conscious of the necessity for it *to act* to make meaning of events. (*Producing Marginality* 165)

Wallace's argument, in one sense, has become conventional as a reading of nonlinear, nonmimetic performance, but what makes it convincing here is the intersection between the structural features that I have been outlining and the subject matter of at least some of the shows, in which social rather than aesthetic concerns constitute the raw material and in which the cultural work performed by Liitoja's chosen structures is most clear. The necessity for an audience to position itself and to "make meaning," not only of performances, actions, and fragments of light, sound, and language, but also of various positions on urgent social issues, shifts the argument beyond the aesthetic and into the social realm. Two productions may serve briefly as cases in point.

The first DNA production that involved Liitoja's writing his own script, *This Is What Happens in Orangeville*, first produced at Toronto's Poor Alex Theatre in 1987, was inspired by the murder in 1984 of two children by a fourteen-year-old boy and his subsequent confinement for insanity.[26] The production, then, replete with the disjunctions and apparently random actions typical of Liitoja's work, such as screwing in and unscrewing light bulbs, timing scenes, bouncing rubber balls, and performing various other stylized activities, was held together by a core group of scenes between the boy and the psychiatrist assigned to his "case." Unlike most such scenes in contemporary plays such as Peter Schafer's *Equus*, however, these sequences devoted to uncovering a satisfactory reason for the boy's behaviour — explaining it away — came to no comfortable conclusion: the boy tells the psychiatrist without regret that he committed the murders to find out what it felt like to kill. Meanwhile, the interview scenes are interspersed with fragmentary, decontextualized portraits of "ordinary" people in Orangeville, some related to the boy and some not, engaged in quotidian activities, describing their lives or their reactions to the murders, or confronting the audience with their views, their commands, or, in the case of the young girl mentioned earlier, their nakedness.

Taken out of context, many of these ordinary activities seem as inexplicable as the murders, and they blur the distinctions between normalcy and insanity on which our abilities to "come to terms" psychologically with violence that is in fact socially produced depend. Many of these activities, moreover, require a response or conscious reaction of some kind from audience members who are uncomfortably confronted by apparently gratuitous nudity, buttonholed by an apparently imbalanced fellow spectator, or ordered about by an "Ominous Presence" or by aggressive "ladderboys," stripped to the waist. The confrontation of these random acts of theatre in the context of a play about what we have learned to call a random act of violence is telling, and it requires that we, as individual audience members, confront a plea of insanity that seems to make no conventional sense: the boy seems, at least, to be the coolest, most rational, most "normal" presence in the room, audience members included, and thereby raises telling social questions about what constitutes the normal in a world that appears to have gone mad. The play ends with the playing of an audio-tape of a psychiatrist talking with Liitoja about the effects of child murders on society, and the flicking on and off of stage lights and camera flashes, before, in Hunt's phrase, "the audience is left in the dark, then thrown into the light" (48).

The politics of the subject matter and the involvement of the audience are even more overt in Liitoja's 1990 production of *The Panel: A Devastation Concerning AIDS*, later incorporated into the 1991 production *Sick*.[27] After all, the construction of a discourse on AIDS, particularly one that requires audience participation and debate, was in 1990 and remains a risky and overtly political undertaking. As described by Mark Ruzylo, the form of *The Panel* is "a stylized forum discussion focussed on the representation of AIDS in popular culture" (58), in which seven panelists representing different positions on AIDS, plus a varying number of audience members, who either replace panelists at the central table or speak from the "house," engage in improvised discussions of the implications of selected written and visual media representations of AIDS that vary from performance to performance and that are not seen in advance by the participants. In an effective parody of the oppressive mechanisms of social control and authority, the discussion is regulated by an outrageously outfitted Moderator who outlines an absurdly rigid and arbitrary set of rules and procedural regimens that structures the performance and by a Judge who makes random and destabilizing interjections and who alone is not bound by the Moderator's regulations. This action is surrounded, interrupted, and further destabilized by various other actions, interludes, vignettes, and conversations with audience members and by a woman who screams poetry and shouts out the ingredients of a holistic healing potion that is later sampled by the cast and willing members of the audience.

Not only does the performance allow for the interrogation of dominant representations of AIDS, and not only does it offer what Ruzylo calls "representational mutability" (57) in its refusal to present a single, dominant, or controlling discourse on a disease that has become a discursive battleground in a political struggle over issues of owner-ship, representation, and control; *The Panel*, as Alan Filewod argues, also "interrogates the politics of the AIDS narrative by restructuring the fundamental relationship of performer (that is, discourse) and audience" ("Acting AIDS" 13). Audience members not only wander the space freely, as in most DNA productions, but they are also invited to participate directly in the show's discussion, incorporated into the structure of the panel, and forced to confront, take into account, and respond to a range of views different from their own in a forum that is determinedly social. As Ruzylo notes, the performance "challenges the spectators' passivity and indifference, no longer allowing them to distance themselves from the social realities of the epidemic" (86), or, in Filewod's words, from "the historical indifference of society to AIDS" ("Acting AIDS" 13).

★   ★   ★

The audience is treated as visitors to an open house in a mental health institution. The audience is required to answer question-naires, given badges, divided into groups and led up and down stairs and in and out of various rooms that make up Theatre Passe Muraille. As tourists, the audience's response is a detached one: moderately bemused, a little bored and occasionally diverted.

There is a . . . frisson of horror, and an evocation of the gas ovens of Nazi Germany, near the play's end when the audience is herded into a darkened elevator and led to the sleep room of the play's title.

— Liam Lacey

As this description of *Sleeproom*, an environmental play written by Sally Clark, Robin Fulford, Daniel MacIvor, and John Mighton and directed by Ken McDougall at Theatre Passe Muraille in January 1993, suggests, not all environmental theatre in Canada functions according to the principles outlined by Schechner, conforms to the practices of Schechner, Schafer, or Liitoja, or sees environmental staging as an enfranchisement of audiences. Indeed, one of Canada's best-known directors of environmental theatre, Richard Rose, follows very different procedures to very different ends.[28]

Rose established his reputation in the early 1980s as an inventive young director with a flare for the innovative use of three-dimensional space. Early in his career, in productions of plays such as Euripedes's *Electra*, he experimented with unusual audience-stage configurations and with devices such as simultaneous staging in order to break down audience complacency about theatre and the world. In *Mein*, a collective creation, Rose and his designer, Dorian Clark, created a black grid-work box in the cramped back space of Theatre Passe Muraille to explore within a single mind the psychology of corporate ambition. In *The Seagull*, he staged a promenade-style production in a temporarily empty shop with a floor-to-ceiling glass wall overlooking Lake Ontario in Toronto's chic Queen's Quay Terminal, while at the other end of the scale he produced the stage version of Michael Ondaatje's *Coming through Slaughter* in Toronto's distinctly downscale Silver Dollar tavern. In John Krizanc's *Prague* and Jason Sherman's *It's All True*, the proscenium stage of Tarragon Theatre was systematically exposed and exploded in complex metatheatrical deconstructions of theatrical space. Until recently, Rose was best known for his production of Krizanc's *Tamara*, a critique of fascism that attempted to deconstruct the totalitarianism of the theatre itself, as audience members were invited to put together their own play by following actors of their choice from room to room in Toronto's historic Strachan House. *Tamara* became an international hit when it was remounted by Rose in Los Angeles, New York, and elsewhere.[29] Finally, *Newhouse*, his exploration of contemporary political morality, was staged in a Toronto hockey arena that stood in allegorically for "the political arena" and borrowed elements of allegorical/environmental stagecraft from medieval pageants and morality plays. In production after production, then, Rose has managed to make the play spring, as one reviewer remarked, "almost spontaneously from the building in which it is performed" (qtd. in Knowles, "Richard Rose").[30]

Although Rose's environmental theatre shares some features with the environmental work of Schechner, Schafer, and Liitoja, it is nevertheless fundamentally different in a number of important ways. Rose differs from Schechner — or at least from the canonical reputation and influence of Schechner's work on environmental theatre — primarily in his understanding and practice of the politicization of space. Where Schechner is interested in enfranchisement, Rose is interested in power; in fact, it may not be stretching the argument too far to suggest that Schechner is engaged in the constitutionally American search for life, liberty, and the pursuit of happiness, while Rose pursues the personal and political implications of Canada's constitutional guarantee of peace, order, and good government.

Schechner's assumption articulated in "The Decline and Fall of the

American Avant Garde" that "frontalism," or proscenium stagecraft, is politically "retrograde," "a conservative retreat" (96), an assumption that has been usefully critiqued by Timothy Murray, is rejected by Rose, who believes that all performance venues, including proscenium stages such as those that he employed in *Mein* and *Prague*, are environments with, in Marvin Carlson's phrase, their own inherent or historically resonant "environmental semiotics" (*Places* 36).[31] Rose's productions put into practice the more politically nuanced position that environmental theatre is most usefully defined by its acknowledgement rather than mystification of the space that it inhabits, whatever that may be. Similarly, while for Schechner participation is fundamental to environmental theatre and liberatory politics alike, Rose's work (among that of others) has prompted Steve Nelson's observation that "There is a misconception among critics that environmental theatre is an intrinsically participatory experience. . . . [N]othing could be further from the truth" (92). "Radically altering the audience/performance contract," Nelson argues, "is no longer the concern. People walk about and get close physically, but the barrier between actor and spectator remains intact" (93).[32] Indeed, for Rose it is crucial that the barrier remain intact: his interest is in allowing audiences to see performance and behaviour clearly, and from close proximity, and he believes that this is impossible both in life and in theatrical productions in which one is too immediately engaged in the self-conscious processes of interaction to see clearly or judge accurately. In Rose's environmental productions, then, with the exception of certain formalized moments of admission to the space, regulation of behaviour, or direct address, actors do not acknowledge the presence of audience members, particularly in intimate scenes, however much they may share spaces. Rose's productions construct their audiences as voyeurs rather than as participants, visitors who exercise some apparent choice, however severely limited, in the selection of what to look at and the piecing together of the story but who have no influence over the action. They tend to experience, moreover, none of the felt sense of control over the gaze, superior knowledge, or objective viewpoint available through standard proscenium stagecraft, and in productions such as *Tamara* they are constantly aware of scenes going on "offstage," as it were, before other audience members, to which they are not privy.

In spite of Krizanc's claims about the democratization of focus in *Tamara*, then, and Alberto Manguel's hyperbolic claims for it as "the first democratic play" (5), giving audiences more freedom than they have ever had in the theatre,[33] Rose's environmental theatre productions do not take place in open, transformative spaces, nor do they create a sense of audience freedom or enfranchisement. On the contrary, like the production of *Sleeproom* described in the epigraph to this section, in which audiences underwent a test at the outset, were divided into three groups, and were herded through the building that housed the show (but unlike Schafer's *The Greatest Show* or Liitoja's environmental work), Rose's productions, which often explore issues such as censorship, house arrest, fascism, and other mechanisms of social control, tend to employ spaces of entrapment and to point up constraint. Thus, in *Censored*, an adaptation of Mikhail Bulgakov's *A Cabal of Hypocrites*, Rose used a former church interior to house the court of Louis XIV and to explore the relationships between the church, the state, and the arts. The production opened with the audience as extras in Molière's acting company, cramped backstage (in the theatre lobby/church foyer) awaiting the king's reaction to the first performance of *Tartuffe*. The last act of *Tartuffe* was actually performed offstage, with the actors "exiting" to the lobby to apply makeup and change costumes. Only when *Tartuffe* ended was the audience herded into the playing space proper for the opening of *Censored* itself.

In *Tamara*, which takes place in simultaneous scenes on 10–11 January 1927 throughout Il Vittoriale degli Italiani, the villa of Gabriele d'Annunzio where the Italian nationalist poet is being held in house arrest by Mussolini, the audience is greeted at the door by Capitano Finzi, dressed in a black fascist uniform and standing behind a lectern asking for their "Carta d'identia," issued as part of the program:

> Papers. (*looks at the passport then hands it back to audience member*) Sign there. You will keep this with you at all times. If you are asked to produce your visa, you will do so and you will be required to know its contents. Read it. Anyone found without their papers will be arrested and deported. (Krizanc 20)

(At the beginning of the second act, a missing passport is found, and a female audience member is taken from the room, "interrogated," and asked to scream, "so that your friends suspect nothing," a scream that is heard in other scenes and contributes to the play's action [181].) The passport device is artificial, of course, and audiences tend to find it amusing rather than threatening, but it does point up the real limitations on audience freedom — "the regulations regarding movement in this house" (23) — that are also articulated at the outset, this time by d'Annunzio's valet, Dante Fenzo: audience members may only move between rooms when following one of the characters in the play/ residents of the house ("If you are not following a person, you are breaking the law" [24]); if a character closes a door, audience members are not to follow him or her, nor are they to open closed doors; they must move quickly and quietly throughout the "villa"; certain areas are off-limits; they may speak only when spoken to; and so on. At the end, they are more or less ousted from the building, and the doors shut against them.

Newhouse, an adaptation by Rose and D.D. Kugler from Tirso de Molina's *Don Juan* (*The Trickster of Seville*) and Sophocles's *Oedipus Rex*, includes interrogations of telemedia representation and the political structure of the Canadian government, all focusing on the crisis repre-sented by an unnamed "plague" that is clearly AIDS. The environmental setting in this case orchestrates audience movement as a representation of the manipulable masses as they respond to political speeches, televi-sion images, reporters, and theatre itself by following the action from platform to platform and large-scale monitor to monitor. "It was fasci-nating to watch the crowd surge in a general wave of movement whenever the action moved," Alan Filewod remarks in his interview with Rose and Kugler, who describe the setting as "a kind of cage," inside which the audience was trapped, "a kind of a beast," in Kugler's words, "Totally present but totally excluded" (Rose and Kugler 39).

The hockey rink in which the action was set evoked the political arena, of course, an evocative metaphor when most political conventions in Canada take place in sports facilities and many of Canada's most momentous political events, such as the first election of the separatist Parti Québécois in 1976, are indelibly associated with hockey arenas (see chapter 5). More importantly, however, the setting also directly evoked medieval allegorical stagecraft in a number of suggestive ways.

Although it was not immediately apparent to the audience, the set was most clearly derived from medieval staging in its evocation of the body politic *as* a body. Indeed, the staging evoked the layout of the medieval cathedrals in which the earliest liturgical dramas took place, with their mapping of the head of Christ (the priest in the apse), his outstretched arms (side chapels), and the congregation as corpus. The arena in which *Newhouse* was staged was mapped out with a platform at one end used by the prime minister (the head of government and the source of reasoned argument, as well as the play's Oedipus/Christ figure as sacrificial victim), flanked by banks of television monitors and a small chapel; a "groin" platform at the opposite end, without screens, where Newhouse, the son of the minister of external affairs and the play's Don Juan and Trickster figure, seduced two of his victims; a central platform, also without screens, as the "heart" of the assembly, where action involving emotion took place; and two side platforms, the "lungs," each divided lengthwise by a large screen and used as public areas, the media centre and embassy on one side, the bar and various other locations on the other. In this schema, as Rose and Kugler made clear in their interview with Filewod, the audience, moving through the space as the action shifted from platform to platform in cinematic "edits," functioned as the veins (39).[34]

The allegorical functioning of all this in a play that pitted reason against passion and public against private morality is clear, and the updating of source elements was cleverly done. Sophocles's Chorus, for example, was replaced by a gaggle of reporters and camera operators who followed the public action, broadcasting it "live" to the play's audience and an implied general public. But the revisionings of ancient and medieval staging had political resonances as well. In the case of *Newhouse*'s version of the Greek Chorus, the audience was forced, as Natalie Rewa has pointed out, "to accept the reporter as their collective spokesperson," together with the perspective on events chosen by the camera operator (41). Rewa's analysis of the production's use of space is perceptive and resonates interestingly with Robert Weimann's analysis of the politicized use of *locus* and *platea* in the medieval and early modern theatre (73–85 and passim). For Weimann, the platforms, stations, or pageant wagons that served as fixed locations in various types of medieval theatre were also *loci* of power, and the *platea*, the areas between *loci*, which both actors and audience members moved through and which served flexibly to signify variable locations, were public spaces. In Michel de Certeau's formulation, the latter represents a (timeless) "space" of authority rather than a (temporal) "place," where meanings can be negotiated rather than simply communicated from speaker to auditor (*Practice* 117–18). In this schema, the *loci* of the medieval theatre — heaven, hell, and allegorical sites such as "the world," "the flesh," and so on — were fixed centres of universal truth and stable, naturalized power structures, sites from which strategy, in de Certeau's terms, could be deployed in attempts to fix meanings and social structures in the interests of the currently dominant. The shifting significations of the *platea*, on the other hand, institutionally powerless, were what de Certeau would consider the tactical (and potentially resistant) social sites of negotiated meaning operating through time and therefore through constantly shifting positionalities (de Certeau, *Practice* 35–39).

Newhouse, in which the relationship between fixed stages and open floor space resembled the medieval relationship between *locus* and *platea*, then, employed some of the social and political significations of this scheme but adapted them to the world of late capitalism in ways that took into account post-modern information networks and the shifting meanings of place and space themselves. Here the sites of institutionalized power, the *loci*, were not fixed in "place" but virtually omnipresent. Scenes occurring on them were (strategically) broadcast throughout the arena on large-scale screens and monitors that intruded on the experiences of audience members wherever they were, required no movement or activity on their part, and mimicked a post-(economic)-border, free-trade world in which power is located in (cyber)space rather than in specific seats of government, in communication networks and international capital rather than in capital cities. "Private" scenes, in this configuration, took place on various stages, were not broadcast, but required audiences to move throughout the arena and act as "live" witnesses to what amounted to private, tactical acts of negotiation with the dominant or even with sexual and physical resistance, however (self-)destructive or manipulative. The extremes of the production — extremes of intellect and desire — were represented, on the one hand, by the neoconservative televangelist, a figure modelled on the physical image and some of the writings of Stephen Hawking, who never appeared in person but inhabited the space only through televised broadcasts calling for mandatory testing for "the plague." His disembodied intellectual position was treated with some seriousness and was opposed in the play, on the other hand, by the resistant but sheer physical irresponsibility of the libertine Newhouse/Don Juan as embodied desire, who never appeared on camera but whose physicality and physical magnetism — his body — challenged and resisted containment by the play's represented mechanisms of social control. Between these poles, negotiating between the extremes and engaging in both public and private scenes, moved the production's everyman, the public's and the audience's political spokesperson and their eventual scapegoat, the prime minister. This character was ultimately caught not only between reason and desire, between his private life and his public principles, but also between his position as national leader and pressure from Washington (as transnational signifier), in a global political economy that, like the disease on which the play focuses, respects no borders between one country and another, one person and another, and one national government and another. And the audience/public was his (tainted) life blood.

Liitoja's environmental AIDS play, *The Panel*, then, confronted audiences with the need to position themselves in relation to representations and constructions of the social and medical issues and the public perceptions circulating around AIDS, as it required them to position themselves physically and aesthetically in relation to the performance space. *Newhouse*, by creating an allegorical representation of contemporary public life in a global political economy, making physical the "role" of the public, was, in Filewod's words, "a significant departure from the norm of Canadian political theatre in Canada. Its treatment of AIDS remove[d] the issue from the politics of personal relationships and medical treatment and place[d] it in the arena of public social policy" (Rose and Kugler 33). It did so, perhaps more frighteningly, through a reconfiguration of public and private space, represented and constructed by the theatrical environment as the virtually antidemocratic space of the manipulable circulation of capital, power, information, and disease across national, legal, and personal boundaries.

7

Dialogic Monologue: A Dialogue
(with Jennifer Harvie)[1]

RIC: Dialogic Monologue;

JEN: Or, The Mikhail Bakhtin lectures.

RIC: Every time I give an academic paper, a little voice inside me says —

JEN: "You're a fraud."

RIC: "Get off the stage."

JEN: (That's an intertext — very dialogic — from Ken Garnhum's *Pants on Fire.* Also his *Surrounded by Water.* And from Geoffrey and Jeffrey's *Get off the Stage*).[2]

RIC: But I continue anyway.

JEN: Dialogism, in its simplest formulation, involves intertext at its most profound — the creation of a textual space in which various voices, styles, languages, or "speech genres" —

RIC: Todorov's translator calls them "discursive genres"[3] —

JEN: contest with one another on equal terms, with no single voice dominating. No voice gains authority by being —

RIC: I've got a right to talk too. They only *seem* —

JEN: more articulate, more intelligent, more erudite.

RIC: "Erudite."

JEN: As Bakhtin describes it in his discussion of Dostoevsky's "polyphonic novel,"[4] a dialogic text consists of *"a plurality of independent and unmerged voices and consciousnesses, a genuine polyphony of fully valid voices"* (*Problems* 6).

RIC: If they can engage in *that* sort of academic obfuscation —

JEN: double talk — very dialogic —

RIC: they can listen to *me* for half an hour. But the voice never shuts up. I've internalized the judgement —

JEN: voices —

RIC: I'm anticipating. "Fraud."

JEN: Double talk.

RIC: Very dialogic.

JEN: In 1993, at meetings of the Association for Canadian Theatre Research in Ottawa, Michael Sidnell drew attention to the potential for dramatic monologue to be dialogic in ways that dialogue in the theatre rarely is, and he pointed to a recent proliferation of dialogic monologue in Canadian theatre.[5]

RIC: (Although his observation, like much of our dialogue, is largely Toronto-centric.)

JEN: This paper will examine the potentially dialogic function of monologue in some contemporary Canadian plays and will ask, "When is monologue dialogic? And what are the — "

RIC: "political — "

JEN: "effects of dialogic monologue?"

RIC: According to Bakhtin's "sociolinguistics," all "utterances," as he calls the basic units of communication, which can range from a single nonverbal sound or gesture to a full-length novel, are made up of a heteroglot polyphony of languages drawn from a variety of "speech genres" — social, professional, and cultural communication systems, formal and informal — made unique by the historical/contextual moment of the utterance, which takes place in the historical body of an individual subject in response to and in anticipation of other utterances by other, real or imagined, but in any case *specific*, communicating subjects.[6] (*Beat*) Whew!

JEN: But some utterances are more dialogic than others. Epic and lyric poems, according to Bakhtin, aspire to a monologic unity of voice and expression that attempts to rise above the marketplace of historically situated social exchange to a level of pure expression and disembodied, ahistorical authority.[7]

RIC: The novel, on the other hand, at least at its most polyphonic —

JEN: (Bakhtin finds this in Dostoevsky and Rabelais; Kristeva in *écriture féminine*, in which she includes works by Joyce, Artaud, and Bataille, as well as by women)[8] —

RIC: aspires to the free play —

JEN: or open contestation —

RIC: of equal and interilluminating voices, in which the authority of author and narrator is invaded by the independent, unmerged voices of the characters, manifesting themselves through indirect discourse, parody, "the word with a loophole" —

JEN: or a "sideways glance" —

RIC and JEN: double voicing —

JEN: "intonational quotation marks" —

RIC: words spoken with a "cringe" —

JEN: *as if* in quotation marks —

JEN (*speaks as Ric mouths the word*): "ventriloquism" —

RIC: hyperbole —

JEN: parody —

RIC: or, not that I'd do this myself —

JEN: (self-consciousness) —

RIC: using self-deprecating or overblown speech that repudiates itself in advance.

JEN: There's also "indirect speaking," "quasi-direct speech," and embedding, in which the speech or accents of another person are —

RIC: inserted —

JEN: into the speaker's utterance —

RIC: the voice of the other internalized —

JEN: but not entirely appropriated —

RIC and JEN: or "merged."[9]

RIC: So what makes traditional theatrical modes of presentation *not* dialogic?

JEN: In Bakhtin's view, the freedom and independence of the authorial voice, the politics of speech reported in indirect discourse, and participation —

RIC: the absence of "footlights," which may be interpreted as anything which "separates the aesthetic event from lived life" (*Art* 217)[10] —

JEN: are essential for dialogism but excluded from drama, which he sees as "alien to genuine polyphony," primarily because it "is almost always constructed out of represented, objectified discourses" (*Problems* 34, 188).

RIC: He argues that "Pure drama strives toward a unitary language, one that is individualized merely through dramatic personae who speak it." "Dramatic dialogue," he insists, "is determined by a collision between individuals who exist within the limits of a single unitary language" (*Dialogic Imagination* 405).[11]

JEN: It's this conflation in drama of character and unitary voice — the sense that a dramatist represents a subject through the use of an individuated voice — on which Michael Sidnell focused in Ottawa. In counterdistinction to this, he argued,

> [Guillermo] Verdecchia's *Fronteras Americanas* is about a fail-
> ure of social integration, and, more fundamentally, about
> the lack of self-coherence that is desired both for its own
> sake and as the condition of communality. The problem for
> performance — a problem that Verdecchia's performance
> confronts head-on — is that these *desiderata* are conven-
> tionally assumed as the very basis of theatre, which may be
> said to celebrate them. (3–4)

RIC: What, then, makes a *monologue* in the theatre dialogic?

JEN: According to Paul Castagno, "dialogizing monologue" involves
three *"dematrixing"* techniques:

RIC: His emphasis. His word too.

JEN: "The actor/character can be *dematrixed* if they (1)"

RIC: "fracture the mould of a specific character"

JEN: "(2)"

RIC: "directly acknowledge or address the presence of the audience"

JEN: (Hello audience)

RIC: "or"

JEN: "(3)"

RIC: "foreground the presence of the actor over character" (137).

JEN: We found that useful —

RIC: And we hope you did too.

JEN: Sidnell argued, moreover, that the "dialogism of theatrical monologue is quite different . . . from the virtuosity of one actor playing
many roles. . . . And . . . is also distinct from the representation of
one character in conflict with himself."

RIC: "It's not," he argued, "a character that the dialogic monologue
represents but a fractured, incoherent or self-alienated subject
through which various *voices* are heard" (5).

JEN: Not all monologues, then, are equal: some, again, are more dialogic than others —

RIC: even if you don't get into generic distinctions involving
storytelling, performance art, stand-up —

JEN (*cutting him off*): which we won't get into. There are, for example,
monologues — or soliloquies — that occur *within* plays whose
central mode is dialogue, and in plays such as Judith Thompson's
these are central, and often dialogic, devices. There is also, for
economic reasons, a current proliferation of Canadian monologues
as plays, in many of which a single character is played throughout

by a single actor. Some of them, such as Michael Cook's *Terese's Creed*, Joan MacLeod's *Jewel*, Wendy Lill's *The Occupation of Heather Rose*, Judith Thompson's *Pink*, and so on, are not notably dialogic, but in the case of work such as Daniel MacIvor's *See Bob Run* or *Wild Abandon*, Michael Cook's absurdist monodrama *Quiller*, Tom Cone's *Herringbone*, or Judith Thompson's *Perfect Pie* (in its first version), the single character is fragmented, her "voice" dialogically invaded and fractured.

RIC: Some monodramas, such as Dan Needles's *Wingfield Trilogy*, involve splitting the link between actor and character by requiring the actor to perform multiple roles. Such performances, nevertheless, remain predominantly monologic — at least from the point of view of the audience — in that the virtuosity of role switching produces the illusion of dialogue among discrete characters for whom the need to create distinct, unitary voices is felt, for reasons of clarity, to be particularly urgent.

JEN: There are also plays such as Michel Tremblay's *Albertine in Five Times* and David Young's *Glenn*, in which several actors collectively play one character, a potentially dialogic device, but one that is often neutralized, as in these plays, by the fact that the actors *represent* the character at various stages in his or her life, employing a unitary voice for each distinct role. A more complex, more dialogic variation on this device occurs in Daniel MacIvor's *2-2-Tango: A Two-Man-One-Man-Show*, which you addressed, Ric, in chapter 2, in which the "characters" are named James and Jim, are identically dressed, and interact with one another in the present.

RIC: Finally, there is a subgenre of "lectures/plays," such as John Palmer's *Henrik Ibsen on the Necessity of Producing Norwegian Drama* and Daniel Brooks and Guillermo Verdecchia's *The Noam Chomsky Lectures*. In the latter lecture/play, the actors/lecturers —

JEN: playing "themselves," incorporate —

RIC: contradictions —

JEN: disagreements —

RIC: and fragments from different genres —

JEN: in a very sophisticated, assertively, and self-consciously —

RIC: and therefore dialogically? —

JEN: monologic dialogue.

RIC: Somewhat like *these* lectures, in fact.

JEN: Except not. . . .

RIC (*looks at her*): In fact, we considered doing for the Association of
   Canadian Theatre Research, in presenting this dialogue, what
   Brooks and Verdecchia did for Theatre Passe Muraille.

JEN: Rather, *Ric* considered it.

RIC: A sexual flow chart. Complete with little arrows saying "You are
   here."

JEN: But I vetoed it.

RIC: Too many straight lines?

JEN: What about a line of stars?

RIC: If you say so:

★　　★　　★

JEN: We are most interested here in a particular kind of monologue,
   plays in which a single character engages in a dialogical accounting
   for a "life" that is in some sense represented autobiographically.
   They include Guillermo Verdecchia's *Fronteras Americanas*; Monique
   Mojica's *Princess Pocahontas and the Blue Spots* (not, strictly speaking, a monologue); Margo Kane's *Moonlodge*; Daniel MacIvor's
   House and *Wild Abandon*; Ken Garnhum's *Beuys, Buoys, Boys, Surrounded by Water*, and *Pants on Fire* (also not strictly a monologue);
   and three plays that are not notably autobiographical, except
   perhaps in form: Margaret Hollingsworth's *Apple in the Eye* and
   Diving (*Willful Acts* 17–32, 113–18), and Sharon Pollock's *Getting
   It Straight*.[12]

RIC: Each one reveals the "salient features of novelization" as Bakhtin
   describes them in "Epic and Novel":

> They become . . . free and flexible, their language renews
> itself by incorporating extraliterary heteroglossia . . . , they
> become dialogized, permeated with laughter, irony, humor,
> elements of self-parody and finally — this is the most im-
> portant thing — . . . an indeterminacy, a certain semantic
> openendedness, a living contact with unfinished, still-
> evolving contemporary reality (the openended present).
> (*Dialogic Imagination* 7)

"In these plays," as Sidnell says, "performance becomes . . .
   theory in action" ("Fronteras" 2).

JEN: This is so because, as a form, autobiography can expose the falsity
   of the concept of the single consciousness, by publicly constructing the "life" of the "self." Bakhtin argues, in *Problems of
   Dostoevsky's Poetics*, that "No human events are developed or

resolved within the bounds of a single consciousness" (288). When a single consciousness stages her attempt to *represent* the development and resolution of her life, the fiction that (auto)biography "discloses" a preexisting character by accounting for its "development" (or its social construction) is made manifest.

RIC: And, as Bakhtin says *else*where, in a different context,

> This is not merely a matter of the author's image appearing within his own field of representation — important here is the fact that the underlying, original formal author appears . . . in a new relationship with the represented world. Both find themselves now subject to the same temporally valorized measurements, for the "depicting" authorial language now lies on the same plane as the "depicted" language . . . and may enter into dialogic relations and hybrid combinations with it. . . . (*Dialogic Imagination* 27–28)

This, in a sense, is what happens in Ken Garnhum's *Pants on Fire* —

JEN: "a one-man show for two people" —

RIC: when the author and represented autobiographical subject, "Ken" (played by Ken Garnhum), tells the fictional character, "Gabe" (played by Andy Massingham), "that's a stupid thing to say," to which Gabe responds, "you wrote it."

JEN: At the centre of the show, which consists in part of a self-portrait that stitches together a *series* of self-portraits, is a portrait of the self as the Tower of Babel —

RIC: which is defined in the show itself as "a confusion of voices."[13]

JEN: The fact that much Canadian autobiographical monodrama — including Garnhum's plays, MacIvor's *House, See Bob Run*, and *Wild Abandon*, and Pollock's *Getting It Straight* — is confessional in form is a complicating factor (see Wilson, "Bored").

RIC: Confession is problematic for Bakhtin.

JEN: In the 1961 appendix to *Problems of Dostoevsky's Poetics*, he discusses confession

> as an encounter of the *deepest I* with *another* and with *others*. . . . But the *I* in this encounter must be the pure, deep I from within oneself, without any admixture of presumed and forced or naïvely assimilated points of view and evaluations from another. . . . Without a *mask* . . . , without loopholes, without a false ultimate word, that is, without all that is externalizing and false. (294)[14]

RIC: From anyone else this would seem like Romanticism, but Bakhtin is referring to the true, internal, *social* self.

JEN: And besides, Bakhtin wasn't always very consistent.

RIC: But, as Dennis A. Foster says, "Introspection is a delusion, since each person has to seek his meaning through the speech of others" (10). "The confessional narrative occurs . . . between two substantial, unsettled subjects" (3). Foster sees the confessional narrative as a site of struggle between writing and interpreting subjects, which "unsettle[s] the listener's sense of self-possession" and thereby "sets the listener to work" (5). It is this capacity to set "the listener to work" that we are interested in here. At least I am.

JEN: *I'm* interested in looking at how the dialogism of monologue in the theatre might *destabilize* subjectivity, given that the actor —

RIC: particularly the solitary actor —

JEN: often stands indexically for an autonomous subject, which is easily conflated with the character whom the actor is playing.[15]

RIC: When this conflation takes place in an autobiographical monologue, written and performed by its subject, the theatrical frisson can be both powerfully effective and representationally confusing. Whom, precisely, are we watching, and what are we analysing as a work of theatre when, in *Come Good Rain* —

JEN: billed as "a true story, written and performed by George Seremba"[16] —

RIC: we see the scars on the actor/character's body through which the bullets passed earlier in the life/narrative, or when Ken Garnhum tells us, in *Pants on Fire* —

JEN: a play that is largely about representation, including the representation of AIDS —

RIC: that "he" is HIV positive?

JEN: And who *is* "he" anyway?

RIC: The question becomes more complicated because "he" has made it clear earlier in the play that he is a liar and that theatre is his favourite kind of lying.

JEN: At one point, the stage floor opens, and a "Trojan Cat" enters, bearing on a slip of paper a one-word invasionary force:

RIC: "liar."

JEN: Fraud.

RIC: Get off the stage.

JEN: One of the functions of *Pants on Fire* is to interrogate what Ann

Wilson calls "the nostalgic belief that theatre involves presence" ("Bored" 35), by drawing attention to the fact that these moments of full confessional presence are rehearsed — "répétitions" — and that the powerful, "forced" confession that "Ken Garnhum" "has AIDS," to which audiences respond with stunned silence,[17] is performed night after night for the length of the run.

RIC: Each of the plays that we are considering, then, is in some sense about what Michael Holquist calls "the Bakhtinian just-so-story of subjectivity," or "how I get myself from the other," since, "In order to forge a self, I must do it from *outside*. In other words *I author myself*" (*Dialogism* 28).

JEN: And consequently, as Bakhtin says, "we have no alibi in existence" (qtd. in Holquist, *Dialogism* 29). He insists that "human being is the *production* of meaning" (Holquist, *Dialogism* 158), and he is careful, in a passage that goes some distance toward explaining his reticence about dialogism in the theatre, to distinguish between "person" — which is dialogic, in process, unique, unpredictable, and constructed — and "character" — which is monologic, completed, generalized, and determined.[18]

RIC: As Michael Gardiner puts it, "For Bakhtin, human consciousness is not a unified whole, but always exists in a tensile, conflict-ridden relationship with other consciousnesses, in a constant alterity between self and other" (28).

JEN: "In fact . . . the very process of acquiring self-consciousness from birth to maturity is, in Bakhtin's eyes, utterly dependent upon discursive interaction with another 'I'" (Gardiner 28).

RIC: "We *are*," as Gary Saul Morson puts it, "the voices that inhabit us" ("Who" 8).

JEN: Consequently, "since this process [of coming into subjectivity] is fundamentally historical," "the subject in Bakhtin's eyes is unfinalized"

RIC: "(and, yes, 'decentered'),"

JEN: "in a perpetual state of 'becoming'" (Gardiner 165).

RIC: What we are witnessing in these monologues, as Wilson says, is "the self-consciousness of the performer producing his identity in the context of a wide range of social forces," a self-consciousness that "disrupts the notion of a coherent self which can be told in a story" (37).[19]

JEN: A play such as Daniel MacIvor's *House*, as Robert Wallace notes, openly and self-consciously presents the *construction* of a character,

Victor, as "the sum of his texts" ("Victor[y]" 8). *House* "draws attention to . . . the audience's overt participation in the creation" and nevertheless "resists their interpretation" (10), finally drawing attention to the incompleteness and inadequacy of coherent and unified concepts of a stable human identity. By becoming aware that we are watching not Victor but "the *performance* of Victor" (13), we are made conscious of both the fragmented, processual nature of subjectivity and what Caryl Emerson calls "the indispensibility of otherness" ("Tolstoy" 155).

RIC: This "indispensibility of otherness" is, in one sense, what Garnhum's *Pants on Fire* is about, as the performance artist who writes, designs, and performs his own work faces the onset of an illness that undermines his self-sufficiency. But it also confronts him with the ongoing need for the Other as a necessary part of representation, whether that Other is allowed onto the stage, as in this play — a self-portrait that requires two people —

JEN: very Bakhtinian —

RIC: or merely *acknowledged* as a necessary part of the construction of the self, requiring the audience's complicity, as in *House* or, indeed, most of the plays under discussion.

JEN: These plays do not shrink, however, from representing the *dangers* of the fracturing of subjectivity. It is not incidental that Victor is "fucked up" or that Eme, the central character in Sharon Pollock's stream-of-consciousness monologue *Getting It Straight*, is represented as schizophrenic, an escapee from her "keepers" —

RIC: even if those plays seem to suggest that schizophrenia is an *appropriate* response to a *world* that's "fucked up."

JEN: Ultimately, however, the plays that we are looking at exemplify Bakhtin's insistence on the *responsibility* of the historically situated subject and what Michael Holquist calls "the need for choice": "At all the possible levels of conflict between stasis and change, there is always a situated subject whose specific place is defined precisely by its in-between-ness. To be responsible for the site we occupy in the space of nature and the time of history is a mandate we cannot avoid. . . . (*Dialogism* 181)

★   ★   ★

RIC: We are interested, then —

JEN: in spite of the danger that dialogism, like carnival (or "the de-

graded carnival of postmodernism," as Michael Gardiner calls it
[95]), will turn out to be —

RIC and JEN: just another liberal humanist form of all-embracing plu-
ralism.

RIC: Ok, ok, not *we*: I'm interested in the potential for social *change*
that the dialogic construction of subjectivity makes possible (see
O'Connor 201), in the free play of voices that disrupts the currently dominant, "socializ[ing] — "

JEN: as opposed to psychologizing —

RIC: "internal conflicts," as Emerson says, "exposing their mechanisms
to the light of day. If enough individuals experience the same
gap," she argues, "it is re-socialized: there develops a political
underground, and the potential for revolution" ("Outer Word"
32).

JEN: And *I* want to consider the potential for dialogism to "deprivilege,"
as Helene Keyssar says, "absolute, authoritarian discourses"
("Drama" 89). How, for example, does the dialogic configuration
of subjectivity affect the construction of gender, and can it be
used to deprivilege the discourses of phallocentrism?

RIC: Bakhtin did not analyse in his writings *any* texts produced by
women, he assumed a male readership for his work, and he chose
to discuss a great deal of overtly sexist writing. As Wayne C.
Booth asks, "Is it not remarkable to discover no hint in such a
penetrating and exhaustive inquiry" —

JEN: "penetrating and exhaustive" —

RIC: "into how our various dialects are constituted . . . of the influence of sexual differences, no hint that women now talk or have
ever talked in ways different from men's?" (154).[20] (*Beat. Looks to
Jen.*)

JEN: Carry on.

RIC: Nevertheless, as Keyssar says, "there is a striking confluence between the attention to the construction of multi-voicedness and
hybridization in much of contemporary feminist writing and in
Bakhtin's criticism" ("Drama" 95).

JEN: The contributors to Bauer and McKinstry's *Feminism, Bakhtin, and
the Dialogic*, addressing "The Dilemma of a Dialogic Feminism,"
tend to focus on the ways in which dialogism "questions the
'normalcy' of monolithic, hierarchical social relations" (Herndl
19) and helps to get beyond the "problematical binary opposition
'in here/out there'"(Schwab 67). As Dale Bauer says, "The feminist

204 / The Theatre of Form and the Production of Meaning

struggle is not one between a conscious 'awakened' or natural voice *and* the voice of patriarchy 'out there.' Rather precisely because we all internalize the authoritative voice of patriarchy, we must struggle to refashion inherited social discourses into words which rearticulate intentions other than normative or disciplinary ones" (2).

RIC: Margaret Hollingsworth's *The Apple in the Eye* and *Diving* illustrate the dissident, as opposed to hegemonic, potential of internalizing, refashioning, and ventriloquizing the voice of patriarchy, as the central characters, Gemma in *Apple* and Viveca in *Diving*, assimilate with a twist words, phrases, and constructions that are explicitly external to them.

JEN: In *The Apple in the Eye*, Gemma picks up words that she has "never heard of" from her husband's crossword puzzle (19), words such as "arcane" (19, 24) and "behemoth" (21, 25), and, eschewing his "first order logic" together with his "artificial intelligence" (23), she internalizes them in a gesture of anti-hegemonic appropriation, recontextualizing them in a dialogic play of associative "little funnies" (27), as her offstage husband condescendingly calls them.

RIC: *Diving* does something similar with a voice-over discourse of command and obedience appropriated from animal training, athletic coaching, and parenting, as Viveca employs a carnivalesque "grotesque inversion"[21] to rewrite herself into the discourse —

JEN: as a sort of "Trojan femme"? —

RIC: and "capture," on a tape that she controls, the instructional voice of authority.

JEN: Finally, Sharon Pollock's *Getting It Straight* discursively carnivalizes patriarchal languages in a textbook exercise in *écriture feminine*. At the end of the play, Eme also "confesses": "I let the briefcase hang from my hand," she says, "as I walk to / the water I sit on the shore and I use the key I tear / the papers to pieces I chew and I swallow" (125). Having chewed and swallowed the words contained in the throbbing and threatening briefcase, the symbol of her husband's patriarchal corporate power, she turns to address the audience, "the egg talkin' to all members as the female / sex," imagining spinning "a gossamer net of women's hands and rapunzel's / hair," and wondering, in the play's final lines, "what would it spell?" (126).

RIC: Appropriately, then, these monologues can be seen to employ

Bakhtinian dialogics for feminist ends, deprivileging patriarchal discourses, internalizing them *anti*hegemonically, and reconstructing them dialogically as wild and whirling words.

★   ★   ★

JEN: Dialogism can also be used to deprivilege other authoritarian discourses, and in Canadian monologues it has been particularly effective recently in deprivileging the discourses of *ethno*centrism or, in English Canada, "anglo-conformity," as Donna Bennett has called it.[22] In Canada, at least, ethnicity itself seems to be dialogically constituted, while ethnocentrism is, of course, determinedly monologic.

RIC: As Bakhtin says (though he wasn't at this point thinking of ethnicities),

> *monologism* denies that there exists outside of it another consciousness, with the same rights, and capable of responding on an equal footing, another and equal *I* (*thou*). For a monologic outlook . . . the *other* remains entirely and only an *object* of consciousness, and cannot constitute another consciousness. . . . The monologue is accomplished and deaf to the other's response; it does not await it and does not grant it any *decisive* force. Monologue makes do without the other; that is why to some extent it objectivizes all reality. Monologue pretends to be the *last word*.[23]

JEN: In doing so, it absorbs, assimilates, and colonizes the discourses of the other (constructed and objectified as stable and unchanging) and thereby reifies existing asymmetrical power relations.

RIC: Ethnographic theorists see the dialogism of ethnicity itself as a potential fissure in ethnocentrist discourse. As Michael Fischer says, "a process of assuming an ethnic identity is an insistence on a pluralist, multidimensional, or multifaceted concept of self [that] can be a crucible for a wider social ethos" (196).[24]

JEN: Although, as Bakhtin says, shifting the ground to discourse and nation, this "verbal-ideological decentering will occur only when a national culture loses its sealed-off and self-sufficient character, when it becomes conscious of itself as only one among *other* cultures and languages" (*Dialogic Imagination* 23).[25]

RIC: Bakhtin's thoughts on these and other issues were influenced, according to Katerina Clark and Michael Holquist, by his having grown up in the multiethnic Vilnius, "a realized example of heteroglossia" (22) and one that in this sense resembled the Toronto of the 1990s, where Sidnell's prime example of dialogic monologue, *Fronteras Americanas*, was first produced and is in part set.

JEN: Written and performed by its Argentinian Canadian autobiographical subject, Guillermo Verdecchia, *Fronteras* is notable —

RIC: quite apart from those things that it shares with most of the plays under consideration: its use of disruptive laughter, its "linguistic carnival" (Spanish and some French as well as various modes of spoken English),[26] its disruptions of subjectivity, its mixture of styles, its use of parodic exaggeration and inversion, and its Bakhtinian employment of a hero, "Wideload McKennah," as jester[27] —

JEN: as I was saying, it is notable for its recognition and development of the idea that, as Peter Stallybrass and Allon White have said, "cultural identity is inseparable from limits, it is always a boundary phenomenon" (200).[28]

RIC: In fact, the play is an example as well as a discussion of cultural production as a boundary or border phenomenon.

JEN: When Verdecchia argues that we all must learn to "live on the border" (77), he echoes Bakhtin's various arguments that "A person has no internal sovereign territory, he is wholly and always on the boundary" (*Problems* 287). The borders, or *"fronteras,"* to which Verdecchia refers are also, in a bilingual pun, a new frontier, perhaps a "new national culture" such as Bakhtin posited in *his* utopian vision,[29] and in this, too, Verdecchia echoes Bakhtin's position that "a cultural domain has no inner territory. It is located entirely upon boundaries. . . .":

RIC: "Every cultural act lives essentially on the boundaries, and it derives its seriousness from this fact. Separated by abstraction from these boundaries, it loses the ground of its being and becomes vacuous, arrogant; it degenerates and dies" (*Art* 274).

JEN: And when Verdecchia issues his "manifesto" — *not* a "plea for tolerance" but a "summons to begin negotiations, to claim your place on the continent" (54) — and asks, "will you call off the Border Patrol?" because "the border is your home" (77, 74), he evokes Bakhtin's call late in life for "benevolent demarcation. Without border disputes" (*Speech Genres* 137).

RIC: Finally, near the end of *Fronteras*, Verdecchia locates himself *on* the border in a way that sounds archetypally Bakhtinian —

JEN: isn't that a contradiction in terms? —

RIC: yes — in its heteroglossia, its insistence on the processual nature of identity as a highway, and its parodic wit:

JEN: I'm not in Canada; I'm not in Argentina.

I'm on the Border.

I'm Home.

Mais zooot alors, je comprends maintenant, mais oui, merde! Je suis Argentin-Canadien! I'm a post-Porteno neo-Latino Canadian! I am the Pan-American highway! (74)[30]

★   ★   ★

RIC: Dialogic monologues can disrupt ethnocentric and other authoritarian discourses in a variety of ways, including what I think of as the *structural* or *formal* heteroglossia of a play such as Monique Mojica's *Princess Pocahontas and the Blue Spots*.

JEN: *Princess Pocahontas* is not, strictly speaking, a monologue, since it includes a musician — Alejandra Nuñez in the original production — who also plays several small supporting roles.

RIC: Nor is it autobiographical in the same ways as the other plays that we are discussing —

JEN: though its *form* is in some sense autobiographical, and — as an antihegemonic revisioning of dominant myths of Native women, written and performed by Mojica out of a strong and resisting subject position, from which its various characters, historical and contemporary, seem to emerge — it can be seen as a kind of spiritual/historical autobiography.[31]

RIC: On one level, *Princess Pocahontas*, like Margo Kane's *Moonlodge*, seems to function counter- rather than antihegemonically in that, like *Moonlodge*, with its transhistorical and perhaps nostalgic mission of recovering a lost sense of self, it posits and asserts a strong, stable, and empowering community of Native women —

JEN: a counterhegemony —

RIC: who share what seems to be an essentialist identity as both Native Canadians and women.

JEN: *Princess Pocahontas* explicitly ties this essentialist identity to the biological marker of the "blue spot at the base of the spine — the sign of Indian blood" (Mojica 20). Even as this authenticating signifier functions —

RIC: like post-colonial nationalisms —

JEN: as an empowering device for a marginalized group, however, the play simultaneously cuts across the boundary lines and "border patrols" of the colonizing dominant, emphasizing that, even though it is counter- rather than antihegemonic, it is nevertheless not normative. *Princess Pocahontas* does not reinscribe or even acknowledge the geopolitical divisions that *Fronteras Americanas* confronts; as you said in chapter 4, Ric, the myths of Native identity that it attacks or constructs are indiscriminately drawn from all of North, Central, and South America; and the hybrid nature of Native and other ethnicities is asserted at every turn and embodied in the author-performer. Mojica's heritage as a Native Canadian born in New York City to a Kuna-Rappahanock mother and a Jewish father positions her as an embodiment of Bakhtin's hybridization and of the Bakhtin/Verdecchia border phenomenon.

RIC: *Princess Pocahontas* uses a truly carnivalesque blending of musical and performance styles, including what Bakhtin calls "extra-literary" and "proclamatory" genres (*Dialogic Imagination* 411; *Speech Genres* 132), together with parodic exaggeration and inversion, to deprivilege both ethnocentric and phallocentric discourses.

JEN: It also explicitly employs a transformational structural principle that (as you said in chapter 4) Keyssar has articulated as being both Bakhtinian and feminist.

RIC: The playwright, then, explicitly rejects what Keyssar describes as the "resistance" to polyphony of traditional Western dramaturgical structures, adopting one based on Native mythologies and "transformation." It "requires not that we remove . . . disguises that conceal us from our 'true' selves," as in Aristotelian "recognition," "but that we imagine men and women in a continual process of becoming other" ("Drama" 92).

JEN: "It is becoming *other*, not finding oneself, that is the crux of the drama," Keyssar argues —

RIC: and she argues further that such "transformational strategies go hand in hand with the dialogic imagination" (92–93).[32]

JEN: Like all of the plays under discussion, then, *Princess Pocahontas* functions in a variety of formal ways as dialogic monologue, emphasizing not simply heterogeneity but also "'social/ideological' contradictions" (Yaeger 244), to destabilize, subvert, or carnivalize authoritarian discourses and to open the way for effective and *ongoing* social change.[33]

★   ★   ★

JEN: As with all utopian visions, there are problems with Bakhtin's. The most apparent have to do with how to construct a space in which dialogue can take place — an arena of free contestation between equal voices — when hegemony dictates that the consciousnesses and voices of marginalized groups are inevitably inflected with the discourses of the dominant.

RIC: *Can* voices be equal?

JEN: Who, and what, *controls* the construction of dialogic space?

RIC: This problem reveals itself clearly in Bakhtin's construction of carnival and carnival laughter as healthy and socially disruptive —

JEN: when in practice both frequently reinforce social stereotypes and therefore aid social control of ethnic minorities, women, gays, lesbians, and others. Heard any good Newfie jokes lately?

RIC: At the heart of this is the question of power and the fact that "communication itself is by nature more coercive and disproportionate than we think," as Aaron Fogel notes, "when we sentimentalize terms like *dialogue* and *communication*" (195) — and, as Deborah Jacobs points out, when we "romanticize marginality" (195).

JEN: And, as Ken Hirschkop says, "dialogue" must be understood to include "not only the liberal exchange of views but also questions of cultural oppression and power" (75)[34] —

RIC: an understanding that will inevitably — and especially in the Stalinist context of Bakhtin's own historical place and time — include coercion, interrogation, force, and unequal societal, grammatical, and rhetorical forms and relationships.

JEN: Shut up, Ric.

RIC: Are you now, or have you ever been, a member of the Association for Canadian Theatre Research?

JEN: Finally, as Michael André Bernstein points out, it is important not to sentimentalize the potential for *genuinely* unstructured polyphony to trap the individual in an "intolerable babble of voices" that is akin to madness or neurosis, as represented in *House* and *Getting It Straight*, or that can produce, in actual (material) practice, a reactionary monologic attempt to shout down and control the "noise."[35]

RIC: The voices of polyphony, Bakhtin would argue, must be firmly grounded in the utterances of an individual and historicized subject.

JEN: In spite of these concerns and of Bakhtin's own awareness of the fragility of "the dialogic sphere" (*Speech Genres* 150), there is surely hope, as well as trepidation, in a model in which dialogic questioning has the potential to "change the consciousness of the individual" (136) and therefore of the culture.

RIC: Even acknowledging the possibility of abuse deriving from unequal power relations in the theatre and in the world, the monologues that we've looked at, as historical utterances in the context of Canadian theatre today, when initiated and controlled by the societally disempowered, can provide a tentative model of contesting and unmerged voices with the ongoing and open-ended potential to change consciousnesses, societies, and social structures.

JEN: The potential provided by dialogism lies, then, in its ability to change, structurally, the ways in which we perceive the world, as Bakhtin believed that Dostoevsky and Rabelais did and continue to do and as we believe that plays such as the Canadian dialogic monologues we have been discussing are able to do.

RIC: Because, after all, as Michael Holquist points out, and as the premise of this whole book asserts, "we experience the world in all its most common and frequent occasions as *forms*" (*Dialogism* 151).

JEN: Perhaps it's appropriate here to give the last but hopefully not closing words of this dialogue to Bakhtin.

RIC: And, perhaps appropriately, they constitute his last, but not closing, writings.

JEN: There is no first or last discourse, and dialogical context knows no limits (it disappears into an unlimited past and into our unlimited future). Even *past* meanings, that is those that have arisen in the dialogue of past centuries, can never be stable[;] . . . they will always change (renewing themselves) in the course of the dialogue's subsequent development. . . . At every moment of the dialogue, there are immense and unlimited masses of forgotten meanings . . . [that] will return to memory and live in renewed form (in a new context). Nothing is absolutely dead: every meaning will celebrate its rebirth. The problem of the *great temporality*. (qtd. in Todorov 110)

Structuring SpaceTime

Toward a Quantum Dramaturgy

> Somehow, after all, as the universe ebbs towards its final equilib-
> rium in the featureless heat bath of maximum entropy, it man-
> ages to create interesting structures.
> — James Gleick (308)

> What is the relationship between reality and its representation?
> — Nick Herbert (122)

This book on contemporary Canadian dramaturgies follows a historical
path. It began in chapter 1 with naturalism, a dramaturgical form that,
however much it derived from Aristotle, Sophocles, and the Bible, was
essentially novelistic in its understandings of individuals and cultures,
particularly in its use of linear time as its organizational principle and
the element within which events happened. Naturalism was consoli-
dated at the height of industrial capitalism, with which it conspired in
its constructions of linear "progress" and the separation that it effected
and enforced between the realms of technology and values, nature and
culture. Naturalism reached its crisis with the turn of the century,
World War I, and the onset of structures, dramaturgical and otherwise,
based on modernism, structures that retreated from time and history
into "pure" (and unchanging) spatial form, that treated space rather than
time as the site of dramatic action, and that are the subject of chapter
2. In spite of an initial antibourgeois radicalism and an emergence out
of anxieties about the fragmentation of modern, technological society,
this modernist retreat into ahistorical space and aesthetic form can also
be seen as a retreat from social responsibility, and modernism itself has
frequently been seen to be complicit with various repressive political

ideologies. Parts 2 and 3 of *The Theatre of Form*, then, have focused on various strategies of multiplication employed in attempts to resist the politically conservative, totalizing impulses of naturalistic and modernist dramaturgies respectively, as they have manifested themselves in Canada. Part 2 has attempted to examine works that multiply, complicate, or subvert temporal structures, part 3 spatial ones, those that had come, by the late 1960s and early 1970s, to seem oppressive. Thus, collective, collaborative, and community work on the one hand and historiographic metadrama on the other focused on democratizations of the making of theatre and history as *process*, while experiments in environmental theatre and in the imbrication of the solo actor with the audience as addressee focused on the potentially politically liberating creation of theatrical and dialogic *spaces*.

But much has been made in the past two decades of another paradigm shift that has made possible and necessary yet again different ways of seeing and understanding in all fields, from cultural and literary theory through new theories of consciousness to new modellings of reality based on developments in information technology. Thus, the multiplications of the post-structuralist and post-modern in arts and culture, globalization (or multinationalization) in political economy, and the shift to the historical moment of *late* capitalism respond to and construct new ways of seeing and thinking that render inherited forms and structures obsolete or ineffective as strategies of intervention.

Analyses of these shifts to a new episteme, moreover, have often associated them directly or metaphorically with the "new science," the nondeterminist, post-Newtonian physics lumped together by Jean François Lyotard in the conclusion to *The Postmodern Condition: A Report on Knowledge* as "parology" and variously identified with relativity theory, quantum mechanics, chaos theory, fractal geometry, and complex adaptive systems.[1] James Gleick, the most prominent popularizer of the new science, quotes an unidentified physicist as saying, "relativity eliminated the Newtonian illusion of absolute space and time; quantum theory eliminated the Newtonian dream of a controllable measurement process; and chaos eliminates the Laplacian fantasy of deterministic predictability" (6).

Both dramatists and drama theory have drawn on these developments, explicitly making links between what have been — since the so-called dissociation of sensibilities in the early modern period — the separate universes of science and theatre. Thus, Tom Stoppard can invoke quantum mechanics, chaos theory, and the second law of thermodynamics as themes in *The Real Thing, Hapgood,* and *Arcadia;*[2] Natalie Crohn Schmitt can borrow her title and analytical approach from Niels Bohr and the Copenhagen school of quantum physics for her book of drama criticism, *Actors and Onlookers: Theatre and Twentieth-Century Scientific Views of Nature;*[3] scholars such as Rosemarie Bank, David George, and (especially) William Demastes can develop models based on post-Newtonian physics for the analysis of theatre history and for dramatic criticism of work with no conscious connection to any version of the "new science"; and Gordon Armstrong, claiming that "chaos theory is a dead end project" (279), can argue the case for analysing theatre itself as a complex adaptive system.

Without attempting to provide an exhaustive explication of relativity theory, quantum mechanics, chaos theory, complex adaptive systems, or the application of any of them to culture, literature, drama, or theatre, I will try to elucidate a few ways in which two Canadian dramatists, John Mighton and John Krizanc, each of whom has explicitly invoked these developments, have experimented with dramaturgical structures that imitate some of the central features of quantum mechanics and chaos theory, in order to explore the potential for such dramaturgical models either to intervene in or to collude with late capitalist hegemonies.[4] Given my focus on the dramaturgical politics of time and space, I am particularly interested in post-relativity theory investigations of what Bank calls "time, space, timespace, spacetime" and their attempts to bridge this book's central divide between temporal and spatial dramaturgical structures. Important for my purposes is Einstein's observation, which Bank views as fundamental to the new episteme, that "time and space are modes by which we think and not conditions in which we live" (A. Forsee, qtd. in Bank 66).

For my purposes here, the central problematics of nondeterministic physics, and those invoked by Mighton and Krizanc, include, from quantum mechanics, Heisenberg's uncertainty principle ("everything we can measure is subject to truly random fluctuations" [Davies 215]); Bell's Theorum and the fact of nonlocality (subatomic particles can influence one another without contact over vast distances); "tunnelling," the ability of particles sometimes to penetrate impenetrable barriers; and various solutions to "the measurement problem" (the fact that measuring subatomic wave and particle behaviour alters that behaviour). These solutions include the "many worlds" theory of branching, parallel universes, and the "many minds" theory, in which John Von Neuman posits that "human consciousness is the site of wave function collapse" (Herbert 148). From chaos theory comes the collapse of the reductionist program in science, "a breakdown of pre-determinable causality leading to bifurcation, chaos, and finally windows of order within the chaos phase" (Demastes, "Reinspecting" 250). Chaos gives us

- "strange attractors," which model randomness within a limited space;
- the "butterfly effect," involving hypersensitivity to initial conditions and leading to disproportionately great effects from apparently inconsequential causes (and echoing the "always-already" of Derrida, together with his insistence on the futility of tracing originary moments);
- feedback loops, in which output feeds back into the system as input (leading to both the butterfly effect and "equivocation" or "what is added to or subtracted from information as it passes through a noisy channel" [Hayles 56]);
- the "carpet effect," through which chaotic processes produce orderly patterns;
- Ilya Prigogine's theories of "order out of chaos" (Prigogine and Stengers), which see entropy as the necessary precursor to self-organization;
- and "fractals," irregular shapes or number systems that repeat themselves on varying scales (and fascinatingly restructure the relationships between the local and the global[5]).

Crucially, in terms of their political implications, both quantum mechanics and chaos theory reconceive science as a study less of things, of fundamental particles, than of processes, less of being than of becoming (Gleick 5). The social and political implications of this as a deep structure are extraordinary. Becoming precedes being in Bohr's notion of *"relational reality"* (Herbert 161), as it does for James Reaney (see chapter 5); and Heisenberg's uncertainty principle "declares the raw material of the universe to be potentia, tendency, possibility — a world, in a word, founded on a wave of opportunity" (Herbert 245). If things *happen* rather than *are*, then, and "the fundamental concepts are the events or changes rather than the objects that are doing the changing" (Rae 108), *change* is configured by the new science as fundamental to existence,[6] and, as Stanley Aronowitz puts it, *"relations, not things, [are] the true object of inquiry"* (250).

If, in addition to this shift, one takes into account the quantum fact, not only that observation alters what is observed (including the past) but also, because *"everything we touch turns to matter"* (Herbert 194), that in a quantum universe we *cannot* observe becoming, only being, then we enter a realm — also reminiscent of Reaney's dramaturgy of genesis (see chapter 5) — in which "The moment of the world's creation is seen to lie, not in some unthinkably remote past, but in the eternal now" (John Archibald Wheeler, qtd. in Herbert 167). In the act of observation, then, our senses are involved in what Michael Talbot calls "a highly complex feedback process whose final result is to actually *create* what is out there" (qtd. in George 173), and "nature, too complex to fit into the Procrustean bed of linear dynamics, can renew itself precisely because it is rich in disorder and surprise" (Hayles 10–11). Even the most conservative accounts of the contributions of quantum mechanics and chaos allow that, "even accepting a strictly deterministic account of nature, the future states of the Universe are in some sense 'open'" (Davies 221), as they acknowledge the need for chaos in order for systems not to atrophy, to resist shocks precisely because they are capable of changing in ways that are not predictable or determinate (Gleick 293). But the question of who *controls* quantum spacetime remains, and — as for similar questions about the democratizing processes of collective creation or the "free" spaces of environmental theatre or dialogism — that question is a political one. As David George argues,

> it is probably less as an epistemological model that the Quantum Theatre has the latent power to transform our attitudes than as an ideology . . . : predicting what *can be* known and the laws of behaviour, it establishes always a social code as much as an epistemological range. . . . [But] the point is . . . that the new physics radically challenges that ideology — discovering and now accepting indeterminacy, chance, and by implication spontaneity, change and, most drastically, seeing the world as one in a perpetual process of creation and transformation. (175)

The political effects of this epistemic shift are clearly potentially liberatory in their inscription of becoming rather than being as fundamental. But if existence is seen as nondeterministic, and reality is created and controlled by its observation or representation, if, indeed, it is a locus of potential, a kind of post–Peter Brook empty spacetime, then the political stakes are very high surrounding the question of who controls representation within the quantum theatre. Like the other apparently "free" or dialogic spaces and exploratory processes discussed in earlier chapters, and like the cyberspace of new technology or the multiplication of "free trade" zones within the late capitalist economy of globalization, if quantum spacetime and the turbulent flows of the universe of chaos theory are uninterrogated, then they can simply work to privilege the currently dominant, undermine identity politics and the strategic essentialisms of societally marginalized groups, and beg the question of who gets to observe, and therefore constitute, the new realities, and from what position. Already, as N. Katherine Hayles has demonstrated, the quantum theatre is very traditionally gendered, at least in its popular representation, its cast list restricted to heroic, individualist male scientists struggling to control chaos (gendered female), "admitting the feminine as an abstract principle but excluding actual women" (174).[7] It is perhaps not surprising, though also somewhat alarming, that in Canada as elsewhere most playwrights who have thus far explored post-Newtonian dramaturgical structures have been middle-class heterosexual white men.

The kinds of analyses that Hayles undertakes, then, might be extended to the implications of the turbulent flow of quantum and chaos realities for post-colonial, queer, and other interrogations of race, nation, gender, class, and sexuality. It is important that, in the rush to embrace the political potential of a scientific worldview based on instability and change, the erasure of places on which to stand and of history effected by the scientific shift from particle to process and on into spacetime not conspire with developments such as the reactionary marshalling of free speech, free trade, and academic freedom by the right, or the alarmingly adaptive emergence of multinational, post-national capitalism in the face of post-colonial nationalisms or political philosophies based on revolutionary historical change. Already works such as Gleick's introduction to chaos theory and Demastes's book-length application of chaos to drama, *Theatre of Chaos: Beyond Absurdism, into Orderly Disorder*, have begun the recuperative process of moving "into orderly disorder." The emphasis in these fundamentally conservative works on the (re)emergence of order out of chaos — the emergence, perhaps, of a "new world order?" — should concern us.

★   ★   ★

We obviously need to be more sophisticated in our choice of possible worlds.

— Nick Herbert (228–29)

If, as chaos pioneer Mitchell Feigenbaum's work demonstrates, "chaos has a deep structure" (qtd. in Hayles 152), then how do the deep structures of chaos and quantum reality become useful or meaningful dramaturgically, for whom, and in whose interests? John Mighton, one of the leading playwrights to emerge in Canada in the 1990s, has BA and MA degrees in philosophy and is completing a PhD in mathematics while teaching both mathematics and physics, and he brings his understandings of the worlds of science and mathematics to bear on his dramaturgy. In his early play *Scientific Americans*, the politics of post-Newtonian physics appear primarily at a thematic level. The central character, Jim, who hears from General Berger when he is hired to work at a military research facility that "Chaos has a bad name. But all natural processes depend on it" (21), eventually uses Bell's Theorem and the quantum concept of nonlocality ("different parts of a quantum system appear to influence each other even when they are a long way apart and even although there is no known interaction between them" [Rae ix]) to design a weapon, a kind of stealth bomber, that can operate at an impossible distance. Structurally, although the play's main action is more or less naturalistically conceived, it is punctuated by lectures delivered by an army psychologist, Bill, to groups such as "Physicians for Peace" (95), lectures that employ elements of chaos theory, influence the action at a distance, provide a kind of feedback loop within the play itself, and point to some of the problems that emerge through the principles of nonobjective observation and investigation. "You too," Bill argues, "can learn to think like a scientist":

> Formulate startling analogies. Make deft generalizations. Notice lawlike behaviour. There's only one danger. Sometimes a person's ability to see connections and analogies becomes abnormally heightened. He begins to think that everything he sees or reads about relates to him in some essential way. We call the ability to see these kinds of connections "paranoia." (28)

The character ends the play with a speech that begins with Freud on aggression and proceeds to invoke feedback, Bell's Theorem, marketing, and desire, a speech that issues in a warning about responsibility, control, and the politics of late capitalist quantum space (or of chaos as interactive theatre):

> I'd like to point out something I've noticed over the years. It's very simple — people change in groups. They regulate each other's behaviour. It happens in highway driving. When you get enough cars on a road there's a phase change from a bunch of individuals driving to a coherent structure. Right now you're responding to the things I say in ways you might not if you were alone. There's a complicated flow of information in this room. Feedback. My words are causing neurons to fire in your brains. You can't help it. But your reactions are changing my speech. . . . Most people think that speaking is one-way. Like advertising. People just passively soak it up. But advertising is based on market research. When it works it's really just a way of reinforcing what we already believe. Like propaganda. Hitler didn't succeed by telling people things they didn't want to hear. . . . Some scientists think that subatomic particles can communicate over large distances instantaneously. They explain ESP and precognition in terms of vast fields of information stretching across time and space. Right now, all across the country, people are spying on each other, gathering information in ways you aren't even aware of. It's no different here. Tonight is an exercise in market research. People are watching you watching. Advertisers, politicians, activists, generals, producers. If you laugh, you're casting a vote. If my speech succeeds, if the papers support us, you're going to hear the same thing over and over until you puke. So be careful. Don't clap too loudly. Otherwise someone is going to find out what you want . . . And you may get it. (95–96; three-point ellipsis in original)

If quantum theory operates primarily at a thematic level in *Scientific Americans*, then it is implicated both structurally and thematically in Mighton's later play *The Little Years*, in which one character, William, who doesn't appear in the play, nevertheless functions as a kind of structural "strange attractor." The published script and the program for the Theatre Passe Muraille premiere in 1995 are introduced with an epigraph from Thomas Nagel:[8] "A man's life includes much that does not take place within the boundaries of his body and his mind, and what happens to him can include much that does not take place within the boundaries of his life" (8). The play proceeds to circle in virtually fractal patterns around the life, and its aftereffects, of the missing William, a reportedly brilliant child at the outset who becomes a famous poet before dying between the play's two acts. The cast list in the published version describes all of the characters in relation to William — his mother, his sister, his wife, his daughter, and his friend, and he is the object of discussion in many of the scenes. Insofar as the action is nonlinear, it imitates the properties of the strange ("butterfly" or "Lorenz") attractor of chaos theory, in that it seems to represent randomness within a fixed, relational space and to construct a dramatic world of relative uncertainty, what chaos pioneer Benoit Mandelbrot calls "deterministic chaos," "deterministic yet unpredictable motion" (122).

This aspect of the play's structure functions in essentially spatial, geometric ways, but as William's sister, Kate, knows, this play and the world that it represents operate in space/time: "A hundred years ago they showed that light always travels at the same speed, regardless of the motion of the earth. Once you accept that you have to abandon absolute time and space. Space contracts and time slows down as you move faster" (18). Early in the play, the young Kate is obsessed with nonlinear time. At thirteen, she tells her mother about relativity and the measurement problem, regales a dance partner with accounts of space/time, and writes assignments on "the future" for her English class about wanting to come back before she was born. Later she tells a famous painter about the shape of his immortality in a world that accommodates relativities: "Did you know that some infinite sets are larger than others?" she asks. "It's an elementary fact of set theory. If time branches you would have more immortality than in linear Newtonian time. Infinitely more immortality" (33). But the play is also structured according to the principles of the second law of thermodynamics, and the girl who asks "Why do we remember the past and not the future?" (14) grows up in a play framed by funerals to understand, as chaos theorist Peter Coveney says, that "Life itself is a non-equilibrium process: ageing is irreversible" (205).

Two of Mighton's other plays, *A Short History of Night* and *Possible Worlds*, published together, explicitly evoke in their titles two of the most prominent popular manifestations of post-Newtonian physics: the former echoes the title of Stephen Hawking's best-selling book about the quantum universe, *A Brief History of Time: From the Big Bang to Black Holes*; the latter conjures up in both title and dramaturgy physicist Hugh Everett's solution to the "measurement problem" in quantum theory, the problem that has most consistently captured the popular imagination: that of parallel universes, which posits the simultaneous existence of an infinite number of possible worlds and predicts, in what sounds like an absurdist quantum version of Murphy's law, that "everything that can happen does happen" (Herbert 175). Or, as the play's central character, George, explains the theory to Joyce, one of the women played by the same actor with whom versions of George have relationships in the play,

> Each of us exists in an infinite number of possible worlds. I'm in one world while I'm talking to you right now but your arm is a little to the left, in another world you're interested in that man over there with the glasses, in another, you stood me up two days ago — and that's how I know your name. (23)

A kind of quantum murder mystery about brains stolen from rooms that have been locked from the inside — "tunnelling," if on an impossibly large scale — *Possible Worlds* combines the investigative structure of the detective narrative (detective Berkley concludes the first scene "running over some possibilities" [12]) with a quantum variation on the early modern comic structure of multiple, parallel plotting and an inventive use of the vagaries of theatrical doubling. Thus, the parallel universes invoked are played out in a number of mutually exclusive, parallel scenes performed by actors who may or may not be doubling the roles of characters who may or may not be the same "people" (in a quantum reconfiguration of human subjectivity and dramatic character). But the plot structure also hinges on another possibility and another answer to the quantum measurement problem: the so-called many minds theory. There is a strong possibility that the action takes place within the brain of George, which has been stolen and is being kept alive by an experimental scientist who tells Berkley early on of the need to "consider every possibility" (27). Structurally, what this comes down to is the playing out of mutually exclusive scenes before audience members who must, by observing the play, make choices (wave or particle?) that *produce* the action, in a theatrical version of the interactive quantum fact that we radically change what we observe. (It has always been a fact of theatrical worlds that a performance doesn't exist without an audience and that it exists and means differently for different audiences. It has also always been true of theatrical relationships between producers and reviewers — not to mention playwrights, directors, and actors — that this issue is the fundamentally political question of who controls meaning.)

A Short History of Night deals not with contemporary scientific discovery but with the life of two pre-Newtonian scientists from the sixteenth century, Johannes Kepler and Tycho Brahe, while drawing directly on the ideas of René Descartes and Marcus Aurelius. The play nevertheless questions the relationships between time, memory, and history in the evolution of theories of the cosmos. It also interrogates the Laplacian idea that "the world is a clock driven by physical causes" (118), a world in which randomness, and therefore change, are unthinkable, and it dreams, with its central character, of a "One day" when "people will see exactly with their minds, not by analogy" (164). The politics of this vision are implicit structurally throughout the play (and much of Mighton's other work), and they are made explicit in his "Author's Note":

> When people think about the future, they tend to imagine a world in which, for better or worse, everyone agrees. In dystopias like Huxley's *Brave New World* the agreement is imposed from above; in utopias it is spontaneous and based on truth. But if the human mind is incapable of understanding the world in its entirety, then people may never entirely agree. Perhaps we should start preparing for a future in which people don't agree, in which tolerance will have to be the chief virtue. (83)

★   ★   ★

> The uncertainty principle fundamental to physics is based on the failure of the empiricist to secure the real. *Fort. Da.*
>
>   — Peggy Phelan, *Unmarked* (167)

John Krizanc, who explores in *Tamara* the politics of space, turns in *The Half of It* explicitly to the politics of spacetime, invoking post-Newtonian physics to construct what David George would call a "quantum theatre." The play is set in permeable space and not always determinable (or determinate) time schemes, but its central actions revolve around Jillson Ashe, whose natural father, as it turns out, Freddie Boise, is an unscrupulous stockbroker who hires her husband,

Peter, to manage an "ethical" environmental investment portfolio. Jill's legal father, meanwhile, has died, having given away much of the family fortune. The family — Jill; her mother, Clare; and her sister, Hillary — have to decide whether to preserve their thousand acres of treed property, "Burnham Wood," or to sell it to a developer who will "turn it into a subdivision in no time" (70). As the naming of the property and of many of the characters suggests, Krizanc tends in *The Half of It* to use a virtually neomedieval allegorical structure that mimics the parallel universe theory, constructs parallel rather than totalizing signifying systems, and draws attention to the materiality of the sign, in counterdistinction to the appropriative properties of metaphor, which engulfs what it represents.[9] Thus, for example, the audience is invited to view the action through a variety of framing grids, ranging from Shakespearean tragedy ("Burnham Wood"), through social Darwinism ("What am I, some bimbo?" asks Boise's opportunistic secretary, Dee. "I don't know from Darwin?" [156][10]), to fairy-tale allegories of good and evil based on Peter Pan: crocodiles occasionally drop from the sky/lighting grid, and Peter Malchuck is pitted against Freddie Boise, whose lost arm has been replaced first by a hook and then by a technologically marvellous computer as prosthetic device.

One strand of the play's complex structure pits Freddie, the masculinist stockbroker before whom the world is laid out "in a straight line. Everything certain" (153), against Jill, who may or may not be his daughter and who is not interested in "what is, or is not, objectively, the case" (142). Boise, on the other hand, instructs Peter that "We're piloting the economy. . . . We have to rely on the objectivity of computers" (106), and he greets the news that the lab technician is "fairly sure" that a blood test reveals that Jill is his daughter with "fairly sure? What kind of fucking scientist is he? I want to know!"

> What's going on here? I gave my goddam blood! Are they reading the entrails of some pig? You tell the son-of-a-bitch to find a bigger microscope.[11] I don't care how much he has to enlarge it, but I want the absolute-irreducible [sic]-fucking truth, and I want it today on this desk on a piece of paper I can staple to the woman's heart!" (104–05)

Jill, on the other hand, is an advocate of the new science. "There's a theory, derived from quantum physics," she argues, "which says that all possible universes exist. . . . Universes could be constantly emerging, branching out, and running parallel to each other with every possibility" (11). Elsewhere (97–99), Jill instructs the character who, in her part of the stage and the play world, is her lover, called Newman, but in Boise's office and world is his spy, Kilman, on the quantum measurement problem, relating it, as scientists occasionally have, to things such as intuition, dowsing for water, and falling in love. In fact, Krizanc refers to Jill as a "quantum character," in counterdistinction to what he calls "Newtonian" concepts such as "the trajectory of a character" and the through lines, rising actions, climaxes, and turning points of traditional "deterministic" dramatic structures.[12] That such concepts are fundamentally masculinist, imitating the structure of the male orgasm, is inescapable: as the spokesperson for the certainties of traditional science, as well as for the corporate world and the principle of self-interest, Boise speaks throughout the play with aggressive sexuality. He tells his offshore agent, Angel, discussing a market manipulation, to "fuck it into the ground and put a stake through its heart" (14), and elsewhere he explains to Peter that "it's not really about numbers. It's about who's got the bigger dick" (93). And, as Dee explains to Jill, "You know about imperialism? Whites penetrating darkest Africa? That's sex, Jill. Penetration is imperialism plain and simple" (157–58).

The Half of It searches for alternative structures in which characters both were and were not drowned (or moved to Rhodesia) when they were ten (or in their late thirties); in which Newman and Kilman both are and are not the same character; in which characters walk through walls and simultaneously inhabit discrete spaces; in which actions take place simultaneously in different locations, mimicking quantum nonlocality by influencing each other simultaneously and tangibly in spite of the apparent impossibility of their doing so; in which the interrelations between objects, characters, events, and audiences do not occur *in* space and time but themselves *create* and *define* — constitute — "space-time" (see Massey 154); and in which the either/or dichotomies of the central action are left for their resolution to an audience constructed as being complicit in the play in much the same way that the scientist is complicit in her or his experiment: the act of watching the play constructs the experience and affects — or perhaps effects — the play's meaning. In a play in which spying is one of the central and most intrusive activities, watching is acting, and the spectator is always and necessarily implicated. Krizanc, not incidentally, quotes Neils Bohr in one of his epigraphs to the play: "In the great drama of existence we are simultaneously actors and spectators" (iii).

The rupture with Newtonian physics and neo-Aristotelian drama-turgies effected in *The Half of It* is, however, more than a matter of coins and crocodiles dropping from the sky and inhabiting both the conscious and unconscious minds of the characters and the stage world(s). If, in a world without objective truths, meaning depends on what you make of it (and some quantum scientists have proposed "that there is exactly one physical world but that . . . there are two [or more] incompatible *stories* about that world . . . which are both somehow simultaneously true" [Albert 115]), then the struggle is on for control over quantum spacetime and over which people get to tell their stories. As Dee, the most successfully self-interested character in *The Half of It*, puts it, "you've got to take all these random events and order them to your own advantage" (156). "The key to survival," she argues, "is to adopt a strategy which turns your weakness into strength" (155). Finally, in relation to both its audience and its represented world, *The Half of It* insists that passive observation is not only impossible but also socially irresponsible, and the play is hardest on impassive liberals, both in the play and in the audience, who maintain their integrity by with-drawal from the world. As Boise asks Peter, "Why do you think they're always putting up statues to people with integrity? Because they're monuments to inaction" (47). Jill ends the play (having given birth to Newman's daughter, moved to Zimbabwe, and adopted the personality of "Kate Riley," who may or may not have been the lover of the man who may or may not have been her father) with the recognition that to have "withdrawn into our own personal chaos" is to have abrogated responsibility for the construction of better "possible worlds" (168). Her withdrawal has been no different in effect from Peter's collabora-tion or Boise's greed. As her sister argues earlier, "People are interested in what you do — *do* — in the world! . . . Feeling is *not* an event, it is *not* an accomplishment, and it is not something people want to know. Good night" (97).

★ ★ ★

The politics of *The Half of It* itself, and the epistemic shifts with which it concerns itself, are perhaps outlined most clearly in Jill's opening monologue, a "history of science" address to her private girls' school primary class, delivered standing before a blackboard on which are written several phrases: "Mind/Body," "Nature vs. Reason," and "Dead or Alive" (1). Jill later tells her mother that the monologue was intended "to teach them [the class] that how we view the world is culturally conditioned" as "a preamble to introducing them to quantum mechanics" (to which Grace replies, "People don't send their girls to private school to meet mechanics" [20]). I will conclude, insofar as conclusions are possible, by quoting from the monologue at length. It cross-fades in beneath the first few verses of Leonard Cohen's song "Everybody Knows," which perhaps evoke Einstein's famous antichaos claim that "God does not play dice":

Everybody knows that the dice are loaded
Everybody rolls with their fingers crossed
Everybody knows the war is over
Everybody knows the good guys lost
Everybody knows the fight was fixed
The poor stay poor and the rich get rich

That's how it goes
Everybody knows . . .

JILL . . . and it wasn't once upon a time, but at a specific time not so long ago, when we still looked upon the world and saw everything in it as equal to ourselves, because everything was alive. If we needed branches for our shelter we would ask the tree's forgiveness before cutting it down. And if a rock didn't move, it wasn't because it was dead but because it was sleeping. . . .

Now, as individuals formed themselves into tribes it was inevitable that hierarchies should develop and that our view of nature should change to reflect this . . . that the tribal chief should make an offering to the chief of all deer spirits, whatever. Thousands of years pass and eventually all these spirits are reduced to one life force — God — and this is called . . . anyone? (*pause*) Monotheism.

Now, if this guy — and it's interesting that we usually think God is masculine and the earth feminine — if this God is up there somewhere, the life force is up there somewhere, then the earth is dead. It's no longer a source of magic and wonderment. We no longer have to thank the tree for its branch because we have it from God, the God that *we* invented, that all this stuff, this nature stuff, is here for the taking. This was, like — the biggest real-estate deal in history. . . . And the great thing about it was

that it made it okay to cut down all the trees because really —
they were dead already. You didn't have to feel guilty now, unlike
before, when the earth was your mother. . . .

Anyway, we got this thing from God — the whole earth —
it's a present from God. So, remember when you were a kid —
what's the first thing you do with a present? (*points*) Ann? Play
with it — a good answer. Unfortunately it may be the reason
girls are discouraged by science. Do you have a brother? What
would he do with his present? Find out how it works. How?
Take it apart? Right. Now, when it comes to the world, the
system that was developed for this purpose was called science.

Science was supposed to reveal the mysteries of creation and
thereby bring us closer to God. . . . The trouble began when it
became apparent to the scientists that what they were finding
didn't jive with what the church was telling them they were
supposed to find. . . . [D]etermined to get to the bottom of all
this, a fun guy named Francis Bacon suggested scientists should
tie nature to the rack and torture her secrets from her. . . . The
boys started playing for keeps. They wanted to find the truth, a
truth which was experimentally verifiable and quantifiable, a one-
plus-one-always-equals-two kind of truth. You'll notice I said the
truth, because for most scientists how something works is equal
to its truth.

In what became traditional science you and I are reduced to
nothing but valves and pumps. Yet surely we have a uniqueness
beyond the mechanisms which give us life.

This term, we'll delve into that question by exploring some of
the ways in which recent science has realized the limitations of
traditional reductionism. . . . Okay, tomorrow we'll start to look
at the collapse of objectivity in contemporary physics. . . . Ann?
. . . Right. Homework. When you go home I want you to ask
your parents . . . "What is reality and how much does it cost?"
(1–4; some ellipses in original)

Notes

INTRODUCTION: The Politics of Dramatic Form

¹ The distinction between form and structure here is somewhat artificial but useful for my purposes. I use "form" in part — as in my title — as a larger category of which "structure" is a subset. However, in using "form," primarily in part 1, I wish to suggest generic organizing systems, such as those employed in tragedy and comedy, that are often taken for granted by playwrights and audiences as "natural" but that can be either silently adopted (an affirmative strategy, in which audience expectations are satisfactorily fulfilled) or foregrounded and (possibly) subverted (a disruptive strategy, in which expectations are disappointed). I use "structure," on the other hand, primarily in parts 2 and 3, to suggest more overtly selected or constructed — and potentially more flexible, innovative, or experimental — organizing strategies that are less likely to draw on preexisting generic expectations of audiences. With the exception of chapter 1, however, I have avoided genre theory as such, though I am aware of the relevance to my argument of many scholars' observations about the use or misuse of genre conventions in respectively upholding or throwing into question traditionally held beliefs and values and in forming, reforming, or deforming social subjects, particularly as traditional genres move toward satisfying, fulfilling, or disrupting socially acceptable closures. For valuable discussions of genre, see Fowler; and Longhurst.
² I will occasionally discuss Québécois plays, but only when they have received significant productions or publication in English Canada and, as translations, have become part of the theatrical tradition of English Canada.
³ I am adapting this idea of form as the unconscious of a dramatic text from Fredric Jameson's entirely compatible concept of "the political unconscious" and ultimately, of course, from Claude Lévi-Strauss's observation that the "road toward the understanding of man [sic] . . . goes from the study of conscious content to that of unconscious forms" (24–25).
⁴ The authorship of this work is disputed. It was first published under Medvedev's name and later claimed for Bakhtin or "the Bakhtin circle." The dispute, the grounds for which are outlined in the introduction to the translation listed in my works cited, does not affect my use of the book here. I am interested, of course, only in dramaturgical elements of the construction of playtexts, not in subjects such as poetic language or other "micro" elements of form that were the first concerns of the Russian Formalists that Bakhtin/Medvedev critique.
⁵ Bakhtin/Medvedev note, moreover, one tendency of "making it strange" in the work of the Russian Formalists that they call its "negative aspect," which, "far from

emphasizing the enrichment of the world with new and positive constructive meaning, simply emphasizes the negation of the old meaning" (60).

⁶ Herbert Blau, however, provides a convincing critique of the position that even performance is somehow "dissociated . . . from the (allegedly) repressive dramaturgy of the oedipal tradition" and that it somehow escapes commodification (11–12). That argument is made most cogently, perhaps, if from a different angle, by Peggy Phelan, who is concerned with the undeniable *presence* of the performance artist and the supposed unrepeatability of the performance event.

⁷ For a full discussion of the recent history of Buddies in Bad Times, see Wallace, "Theorizing."

⁸ I am not analysing productions of the plays, however, simply the structures and deep structures of one portion of what constitutes the performance text: the script.

1   ARISTOTLE, OEDIPUS, AND THE BIBLE: FORMS OF NATURALISM

¹ The standard studies of closure are those by Frank Kermode and Barbara Herrnstein Smith. In relation to Shakespeare, the field on which theories of dramatic form were most directly played out in high school and university classrooms in the 1960s, see Barbara Hodgdon's complex analysis of the history plays in *The End Crowns All: Closure and Contradiction in Shakespeare's History*.

² Catharsis, of course, requires a degree of empathy or identification. Both concepts are usefully interrogated by Elin Diamond, who, noting the fears potentially called up by identification as introjection, and the potentially destabilizing conception of identity as itself a "crucible of identifications" (particularly in Plato), claims that "Aristotle tamed such fears, making imitation the central and enabling heuristic of the developing human": "For Aristotle, then, identification combines catharsis with social discipline: built on the universally upheld virtues of consistency and causality, catharsis adjusts its spectators to accept the truth and rightness of the hero's destiny and the play's action. In such acceptance the spectator reaffirms his place — his role — in the polis" (392).

³ Jewinski's article opens with the following (almost textbook) summary of the educational tradition that I have been describing:

The lack of the tragic hero in modern drama has become an accepted fact. One no longer seeks, or expects, the noble character whom Aristotle described, whose fall from great heights is balanced by his spiritual strength and growth, whose suffering is in excess of his deserts, but whose fall is due, in part, to his own character. The tragic hero, victim of fate and of himself, carrying within him the seeds of his own doom and of his spiritual triumph, the Prometheus of Aeschylus, the Oedipus of Sophocles, the Hamlet of Shakespeare, has been replaced in modern drama by a series of victims of accident, society or heredity, a series of little men whose fall (if there is one) is not far, whose dignity is questionable, and whose insights — introspective or otherwise — are negligible. (92)

⁴ These naturalistically represented oedipal dramas, not surprisingly, by "reflecting" what Canadians are "really like" (see Johnson, "Is That Us?") *as* a post-colonial nationalist gesture that consisted largely in mimicking the naturalist dramas of our theatrical parents (British and American), may be considered to have served the centralist agenda of the Trudeau government, itself elected in the wake of Expo '67 and Canada's other "coming-of-age" centennial celebrations in 1967 (Wasserman 21). Trudeau's attempt to carve out independent foreign and economic policies from the American "father" can

be seen to play out the "leaving home" drama that constitutes the plots of many of the naturalistic plays of the period — Jerry Wasserman suggests that these plays embody "a kind of national autobiography" (21) — plays that, like Trudeau's policies, were nevertheless heavily dependent on American models. It is important to note, too, that the genre of oedipal father-son plays, in some cases involving nationalist allegories, did not die out in the 1970s. George F. Walker's *Nothing Sacred*, discussed below as a perversion of the tradition, was produced at Toronto's Canadian Stage in 1988 under the direction of Bill Glassco, who also directed the premieres of *Leaving Home*, *Of the Fields, Lately*, and almost all of David French's subsequent work. Also in 1988, Richard Rose and D.D. Kugler wrote and produced *Newhouse* (discussed in chapter 6), a rewriting of Molina's *Don Juan* and Seneca's *Oedipus*, in which the oedipal figure is the Canadian prime minister.

⁵ Not incidentally, Freud turns his attention in *The Interpretation of Dreams*, immediately following his discussion of *Oedipus Rex*, to that other staple of classroom drama, Shakespeare's *Hamlet* (see 366–68). (For an excellent discussion of Freud on *Hamlet*, see Marjorie Garber's "*Hamlet*: Giving Up the Ghost" [*Shakespeare's Ghost Writers* 124–76].) Freud's fullest account of the Oedipus complex is in *The Ego and the Id*.

⁶ On the hegemonic inscription of narrativity, and therefore of oedipal structures, as a cultural mode, see Teresa de Lauretis's delightfully titled "Oedipus Interruptus." Because my focus is on dramatic structure, I have omitted here the role that post-Stanislavksi "method" acting — particularly as represented in handbooks such as Sonia Moore's *The Stanislavski System: The Professional Training of an Actor* — has played in the construction and definition of dramatic character and action through the construction and playing out of linear objectives and superobjectives in a central Aristotelian action based on conflict and resolution. As the dominant influences on actor and director training in Canada as elsewhere, the Stanislavski "System" and its North American counterpart, the "American Method," are completely congruent both with neo-Aristotelian dramaturgy and with Freudian psychology.

⁷ It is important to remember that Freud's theories were based on his psychoanalytical practice and that his object was to return maladjusted patients to a socially acceptable norm. His influence on North American drama and theatre, in particular, is allied with North American practices of psychoanalysis that are still more socially normative, designed to construct subjects who are "well adjusted": that is, subjects who are capable of "coping" with "the way things are." This process involves accepting that their inability to cope is by implication a function of their own maladjustment rather than of social problems that could themselves be addressed — and this implication is inscribed in plays that employ the Freudian/oedipal model. The analogy between the psychoanalytic experience and the theatre audience's experience of neo-Aristotelian catharsis — the purging of socially disruptive passions — is clear. The reader might also want to refer to Volosinov/Bakhtin's Marxist critique of Freudianism on the social and ideological construction of the psyche (Volosinov, *Freudianism*) and to Deleuze and Guattari's *Anti-Oedipus: Capitalism and Schizophrenia*.

⁸ Entry into the Symbolic Order involves the construction of subject positions through difference and the construction of desire through "lack." This difference, deferral, and lack become for our purposes here the driving forces in linear narrative. Terry Eagleton and Janelle Reinelt, respectively, provide useful summaries for the uninitiated of the related Lacanian concepts of the imaginary, the mirror stage, and their relevance to critical theory. For Eagleton,

The "imaginary" is a technical term in psychoanalytic theory to denote that narcissistic state, typical of early childhood but influencing all adult life, in which external reality seems merely a mirror in which the individual can harmoniously identify with an idealized self-image, in which there is as yet no fully independent subjectivity and no firm borderline between subject and object. At the point of Oedipal crisis and the acquisition of language, this imaginary unity is ruptured: the child must come to acknowledge itself as merely one "signifier" in an impersonal structure of relations which assigns it its allotted place. This structure of relations is known as the "symbolic order," in which each place of "subject position" is defined merely by its difference from the others, and in which, because of the absence or removal of the desired object, the fullness of the "imaginary" image gives way to the "lack" of desire. (105–06)

And, for Reinelt,

This notion of the mirror stage has been especially useful for performance studies because of the analogy between it and the mimetic mirror of the stage, which reflects representations of the self and its world. The social construction of the representations leaves no doubt that the reflection in the stage mirror is also Other, not identical to any viewing selves, and not "accurate" about any so-called human nature but, rather, a socio-cultural construct of ideal images. Besides demystifying the nature of such representation, however, Lacan provides an explanation of why spectators are in thrall to these representations, why their desiring apparatus is set in motion each time a stage mirror simulates this experience. Many of the basic theoretical questions of dramatic theory touch on this psychological process: the role and purposes of aesthetic experience, the Aristotelian notion of catharsis . . . , the Platonic/Aristotelian debates about the danger/good of mimesis, the question of presence in acting theory . . . , the modern discourse on the role of empathy, and the benefits of alienation in receiving representation. All these topics can be seen as intimately linked to the paradigm of the mirror stage. . . . (385–86)

See Lacan's essay "The Mirror Stage as Formative of the Function of the I" (*Écrits* 1–7).

[9] Canadian playwright Betty Lambert, for example, said in an interview in *Room of One's Own* in 1983:

I wanted a new form of tragedy. I wanted to battle Aristotle['s assumption that,] when Oedipus tears out his eyes, that's it. Even though Sophocles is going to write *Return to Colonus*, you've got this tragic moment. Women know something that maybe men don't know. We know that after the death, somebody cooks bacon and eggs. And that suicide is not an answer, because life bloody goes on. And on some fundamental level I wanted to break the tragic code. (qtd. in Hale 78–79)

For feminist analyses of Freud and Lacan that are relevant to this inquiry, see de Lauretis, *Alice Doesn't*; and Silverman. Christine Rochefort, in an autobiographical polemic delivered at the University of Wisconsin in February 1975, concisely accounted for the feminist suspicion of therapy as return to a (neo-Aristotelian) patriarchal "norm" or "reality": "In the world of appearances, I didn't feel real. Schizophrenia? I was lucky that my parents were not in a position to take me to a therapist: he would have discovered my trick, brought me back to "reality" and it would have been the end of me" (184).

[10] Aristotle's structural analysis was developed and applied to comedy (though the relationship is not acknowledged and is not precise) by Donatus in his threefold

division into protasis, epitasis, and catastrophe and by Horace in the *Ars Poetica*, which prescribes a five-act structure for any play, comic or tragic. See Herrick 89–129.

[11] My discussion of Frye and Barber is indebted to Bristol, who, however, treats Frye as an American scholar.

[12] This analysis of Barber is primarily of the impact on criticism of *Shakespeare's Festive Comedy: A Study of Dramatic Form and Its Relation to Social Custom*. Barber's later work and his personal influence were nevertheless important, as Bristol notes, "in fostering the emergence of the feminist critique of Shakespeare" (184) and in the development of psychoanalytic criticism.

[13] The foundational guarantee in the Canadian Constitution of the right to "peace, order and good government" (as opposed to the American right to "life, liberty, and the pursuit of happiness") may be significant here.

[14] French describes the process of writing the play as a problem-solving one, working his way through to a knowledge of the characters, to a finding out of their motivations and their goals. He describes "logging fifteen to eighteen hours a day. . . . I don't remember a day when I wasn't eager for the typewriter and not a night I didn't resent the necessity of sleep":

> It was the most cathartic experience of my life. The more I began to understand the relationships in the family the more moved I became. There were times I couldn't see the keys of the typewriter for tears, and times I would almost topple my chair howling with laughter. . . . ("David French" 246)

[15] I am indebted to Forte and Sumption 39–41 throughout this discussion of Barthes and de Lauretis.

[16] Jacqueline Rose, in her discussion of what "psychoanalytic and literary criticism share with the literature they address" (95), shows how, in T.S. Eliot's readings of *Hamlet*, "It is as if the woman becomes both scapegoat and cause of the dearth or breakdown of (Oedipal) resolution which the play enacts, not only at the level of its theme, but also in the disjunctions and difficulties of its aesthetic form" (103). Making women scapegoats is a typical (and oedipal) strategy of both modernist art and structuralist criticism, as I will discuss in chapter 2.

[17] Volosinov/Bakhtin's critique of Freud based on the centrality of the social and discursive construction of subjectivity is relevant here (see Volosinov, *Freudianism*).

[18] It is interesting, however, while writing a book that perhaps problematically takes a *national* drama as its focus, to note that, as Kass Banning says, "Not coincidentally, feminism's Other, patriarchy, often behaves indistinguishably from Canada's Other, the United States" (149).

[19] The famous symbolic excess of the conclusion of *Jacob's Wake* is perhaps illuminated by a Lacanian reading of Cook's remarks here, of his "poetic" treatment of language throughout his work, and of his frequently expressed sense of groping toward — desiring — a clarity and completeness of meaning that is always unattainable. In *William Shakespeare*, a work that concerns itself with the subject of excess throughout, Terry Eagleton makes several observations that are relevant here:

> it is part of the very nature of a sign to "absent" its referent. The symbol, as Jacques Lacan once remarked, is the death of the thing. In language we deal with the world at the level of signification, not with material objects themselves. In this sense, the estrangement of sign from thing . . . is structurally essential for the sign to function at all. . . . Lacan also writes enigmatically that "language is what hollows being into desire": because it works by difference, metonymy, a perpetual play of presence and absence, language divides and diffuses whatever lies

in its path. A "linguistic body" would thus seem something of a contradiction in terms: the solid, unified entity we call a body is fissured, rendered non-identical with itself, by the language which is its very breath.

Language, and the history of which it is the medium, extends and transforms the body's limits, as is obvious enough in the history of technology. . . . [I]t is this capacity to transgress or go beyond which is the very mark of human creativity, the reason why we have history rather than just biology. (97)

[20] Cook's work, perhaps not surprisingly, has received little attention from feminists. A passage by the "new French feminist" Annie Leclerc, however, provides a brutal gloss on the absurdist/tragic worldview that Cook articulates in his interviews and essays and inscribes in his plays. In a passage that could easily refer to Cook in general and to *Jacob's Wake* in particular, Leclerc also draws attention to the absence of the social, and of the impetus for social change, in visions such as Cook's:

Listen to him for once with a sound ear. He says that life is absurd. Life absurd! And all because his reason cannot manage to account for it. And he submits life to examination and to the judgement of his imbecile reason. And it simply never occurs to him that there is something unhinged, something *monstrous* in a reason that enunciates such absurdities!

Hence the question: "Is life worth living or not worth living?" is not the most basic of human questions; it is the most profoundly stupid expression and as it were ultimate image of a thinking corrupted by reason.

As if anything could be worthwhile outside of life or allow anything to be appreciated outside of life —

As if thought, that life alone makes possible, could have any other task than serving life.

There is only one just form of thought, the living thought that can revive the smothered fire of life and sow revolt against the poisoners, the pillagers, the profaners of life.

To revolt: that's the right word. Yet it's still not quite strong enough. Let the bell toll the end not only of those eminent possessors but also their carrion-eating values that have polluted the whole world. (85)

Courage is worthless in itself. Less than worthless. Courage is not beautiful. Courage is not great.

It is wretched, hateful, swollen, puffy, deathly, since its mission is to subdue, oppress, and repress all living things.

And courage is nothing but that pain, that harsh violence wrought upon the self when one must pass through it into the fight against oppression.

No, it's over, finished. I pity the masquerades of the hero. And I laugh at him, with his important airs, his tragic antics. He may count on me no longer to help him in the way he asks, in the way he demands, to establish his rule. The rule of human greatness. Because I don't give a damn. (86)

[21] See Wallace, *Producing Marginality.*

[22] Bakhtin uses "dialogic" to suggest a "polyglot" polyphony of voices, opposing it to the "monologic," in his discussion of alterity and polyphony as revolutionary in potential. See chapter 7 of this book and Bakhtin, *Dialogic Imagination*, and *Problems.*

[23] Used in conversation with the author, 29 October 1987.

[24] In conversations and classroom visits 1984–90 and in Johnson ("George F. Walker Directs" 170), who says that "'Parody' is anathema to Walker as a description of his

work." Walker is thinking of parody in the usual sense as ridiculing imitation rather than in the specialized sense of "repetition with critical difference" that Linda Hutcheon uses in *A Theory of Parody* (7). Hutcheon's "parody" is related to what I am calling "perversion," but I am focusing on intertexts that operate on the level of structure and semiotics without necessarily conjuring up any conscious reflection of specific texts.

[25] The classic case for schizophrenia as an entirely appropriate response to a capitalist society is Gilles Deleuze and Felix Guattari's delightfully anarchic and distinctly perverse *Anti-Oedipus: Capitalism and Schizophrenia*, a book that resonates with Walker's plays in a variety of ways (including its anger, its love, and its intriguing observation that "Schizophrenia is like love" [5]). At one point, for example, Deleuze and Guattari offer a discussion of schizoid behaviour that reads like a commentary on the character of Sarah, particularly her strategies for coping with the play's "greedy pricks":

> The schizo has his own system of co-ordinates for situating himself at his disposal, because, first of all, he has at his disposal his very own recording code, which does not coincide with the social code, or coincides with it only in order to parody it. The code of delirium or of desire proves to have an extraordinary fluidity. It might be said that the schizophrenic passes from one code to the other, that he deliberately *scrambles all the codes*, by quickly shifting from one to another, according to the questions asked him, never giving the same explanation from one day to the next, never invoking the same genealogy, never recording the same event in the same way. When he is more or less forced into it and is not in a touchy mood, he may even accept the banal Oedipal code, so long as he can stuff it full of all the disjunctions that this code was designed to eliminate. (15)

R.D. Laing, in *The Divided Self*, which concerns itself specifically with female schizophrenia as an intelligible response to the "double bind" of invalidation within the family, includes an account of Ophelia that is also compatible with Walker's Sarah.

Sharon Pollock's *Getting It Straight* also presents a scathing critique of patriarchal structures from positive, feminist, and schizophrenic perspectives, in ways that are considerably more sophisticated and subversive than those of her earlier oedipal drama, *Doc. Doc*, of course, has reached a much larger audience than has *Getting It Straight*, in part because, although it regenders the central character(s), as an autobiographical therapeutic memory play in the tradition of *Of the Fields, Lately*, it presents no *formal* or deep-structural challenge to a mainstream audience.

[26] I am indebted in my discussion of Sarah and Walker's characterization to Mary Pat Mombourquette 130–35.

[27] See Eagleton 64 and 107, note, where, however, he notes that "It need not be supposed . . . that when Lear asks Cordelia what she can say to win his favour, she replies 'female genitals, my lord.'"

[28] It is significant that most of the play's men are obsessed with, or "in love" with, Anna, who (as both a woman and a nihilist) has an overcoded connection with "nothing" and who (as a terrorist, we are told) has used "one or two" bombs and plans to use more (81).

[29] "Oedipus" is the term that Deleuze and Guattari use, *tout court*, as a conflation of the various functions played in psychoanalysis and society by the Greek myth of Oedipus, "the" Oedipus complex, and various oedipal mechanisms, processes, and structures. See their translators' note (3).

[30] The most explicit statement of the nature of Pavel's obsession comes from the character himself, in a letter that he reads to Anna in an attempt to explain the emotional "terrorism" (another connection to the Bazarov/Anna plot) that he had carried out on her mother and is now directing toward her:

> "The love I felt for your mother was my life. It came to be my entire life. No thoughts in my head. No world in front of my eyes. No friends. Or family. Or profession. I only lived in my love for your mother. Which drew me to her, so close that everything in the world came through her and I was just an aura, not solid, not heard . . . and finally not felt. And when she was gone from me . . . I began to dissolve . . ." *[He looks at her]* And then I saw you and I stopped dissolving and after I stopped dissolving I began to hope that I could become real again. (75; ellipses in original)

[31] In a panel at Harbourfront in Toronto, 5 June 1990. Reviewer Robert Cushman similarly called the play a "daisy-chain drama," loosely comparing its structure with that of Arthur Schnitzler's *La Ronde*.

[32] I am using the 1985 revised edition, but Thompson revised the text again for the tenth-anniversary production at Tarragon Theatre in April 1994, making significant changes to the opening and closing of the play, further clarifying the symbolic structure but omitting the passages at the end that I discuss below.

[33] Thompson, in conversation with the author, 16 January 1985.

[34] Cape tells Glidden that the dachshunds were buried the previous week, but before doing so he smells the cup into which Pony claims to have thrown them up (94). The uncertainty here about what "actually happened" has an effect similar to that of the more radical uncertainty used in *Lion in the Streets*, described above.

2 MODERNISM AND ITS CONTAINMENTS

[1] Edward Mullaly, for example, who has always been good at tracking down influences, wondered in 1975 of *Ambush at Tether's End* "why Walker has spent his time on a script Beckett had already written with much greater discipline, intelligence, and skill" (qtd. in Johnson, "George F. Walker: B-Movies" 91). The tendency to dismiss Canadian modernist experiments in the 1960s and 1970s is related to the Canadian nationalist tendency to find "the Canadian identity" in rural experience ("typical" Canadian plays for decades being considered proverbially to be Prairie or Maritime realism), while modernism has typically been an urban phenomenon. (For a discussion of the centrality of the city to modernism, see Bradbury.) In English Canadian theatre, modernism has surfaced almost exclusively in Toronto, Vancouver, and Montreal (at Playwrights Workshop), though there is an interesting association in Canada between modernist formalism and the North, notably in the work of Glenn Gould, the Group of Seven, and, in theatre, Herman Voaden.

[2] Jonathan Dollimore and Alan Sinfield, in the context of Jan Kott, *King Lear*, and *Endgame*, discuss the ways in which "modernist and existentialist writings which offer as profound studies of the human condition a critique of progressive ideals and an invocation of 'spiritual' alienation," together with the structuralist understanding of the theatre of the absurd, work primarily to construct political action as "essentially futile" and focus on "an inevitability in historical process" that I suggest is like the cultural work done by the classical conception of fate ("History and Ideology" 208–09).

[3] Frye's observation is not isolated, of course, but is a part of his overriding principle of literary autonomy, which Michael Bristol has called an "ethical imperative" (173). The observation itself has been usefully deconstructed by James H. Kavanagh (164–65).

[4] The iconic status of these plays is apparent in Ken Garnhum's *Beuys Buoys Boys: A Monologue*, which uses a running gag, "Barbie's Beckett," in which a Barbie doll appears in the completely recognizable settings of different Beckett plays, conjuring up the worlds of those plays with absolute precision, if also with a delightfully perverse and disarming incongruity.

[5] Kermode notes the links between modernist formal and aesthetic closure and "the formal elegance of fascism" (114), between "the spatial order of the modern critic [and] . . . the closed authoritarian society" (111). In Canada, the best-known explorations of the relationship between modernist art and fascism are the works of Timothy Findley, particularly his novel *Famous Last Words*, which is framed as a history of the fascist cabal of artists and others that centred on Prince Edward and the Duchess of Windsor in World War II, written (the novel within the novel) by Hugh Selwyn Mauberley, a fictional character originally created by Ezra Pound. The earliest plays in Canada to draw explicitly on modernist forms, the "symphonic expressionist" works of Herman Voaden (see back cover of Voaden), silently conflate formal experimentation, nationalism, and an implicit fascination with power in ways that are consistent with the ideologies of aestheticism that I am outlining here. I am indebted in my discussion of modernism to the essays in Bradbury and McFarlane and to Astradur Eysteinsson, whose analysis, nevertheless, is concerned more with the contradictions of modernism as a historical movement than with the formal approaches of modernism and does not acknowledge the possibility of a link between "aesthetically elaborated form (*as form*) [and] a specific ideology" (15). Raymond Williams, on the other hand, provides in his attack on "a selective view of modernism" (*Politics of Modernism* 65) a careful historical account of modernism that traces the loss of "its anti-bourgeois stance" and its "comfortable integration into the new international capitalism" (35), to the point that his editor can refer to "Williams's thoughts on advertising as the final home of Modernism" (Pinkney 2).

[6] MacLeish's famous argument, of course, in *Poetry and Experience*, which summarized modernist poetics and served as a kind of manifesto for much modernist criticism, was that a poem does not mean but be (see 3–88). In reference to Michael Hollingsworth's plays as theatrical images, Geoff Hancock notes the playwright's sense of the importance in contemporary theatre of the visual (versus verbal) image.

[7] Cone's experiments with a modernist dramaturgy of the visual arts have left little legacy in Canada, except perhaps in the upper-class modernism of the work of Lawrence Jeffery, in many ways one of Canada's most underrated playwrights of the 1980s. Although his plays are rarely produced, *Lawrence Jeffery: Four Plays*, a kind of retrospective of his work, includes *Clay* (1982), *Tower* (1983), *Precipice* (1987), and a more recent, unproduced work, *Children*. Each script is carefully crafted, visually and aurally evocative, and highly theatrical. *Clay*, about a death in the family, is the theatrical equivalent of impressionism. It opens with a woman swinging onto the stage on a playground swing through a "burning" column of white light, and it incorporates with stunning theatricality the chopping of wood and the clipping with scissors of the heads of paper men. *Tower*, the first of what became much later a series of plays on British and North American stages about middle-aged corporate executives, similarly employs the sounds of clinking billiard balls, the onstage mowing of a lawn, and the

image of a woman eating the ashes of her husband. *Precipice* opens with a seventy-five-year-old man in white pajama bottoms pouring a bucket of water over his head and then wiping the water off his body with his open hands; the play moves on to treat the resulting puddle, "a startling intrusion on a bare stage," as urine leaked from a catheter drainage bag. A family drama about a domineering father and a dying mother, the play uses texture — of everything from cookie crumbs to crinkly paper — with the sensitivity of a sculptor with a good ear. In the new play, *Children*, Jeffery paints the raked stage in shades of white or eggshell, introducing splashes of colour that are purposefully "sharp, pure, startling" and that punctuate the plot of a disintegrating marriage. Jeffery is a careful and elegant writer and a close observer of families, with a special interest in in-laws and — not surprisingly in a modernist playwright — in the intricate lives of the upper classes. In each play, though, the real impact lies in startling, iconic, and self-sufficient visual images, as inscrutable and evocative in their ways, and in their sharp-edged clarity, as the bleaker but equally totalizing images of Beckett are in theirs.

[8] See also Knowles, "Reading Material" 276–86.

[9] Again, for an explication of dialogism, particularly as it pertains to single-character and single-actor plays, see chapter 7.

[10] Other works in the contemporary Canadian theatre featuring or inspired by Pound include Timothy Findley's *The Trials of Ezra Pound* and the work of R. Murray Schafer and Hillar Liitoja discussed in chapter 6. See also note 5 above.

[11] This, of course, is Kristeva's revisioning of what Lacan calls the imaginary. See chapter 1, note 8.

[12] Asian drama has not been as directly influential on modernist dramaturgies in Canada as it has in Europe in the work of artists such as Ariane Mnouchkine, Peter Brook, and Robert Wilson and where there has been a kind of wholesale "orientalist" (Said) appropriation of the "inscrutable" (and feminized) East in the interests of Western renewal that parallels the appropriation of "primitive" African art by modernist painters and sculptors. Asian music and philosophy, however, have been used in the structuring of plays such as Ken Mitchell's *Gone the Burning Sun* and *The Great Cultural Revolution* (both in *Rebels in Time*); the latter play, like Druick's *Where Is Kabuki?*, draws metatheatrically and metaphorically on Asian theatrical forms and traditions. The most direct employment of Eastern theatrical traditions in *modernist* dramaturgy in Canada, however, occurs in *Where Is Kabuki?* and in Standjofski's *No Cycle* (both of which are discussed below) and in a number of other plays by Druick, Springate, and Standjofski workshopped at Playwrights' Workshop Montreal, particularly during Springate's tenure there as artistic director (1985–88).

[13] See Keyssar, *Feminist Theatre*, particularly xi–xvi.

[14] Hollingsworth describes her plays as "presenting the inner world" ("Margaret Hollingsworth" 157).

3 THE STRUCTURES OF AUTHENTICITY: COLLECTIVE AND COLLABORATIVE CREATIONS

[1] Sinfield argues that

The twin manoeuvres of bourgeois ideology construct two dichotomies: universal versus historical and individual versus social. In each case the first term is privileged and so meaning is sucked into the universal/individual polarity, draining it away from the historical and social — which is where meaning is made by people together in determinate conditions and where it might be contested." ("Give" 141)

[2] Bert States, talking of surplus of presence (beyond signification) in the theatre, notes that, for example, "with running water something indisputably real leaks out of the illusion" (31). See also Gail Kern Paster on "Leaky Vessels."

[3] Alice Rayner usefully makes distinctions between acting and doing and, drawing on Hayden White, between the epic and the annal that are useful to the analysis of collective creations in Canada:

> Doing does not have the kind of linear temporality of Aristotelian action because it is not shaped by the extension between intentions and ends, with delay in the middle. For both performer and audience the temporality is the same. In doing there is no dilatory space or delay. At most, the intention and the gesture are simultaneous and therefore shapeless. Doing is emphatically in the present and has no duration through time. Though it may take time, it does not make time, insofar as it has no residue. It thus requires no pre-, con-, or re-figuring of time: doing is the figuring itself. . . . Doing can thus be aligned with epic time rather than tragic, for it concerns events more than intentional actions, and epic is the form for relating deeds. The annal is perhaps the closest historical record of doing in the way that it exhibits a peculiar kind of emptiness in pure facticity, as though there were no context for facts. As Hayden White describes the annal:
>
> > It possesses none of the attributes that we normally think of as a story: no central subject, no well-marked beginning, middle, and end, no peripeteia, and no identifiable narrative voice. . . . [T]here is no suggestion of any necessary connection between one event and another. . . . (23–24)

(Rayner is quoting from White's article "The Value of Narrativity in the Representation of Reality," *Critical Inquiry* 7 [1980]: 11–12.) Rayner's analysis of "doing" in the pages that follow this passage has particular resonances with the acting method developed by Theatre Passe Muraille, in which motivation is subordinated to a kind of mimicry and emotion, thought, and meaning occur as a *result* of "doing" rather than as a motivation for "action."

[4] Renate Usmiani contests this description of the structure of *The Farm Show*, finding "a definite design in its inner structure": "The episodes of the second act deal with the more serious issues of farm life and, therefore, have a greater dramatic impact on the audience. There is a definite heightening of tension and emotion as the play progresses, a heightening which leads up to a climactic final scene" (52). Thompson's description is somewhat disingenuous — some shaping of the material clearly goes on in all collectives — but Usmiani seems unduly constrained to find "in" a play that she admires a structure that in her description sounds Aristotelian. Having "uncovered the shape," moreover, Usmiani then finds that "the subtle emotional manipulation of the public through the inner structure of the play is one of the reasons for its success" (52). The most detailed structural analysis of *The Farm Show*, which works from the premise that it is "episodic and anecdotal," is in Bessai, *Playwrights* 67–78.

[5] Beyond the scope of this chapter, but also well worth looking at in its terms, are the complex truth claims of what Philip Auslander (following Baudrillard) calls "mediatized" performance (see "Live Performance"), perhaps best represented in Canada by the early work of Michael Hollingsworth and the Hummer Sisters at Videocabaret.

[6] Alan Filewod employs a different but extremely useful model for the analysis of the "process, politics, and poetics" of collective creation in Canada in his 1982 article "Collective Creation."

[7] This paradox, and the complexities of its playing out, are revealed in the history of "Crab," the untrained dog used to play her (male) namesake on several occasions at the Stratford Festival in productions of *The Two Gentlemen of Verona*, a play clearly written in such a way that whatever the dog playing Crab does will be both appropriate and funny. The first time that she played the role, she was the as yet unnamed pet of one of the actors, and she simply assumed the name of her character — or continued to be called by that name — when the run was over. Clearly, apart from some awkwardness about gender, she was not acting but simply "being" herself in the production, as character and actor were "contained" in the same name. Over time, and in the home of Heather Kitchen, the production's stage manager and her new owner, her name was corrupted, or evolved, as pets' names often do, and Crab was referred to affectionately as "Crabapple." The next time that she was cast in the role, congruent with her professional status and experience and in order to preserve theatrical decorum, the program indicated that the role of Crab was performed by Crabapple. There was some controversy, however, when one (human) member of the acting company objected to her portrait being hung in the theatre lobby among those of the rest of the cast. He felt that his artistry was slighted by the inclusion in the gallery of what was clearly an untrained animal and certainly not an artist. US immigration officials, however, didn't agree. When the show toured to the United States after the Stratford season closed, there was some difficulty about Crabapple that was only resolved by giving her an "extraordinary artist" contract. A few years later, in a production of the play that I directed, I was offered Crabapple but used a flexible amusement-store leash without the dog, absence rather than the surplus of presence, as a theatrical sign.

[8] The most thorough phenomenological explorations of the phenomena that I am describing are in Handke and, especially, in States, particularly 19–47. I am indebted to States throughout this section.

[9] Passe Muraille collectives from the 1970s are typically grouped as "sociological," shows created in and about a particular local community that the company visits and mimics, and "historical," revisionist re-creations of documentary history (see Johnston, "Playwrights" 67, 69). Filewod contests the usefulness or accuracy of this distinction and suggests that Thompson's "folk theatre" is a more useful term for both types (*Collective Encounters* 26), but I think that the distinction remains useful. A third common type of collective creation, the "psychological," in which the collective builds a show around shared personal experiences of a particular topic, was not often used by Theatre Passe Muraille but was employed by many feminist collectives, particularly in the early, consciousness-raising days of the feminist movement of the 1970s. Traces of this approach remain in the works discussed below.

[10] That Theatre Passe Muraille seemingly stumbled upon this focus may have been fortuitous insofar as the split focus — as a community looking at a community or an "encounter of communities" (Filewod, *Collective Encounters* 38) — of its best work has generally been regarded as the work's greatest strength.

[11] Alan Read 228–36 brilliantly discusses theatrical risk and the propensity of pre-twentieth-century theatres to burn down — "it is the absence of fire from the contemporary theatre which marks it off from the past" (236) — in ways that echo in Paul Thompson's aside in his introduction to *Doukhobors* that the company's use of fire was "illegal I suppose" (i). Read notes that "Hotel fires cut to the quick because of the

expectation that a place to sleep is a safe place to sleep. But what of theatre? We have come to expect theatre to be a safe place to sleep — but should we?" (234).

[12] See Bessai, *Playwrights* 53, for a more conventional literary analysis of the play's use and development of fire and nakedness as stage images.

[13] *The West Show*, mounted in Saskatoon, shared many of the features of the collectives under discussion here and is one of Theatre Passe Muraille's most effective shows. It differs from the others, however, in addressing a less specific geographical community — "the west" — and in including previously written material, such as a section based on novelist Rudy Wiebe's "The Vietnam Call of Samuel K. Reimer."

[14] The authentication deriving from the immediacy of assent of the subject community as audience, and from the actors' connection with scenes that they researched and created, narrows that gap between the ghost and the machine, and between acting and doing, in Rayner's sense. The movement from rehearsal to (repeatable) performance, however, reinstates some of that gap in ways that have always dogged theatrical followers of Artaud and others. See Read's discussion of Derrida's analysis of Artaud on 214.

[15] The map in this version of the script could be seen to stand in for the "actual presence" of the performers and their subjects as audience when the play was first performed in Ray Bird's barn — or when *Oil* and *Under the Greywacke* were performed before their host/subject communities. For a discussion of the dual function of stage as map in *The Farm Show* as "a non-representational playing space [that] is capable of being transformed into barns, fields, homes, the town square in Goderich, and so on" and yet "maintains its relation to fact, as a map," see Nunn, "Meeting" 43.

[16] According to Nunn,

The dual focus on the actual world and on the actuality of performance appears to be the structural principle of documentary theatre. The two are intimately related in performance by a powerful sense of the analogy between them. As the performers reveal the truth hidden within the facts, they lay bare their own activity as performers. As in Brecht's epic theatre, their primary gest is showing. . . . The form of documentary theatre is generated by the relation between these two actualities. ("Performing" 52)

Nunn's "truth hidden within the facts" is, I think, what I am referring to as "meaning," and it is the relational production of structure and meaning, to which Nunn points, that I suggest provides these plays with their potential to mean *politically*.

[17] The necessity of the gap between representation and reality is best represented by a passage from Jorge Luis Borges's "Of Exactitude in Science." The passage resonates with the history of documentary theatre in Canada:

In that Empire, the craft of Cartography attained such Perfection that the Map of a Single province covered the space of an entire City, and the Map of the Empire itself an entire Province. In the course of Time, these Extensive maps were found somehow wanting, and so the College of Cartographers evolved a Map of the Empire that was of the same Scale as the Empire and that coincided with it point for point. Less attentive to the Study of Cartography, succeeding Generations came to judge a map of such Magnitude cumbersome, and, not without Irreverence, they abandoned it to the Rigours of sun and Rain. In the western Deserts, tattered Fragments of the Map are still to be found, Sheltering an occasional Beast or beggar; in the whole Nation, no other relic is left of the Discipline of Geography. (141)

For different readings of the gap and its bridgings, see Arnott 107; Bessai 71–72; Nunn, "Meeting"; and Paul Thompson, Introduction ii.

[18] Nunn, "Meeting" 50, 54, cites Turner's *The Ritual Process: Structure and Anti-Structure* (Chicago: Aldine, 1969) and *Dramas, Fields, and Metaphors: Symbolic Action in Human Society* (Ithaca: Cornell UP, 1974). He quotes from Schechner's "From Ritual to Theatre and Back," *Ritual, Play, and Performance: Readings in the Social Sciences/Theatre*, ed. Richard Schechner and Mady Schuman (New York: Seabury, 1976), 196–222.

[19] The show's last speech refers to the "force of sex" as "the same force that brings anywhere from 200 to 700 people here every night to see this show" (76).

[20] The essay, "Gramsci Notwithstanding: Or, The Left Hand of History," was first published in *Heresies: A Feminist Publication on Art and Politics* 4 (1978), under the title "The Left Hand of History."

[21] My position in relation to the material discussed in this section is significantly different than it is in other sections and chapters in ways that may affect its unusual focus on the material conditions for the production of the plays in question. The section is both a product of and an intervention external to the workings of Mulgrave Road and the larger communities of Guysborough and the Maritimes. As a man from urban Ontario, I have an outsider's tendency to romanticize my own discursively constructed pastoral understandings of both "the Maritime sense of community" and "the community of women" and thereby potentially to gloss over practical problems and less than ideal (or even adequate) material circumstances surrounding and shaping the production of theatre in an impoverished and isolated area. As a playwright, director, and longtime member of Mulgrave Road, moreover, who has lived and worked in the Maritimes, and as an academic who has written about the theatre company, I have a stake in celebrating and perpetuating the work of the co-op. I hope, nevertheless, that there is a limited liminal role for a discussion such as this one in reproducing (with an inevitable and perhaps salutary shift) the work of co-op women in the frame of another discourse, in supporting (and publicizing) the production and reproduction of cultural work by the women of Mulgrave Road, and in transmitting and transforming cultural values in the Maritimes.

[22] For a history of the early years of the company, see Knowles, "Mulgrave Road Co-op"; for a discussion of one representative version of the company's administrative structure, see Knowles, "Voices" 108–09.

[23] Smyth's description of quilting provides a remarkable parallel to the process of play production at Mulgrave Road that I am outlining:

It was their quilt now, a thing they were doing together. . . . As the design became clear, so did all the stories. . . . They'd told each other these stories, all the time working and stitching. Watching how it fit together, becoming something other than the pieces they held in their hands. (49)

The breakdown between male "art" and female "craft" has been actively pursued, of course, by visual artists such as Joyce Weiland, whose famous *Reason over Passion* quilt provides a particularly apt example.

[24] "Women's plays" at Mulgrave Road prior to 1994, when the company's administrative structure changed, include, with dates of first productions, *One on the Way* (collective, 1980, unpublished); *Another Story* (collective, 1982, unpublished); *Holy Ghosters, 1776* (by Mary Vingoe, 1983, unpublished); *Spooks: The Mystery of Caledonia Mills* (by Cindy Cowan, 1984, unpublished); *A Child Is Crying on the Stairs* (collective with writer Nanette Cormier and based on her book of the same title [Windsor, ON: Black Moss, 1983], 1985, unpublished); *A Woman from the Sea* (by Cindy Cowan, 1986,

published in *Canadian Theatre Review* 48 [1986]: 62–110; and in Filewod, ed., *CTR Anthology*); *Beinn Bhreagh* (by Cindy Cowan, 1986, unpublished); *Idyll Gossip* (by Carol Sinclair, 1987, Playwrights Union of Canada copyscript, 1987); *Battle Fatigue* (by Jenny Munday, 1989, published in *Canadian Theatre Review* 62 [1990]: 50–74); and *Safe Haven* (by Mary Colin Chisholm, 1992, published in *Theatrum* 38 [1994]: S1–S15). This list is somewhat arbitrary in that other collective creations were predominantly the work of women, were directed by women, and/or cast women in central roles. I have, however, selected productions of plays that were identified by their creators as plays by, for, or about women.

²⁵ Mulgrave Road has initiated or hosted many community-based projects within its theatre building, around which theatrical activities revolve. These projects include hosting meetings of GLOW (Guysborough Learning Opportunities for Women); initiating and hosting the meetings of a weekly creative writing workshop open to anyone in the community; producing the interventionist play/workshop on child abuse, *Feeling Yes, Feeling No*, in local schools; undertaking school tours of Christmas shows; and putting on Roadies, a theatre camp for children offered each summer. Interestingly, writing about the co-op, including my own here and elsewhere, has tended to focus on the so-called major productions and to marginalize these other, equally important, projects, many of which have to do with areas traditionally seen as "women's issues."

²⁶ Many of the women in the community who have forged friendships with theatre workers have been of sufficient economic means to afford homes with extra rooms to billet actors. This situation has often (but not always) meant that the theatre's connections have been with women in positions of leadership in the community — doctors, schoolteachers, and so on. There have been fewer direct associations with working-class women and fewer still with the relatively large black community at the edge of town. For a less sanguine account of the material conditions for the production of theatre in Guysborough than the one here, told from the perspective of an artistic director of the company, see Munday.

²⁷ A group of plays including the collective collaboration with Nanette Cormier, *A Child Is Crying on the Stairs*, and Cindy Cowan's three plays, *Spooks*, *A Woman from the Sea*, and *Beinn Bhreagh*, are partial exceptions to the patterns that I am examining here and require separate treatment. Cowan's plays, moreover, especially *A Woman from the Sea*, seem both to take and to invite a radical or cultural feminist approach that I don't think is appropriate for or available to me as a male critic, unlike the materialist feminist theory on which I am drawing (but that I hope I am not appropriating). For a radical feminist reading of *A Woman from the Sea*, see Hodkinson 133–58.

²⁸ See de Lauretis, *Technologies* 92. Interestingly, again, Cowan's *Spooks* and *A Woman from the Sea* seem to be the only exceptions to the general rule that plays by women at Mulgrave Road have avoided mysticism and mythologizing. In the former play, Cowan attempts to deconstruct media manipulations of the story of a young girl accused of setting fires in her parents' home in 1921; in the latter play, she tries to construct a radical feminist and socially conscious myth of origins and other things.

²⁹ Cowan notes that *Another Story* was instrumental in leading Vingoe "to initiate her own production, *Holy Ghosters*" (108).

³⁰ For a more detailed discussion of *Holy Ghosters*, see Knowles, "Sense."

³¹ The primary source of *Holy Ghosters* is Thomas Raddall's novel *His Majesty's Yankees*, but Raddall is famous for his original and detailed historical research, and Vingoe also drew extensively on primary sources, notably John Robinson and Thomas Rispin's *Journey through Nova Scotia* (1774).

[32] The co-op has addressed some of these issues in productions such as *Victory! The Saga of William Hall, V.C.* (1981), which told the story of the first Nova Scotian, and the first black man, to win the Victoria Cross, in the battle of Lucknow; Chisholm's *Safe Haven* (1992), which treated the intrusion of AIDS into the community; and *Another Story* (1982), in which class is at least implicitly at the heart of the play. These interventions have been important and, if vestigial, are in no way insignificant. Rarely, however, has the co-op faced racism, classism, or homophobia in the community itself head on.

[33] *Aphra* was collaboratively written by the company's founders, Nancy Cullen, Alexandria Patience, and Rose Scollard, "with" Aphra Behn.

[34] The Anna Project consisted of Suzanne Odette Khuri, Ann-Marie MacDonald, Banuta Rubess, and Maureen White, with contributions at early stages of the process from Patricia Nichols and Aida Jordao.

[35] Peggy Phelan, "Reciting" 16–19, discusses Tania Modleski's argument that feminist critical writing is itself performative insofar as it *enacts* rather than describes or analyses, drawing on J.L. Austin's distinction between constative and performative speech acts. I would suggest that all politicized critical writing aspires to the performative in the sense seemingly intended by Modleski and virtually despaired of by Phelan (who nevertheless, in *Unmarked* 146–66, has what seems to be a naïve faith, for so sophisticated a theorist, in an unrepeatable presence of performance itself).

[36] See Hart and Phelan for discussions of several such artists.

[37] I am indebted for this observation to Varley 74.

[38] According to Khuri, one of the creators,
Many people ask us what the images of the nails and the milk mean. The only true answer is that they do not mean one thing; they are not to be read on one factual level. Like images in poetry, they will have a different story, a different resonance, for each reader, each viewer. Almost every night when we talk to the audience, we hear a fresh response to those images. The final milk image is, for me, on the simplest level, an image of absence. The woman at the fridge pours and pours. Anna never takes the milk because she isn't there. In her absence, the milk overflows and spills as we say "I did it for you Anna." This image simply emphasizes the silence. There is that much space round a few words. (Anna Project, "Fragments" 167)

[39] See note 2 above.

[40] *Mary Medusa* seems in this way to adopt a mediative position in the debates that surround the politics of visibility for women, particularly for lesbians. See Lynda Hart's account of these issues in "Identity and Seduction."

4 The Unity in Community

[1] Statistics Canada figures detailing overall population growth in Eramosa township between 1901 and 1986 are reproduced in Little and Sim 5–6. Organizers of the community play, using figures from the year-end analysis of population and households in police villages contained in the Ontario Assessment System "Wellington County Study," placed the population growth of the village of Rockwood between 1987 and 1988 at an unprecedented 37%.

[2] The most comprehensive account of the Colway process is Ann Jellicoe's *Community Plays: How to Put Them On*. See also Baz Kershaw's analysis of the community

play's political efficacy (168–205) and *Canadian Theatre Review* 90 (1997), a special issue edited by Edward Little and Ann Wilson and titled *Community Plays*.

   [3] Many of these plays are unpublished, there are few traces at all of many community-style plays and pageants, and where there are scripts they are even more inadequate as representations of process or even of theatrical product than is usually the case in the theatre. Nevertheless, see Brookes; Fennario; Middleton; Mummers Troupe of Newfoundland, *Buchans*; Reaney, *King Whistle*; Ridout; Ryan; Theatre Passe Muraille, *The Farm Show*; 25th Street Theatre; Winslow; and Wright and Endres.

   [4] Invoking Raymond Williams and focusing on race, Bruce McConachie explores a similar tension and a similar political continuum in similar types of theatre in the United States that he prefers to call "grassroots theatre."

   [5] The phrase "dignity and grace" is taken from the conclusion of the James Gordon song that recurs in the play:
We all know
That this old town has gotta grow
But can't we do it with
Some dignity and grace.

   [6] This larger body includes the worker's Theatre of Action in the 1930s, the interventionist theatre of the Mummers, Theatre Passe Muraille's collective sociological documentary theatre, the revisionist historical agit-prop of David Fennario's Black Rock Community Theatre, and the increasing body of work in the 1990s by gay, lesbian, feminist, and ethnic theatre companies that relate to specifically defined relational communities. Like all community-oriented theatre, these forms originate with a localist impulse — the presentation or representation of community experience to and for its constituent members. In overtly seeking to expand their spheres of influence to be regionally or even nationally interventionist, however, such forms delineate a further continuum of community-oriented theatre practice — one concerned with issues of local, regional, or even national expression and intervention.

   [7] The Green Paper, for example, a guide to rural land use prepared by a citizens' action group formed in conjunction with the Eramosa community play, has been cited as a model by the provincial Ministry of Municipal Affairs. For a more detailed account of the impact of *The Spirit of Shivaree* on local and regional planning, see Little and Sim. It is also worth noting that community plays are not designed for tours or remounts outside the communities that create them, and the remounting for a second year in the same community of the Fort Qu'Appelle community play *Ka'ma'mo'pi' cik/The Gathering*, 1992, 1993 (the first time that a Colway-style play was remounted), provoked controversy both among community play practitioners and within the community.

   [8] Of the Colway-style community plays produced in Canada to date, *The Spirit of Shivaree* was conceived by Dale Hamilton as a means of provoking a local response to increasing pressures of suburbanization (see Little and Sim); Blyth's *Many Hands* (1993) was created to celebrate a theatrical tradition in a community described as experiencing communication problems between a transient summer theatre crowd and the resident community; and Fort Qu'Appelle's *Ka'mo'mi'pi' cik* (1992, 1993, published in Little and Wilson) was designed to help reconcile differences between white and Native "communities." Since then, the phenomenon has taken off in a variety of directions, including the creation of urban versions and productions that combine the community play format with various kinds of social action and popular theatre. These later developments, however, often adapt the Colway format beyond easy recognition.

⁹ In Eramosa township, for example, this network involved groups such as the Local Architectural Conservation Advisory Committee, the Junior Farmers, two women's institutes, church congregations, heritage and environmental groups, the Rockwood School, the Lion's Club, the Grand River Conservation Authority, the Rockwood Recreation Committee, and eventually the township council.

¹⁰ Anderson's concern is with the construction of nationhood and nationalisms, but his concept of "imagined communities" applies to the micropolitical level as well. Of particular interest to the community play's construction and authentication of historical narrative is his discussion of the construction of continuity through the remembering of "forgotten" histories. See, especially, 87–206.

¹¹ In addition to Lay as Mackenzie, members of the Benham, Harris, and Hamilton families played their ancestors in *The Spirit of Shivaree.*

¹² We are quoting from the videotape; see Fox and Hamilton. The final phrase is not included in the published compuscript (Hamilton 56).

¹³ For a political analysis of the distinction between *locus* and *platea*, see Weimann 73–85 and passim.

¹⁴ This winning of the imaginative assent of the audience in the making of history as myths of origin is the typical technique of James Reaney in his Donnelly cycle and elsewhere (see chapter 5). The term "carnivalesque" and the concept of carnival derive from M.M. Bakhtin and are most fully articulated in his book *Rabelais and His World.*

¹⁵ These "testimonials" mixed "actual" statements by community members with scripted perspectives prepared by Hamilton, but the different sources of these materials were not noted in the production.

5 REPLAYING HISTORY

¹ See the works by Hayden White, the leading proponent of this school of historiography and narratology. See also Michel de Certeau's provocative and subtle study *The Writing of History.*

² The published version of *1837: The Farmers' Revolt* is the script of the second version of the play. The first, *1837 tout court*, was mounted in Toronto in January 1973; the second toured southwestern Ontario under the expanded title in the spring, summer, and fall of 1974.

³ I am concerned with the play's structure rather than its content here, but in the title, as elsewhere, Salutin and Theatre Passe Muraille were careful to frame the events of 1837 as a *collective* movement, the result of historical forces and popular will rather than heroic or exceptional leadership. Similarly, the play's content concerns itself with economic forces of production, centring on land use and ownership, in 1837 and, implicitly, in 1973. (Perhaps the title *1837* was chosen rather than the more usual 1838 in reference to the historical events depicted in order to invoke its inversion, 1973, as Orwell's *1984* was designed to invoke 1948.)

⁴ As I note elsewhere, however, this scene is framed in such a way that, when the dummy finds its voice, legitimate questions are raised about where that voice is coming from (see Knowles, "Post-").

⁵ The series has continued beyond the original eight published as *The History of the Village of the Small Huts*, but under different names.

⁶ Michèle White provides an excellent account of the visual, multimedia dimensions of the production in her introduction to the published script.

[7] For a very different reading of *The History of the Village of the Small Huts* that focuses on the construction of Canadian nationhood, see Filewod, "One Big Ontario."

[8] Reviewing the Stratford Festival production of the play in 1974, the production for which the prologue was written, Herbert Whittaker described its effect differently: "We worry that the drama of Walsh will not get started, only to discover it already has, and that we are now becoming aware of the dreadful inevitability of it. We are offered no false hope, only solemn steps toward a kind of doom" (138–39). Malcolm Page 105 has pointed out that in the original version of the play documentary speeches from contemporary sources were read aloud before each scene. These speeches were cut and replaced by the prologue for Stratford and in the published script.

[9] See Scholar 334. See also Deverell's "Author's Statement" about *The Riel Commission*, in which Deverell admits that he accepted Schmalz's invitation to work on the project "too blithely . . . because the next few months would prove the most difficult of my writing career." "We found," he says, "that we were on delicate ground as a couple of white guys from the CBC who could be viewed as exploiting indigenous people for our own ends" (138).

[10] This event prompted the writing and production of Janice Acoose-Pelletier and Brenda Zeman's radio play *Acoose: Man Standing above Ground*, about Acoose-Pelletier's grandfather, a famous Salteaux long-distance runner who set a world record in 1909. See Schmalz viii, 81–94.

[11] The question of "investment" recurs in the play, emerging initially from the financial investment that each of the three central characters has made in the project and expressed by the producer, Burns, in terms of the particular "investment" that westerners — and by extension, presumably, the Métis and others — have "in being Canadians" (98). Gradually, it surfaces that the kinds of personal and political stakes that each character has invested in the story of Batoche are both crucial and problematic. Early on, Matt addresses "Riel," saying "I have so much invested in you" (93), and, when the conflicting investments of Riel's descendants in their history finally drive him from the project, in part at his wife's instigation, he complains: "it's all academic for you. You never had anything at stake, here. You've just watched the whole thing from the outside. You don't care if the whole thing collapses. It's not going to affect you. You're just going to go get your hair done, and maybe get a facial . . ." (130).

[12] The fragment that we see, of course, remains the representation by a white male playwright — one who is, not incidentally, an ordained minister — of Métis history and reality as he imagines a Métis woman would construct it. (It sounds, particularly in its closing emphasis on unity, suspiciously like something that Matt himself would have written.) As Riel walks to the gallows, having sacrificed to his God the opportunity to make a final (and possibly polemical/political) speech, *"Yvonne walks into the scene watching after them"* and speaks the television play within the play's final lines:

Pray for us Louis. Pray for us who come after. Pray for us in your distant future. We are proud to be called your children. Pray for all of us. Pray for those who have forgotten we are Métis. Pray for those who have grown up speaking our own language and those of us who know what it is to be Métis and are joyful. Pray for us who are still searching, still struggling to find out. Pray for us in our politics, in our struggles with the children of John A. Macdonald. Pray for us in our struggles with one another. Help us to be strong and may we be one. (133)

This is, of course, at some remove in tone and content from the work of Métis writers such as Maria Campbell that has emerged in recent years or from the work of playwrights such as Monique Mojica and Daniel David Moses, discussed below.

[13] I do not wish to suggest, here or elsewhere, a simple or causal (in either direction) relationship between dramaturgical forms and social formations. Like other forms of cultural expression (and other sites of social negotiation), Native dramaturgies are both culturally produced and culturally productive, and their relationship to both Native and dominant social formations is necessarily complex.

[14] The play's first production was at Ottawa's Great Canadian Theatre Company in 1991, where it played to predominantly white audiences; its second production was at Native Earth Performing Arts's Native Canadian Centre in Toronto in 1992, where the audience was mixed. Whatever the actual makeup of the audience, however, the play's second act clearly constructs a white audience for its metatheatrical performance within the play.

[15] For an analysis of the pressures and ironies of the playing of Indianness for white audiences in *Almighty Voice and His Wife*, see Appleford.

[16] Rob Appleford provides a different reading of this scene, which he finds "poignant":

we realize that what we have witnessed is not a simple statement of identity but an on-going battle for a soul. In this way, the play conforms to the comic tradition, in that lovers must transcend obstacles put in their path in order to find each other once again. In this case, the obstacles are texts which reify themselves at the expense of the bodies which enact them. (25–26)

[17] On the Western writing of history as "inscription," its reliance on the "otherness" of the past, and its links to ethnography, see de Certeau, *Writing*, particularly 19–113 and 209–68.

[18] Again, see de Certeau on history's functioning to construct and police borders between the dead and the living, conquering both time and distance by asserting closure (passim, and, particularly, in the context of his analysis of Freud's *Moses and Monotheism*, the subsection entitled "The Tradition of Death, or Writing" [*Writing* 322–28]).

[19] See de Certeau, *Writing*, especially his analysis of the "primal scene" of the encounter between writing and speech in Jean de Lery (209–43) and his discussion of "the possessed woman" as a disturbance of discourse (244–68), which resonates directly with *Birdwoman and the Suffragettes* in its use of a multiplication of proper nouns (names) and its analysis of the orality of (demonic) possession as opposed to the *inscription* of control. See also the discussion on the relationship between voice and writing as repression in the context of Freud's *Moses and Monotheism* (341–42).

[20] Acknowledging that "historiography is 'familiar' with the question of the other," de Certeau argues that

its discipline must create proper places for each, by pigeonholing the past into an area other than the present, or else by supposing a continuity of genealogical filiation (by way of a homeland, a nation, a milieu, etc; it is always the same topic of history). Technically, it endlessly presupposes homogeneous unities (century, country, class, economic or social strata, etc.) and cannot give way to the vertigo that critical examination of these fragile boundaries might bring about: historiography does not want to know this. In all of its labours, based on these classifications, historiography takes it for granted that the place where it is itself produced has the capacity to provide meaning, since the current institutional demarcations of the discipline uphold the divisions of time and space in the last resort. In this respect, historical discourse, which is political in essence, takes the *law of place* for granted. It legitimizes a place, that of its production, by "including" others in a relation of filiation or of exteriority. It is authorized by this place which allows it to explain whatever is different as "foreign," and whatever is inside as unique. (*Writing* 343)

[21] Diane Bessai, in "Sharon Pollock's Women," notes that *Blood Relations* was at that time the one play that Pollock conceded "to be 'feminist'" (127), a concession that Bessai herself also makes, if somewhat reluctantly (130–32). I am using the version of the play published in the 1981 collection *Blood Relations and Other Plays*. An earlier version was published in *Canadian Theatre Review* 29 (1981): 46–107, and slightly different versions have been published in Plant, ed.; and Wandor. For information on the evolution of the play, see Stone-Blackburn, "Feminism."

[22] I am grateful to Harry Lane for pointing out to me that the implication of the audience in these lines is not as clear as I earlier thought, when I misread the play's stage direction in my article "Replaying History: Canadian Historiographic Metadrama," on which the present argument is based. Lane, however, sees the conclusion as less effective than I do, arguing that,

> because the play's metatheatrical perspective is allowed to fade from view during the course of the play, as Miss Lizzie becomes increasingly merely Bridget, the play's major point is made to devolve onto that final line: "I didn't . . . You did." It is a fine shock-effect, but demands a great deal of the audience before the blackout that immediately follows. Brecht or Pirandello would undoubtedly have sustained the metatheatrical ironies throughout. (13)

[23] Nancy Copeland, in an article that compares the Maenad's *Aphra* with Herst's *A Woman's Comedy*, takes quite a different view from the one that I present, arguing that Herst's play is, "up to a point, an example of what Jill Dolan calls 'liberal feminism,' which resembles liberal humanism in being 'radically individualistic' and asserting universal human values" (135).

[24] I am indebted to Godard's article throughout my discussion of *Jehanne of the Witches*.

[25] Godard's argument is framed by a discussion of the play, together with Clark's *The Trial of Judith K.*, as adaptation, using resistant translation theory to analyse its reappropriation of the Joan story as told in Michel Tournier's 1983 novel *Gilles and Jeanne*. Clark subsequently denied that her play is an adaptation of the Tournier novel and in fact denied having read the novel before writing the play (letter). She told Judith Rudakoff in an interview that the play was inspired by a bookseller who told her of the friendship of Gilles and Joan (and who had perhaps read Tournier) and showed her a copy of Margaret Mitchell's *God of the Witches* ("Sally Clark" 83). The degree of overlap between Tournier's version of Gilles and that of Clark is surprising, but the debate is not significant insofar as Clark's intertextuality is fairly free ranging, and the Joan and Bluebeard stories resonate freely among audiences in any case.

[26] Oddly, the play's original director, Clarke Rogers, whom Clark credits with providing the impetus for writing the play ("Sally Clark" 82), argues in his preface to the published script that "*Jehanne of the Witches* is misnamed. The play, both in story and central thematic dilemma, is as much about Gilles de Rais as it is about Jehanne" (11), and he proceeds to devote much of his preface to the rehabilitation of the Bluebeard figure. I think that this view is, to say the least, ill conceived.

6 ENVIRONMENTAL THEATRE

[1] I am using the terms "post-naturalist" and "post-modernist" here and throughout this chapter in their hyphenated forms in an attempt to limit the meaning, particularly of the latter term, to formal experiments that develop out of, though they may overlap chronologically with, naturalistic or modernist predecessors and that take place primarily since the inception of "late capitalism" (c. 1970), as opposed to the period of industrial capitalism out of and in response to which modernism emerged.

[2] Schechner published his "Six Axioms for Environmental Theater," coining the term, in *Drama Review* 12 (1968): 41–64, and his book *Environmental Theater* in 1973. They were revised, reintroduced, and reissued together in 1994 as *Environmental Theater: An Expanded New Edition Including "Six Axioms for Environmental Theater."* The other major theorist of the period was Michael Kirby, whose influential "Happenings: An Introduction" and "The New Theatre," together with his and Schechner's "Interview with John Cage," are usefully republished in Sandford. The most thorough taxonomy and history of environmental theatre, (too) broadly defined as "staging that is non-frontal" (1), is Arnold Aronson's *The History and Theory of Environmental Scenography*. Criticisms of these histories might usefully and accurately be levelled in the way that criticisms have been levelled at America- and Eurocentric histories of performance art, with which they overlap.

[3] For ritual shamanism and magic, see especially Schechner, *Environmental Theater* 174–92. In "The Decline and Fall of the (American) Avant-Garde," he argues that "to experiment with the space of the whole theater, and to bring the theatrical event into the world outside the theatre building, is to investigate most directly the relationship between performers and spectators, and between theatrical events and social life" (29). However, Steve Nelson's 1989 reassessment, "Redecorating the Fourth Wall: Environmental Theatre Today" (which treats John Krizanc's *Tamara* as an American play of the late 1980s, without mentioning the author or the show's 1981 origins in Toronto), questions the political efficacy or even intent of most American environmental theatre in the 1980s. Timothy Murray's "The Theatricality of the Van-Guard: Ideology and Contemporary American Theatre" offers a very different critique, based on Althusser, of what Murray sees as Schechner's somewhat simplistic equation of proscenium stagecraft, or "frontalism," with political conservatism, while simultaneously throwing into question the automatic assumption that the "avant-garde" (or the "van-guard") and nonfrontal staging are by definition politically interventionist.

[4] This is my own account of *Stage* (or *Groove*; its name changed between the conception, including the publicity, and the act, but it never became clear whether confusion about the change was part of the show), written and directed by Wendy Agnew and Darren O'Donnell with Dr. Josef Raza and produced by Pow Pow Unbound at Buddies in Bad Times Theatre in March 1993.

[5] Everett-Green quotes Schafer as saying, "I love the natural environment of Canada. I'm not so pleased about the society, which is becoming increasingly vulgar, and hostile to quality. . . . That's why I like to go to Europe, where they still understand what quality means." He also objects to "a slippage towards funding multicultural entertainments rather than Canadian entertainments [sic]. . . . I'm not in favour of multiculturalism. I think you should forget wherever you came from, and live where you are, and build a culture based in Canadian social and climatological experiences" ("Polemics").

⁶ The most thorough account of Schafer's theatrical work is his own, in *"Patria" and the Theatre of Confluence*, which includes copious illustrations ranging from scores that incorporate the composer's doodles, through environmental plans, to production photographs. David Burgess notes the similarity of the "theatre of confluence" to Richard Wagner's *Gesamptkunstwerk* (35), and Everett-Green cites Wagner, together with Richard Strauss and Benjamin Britten ("Schafer") and Alban Berg ("Undisciplined"), as analogues and influences. Schafer himself acknowledges Wagner (*Patria* 22–23 and passim; "Princess" 25). He also cites Rheinhardt (*Patria* 67), D.H. Lawrence ("Princess" 27; "Theatre of Confluence II" 19), Joyce (*Patria* 23, 141), Eliot (*Patria* 141), and Eliot's mythological source, Frazer's *The Golden Bough* ("Theatre of Confluence II" 10). He links himself with Kandinsky, Klee, and the Bauhaus (*Patria* 23; "Theatre of Confluence" 33), as well as with Dada (by way of Tzara, Breton, and Schwitter) (*Patria* 79; "Theatre of Confluence" 36), the Russian constructivists (*Patria* 126), and the Italian Futurists (by way of T.F. Marinetti, whom he quotes at length on "variety theatre" as an analogue to his own "theatre of confluence") (*Patria* 132–34). His director, Thom Sokoloski, indicates in an interview with Burgess that Schafer has talked about Rheinhardt, Meyerhold, Vahktangov, Artaud, and the Russian constructivists (39), and Ulla Colgrass cites among Schafer's influences and interests Cocteau, Klee, Fuller, Schoenberg, Webern, and Eliot, as well as Pound (35).

⁷ My *Cassell's Latin English/English Latin Dictionary* defines *patria* as "fatherland, see *patrius*." *Patrius*, in turn, is defined as "of or relating to a father, fatherly, paternal."

⁸ "Immigrants" are the subject of *Patria 1: The Characteristics Man* (renamed *Wolfman* in 1991 in *"Patria" and the Theatre of Confluence*), in which the central character, "D.P.," is reduced to despair and suicide. In his discussion of this work in *Patria*, Schafer feels obliged to make clear his opposition to immigration, on the ground that "the country [is] already overpopulated" (58). For other critiques of democracy, see "Theatre of Confluence" 37–38.

⁹ See also Schafer, "Princess" 23–26, on his borrowing, as he calls it, from Native legends and languages; "Princess" 26, together with "Theatre of Confluence II" 15–17, on Japanese ritual, including the tea ceremony; and *Patria* 65–66 and "Theatre of Confluence" 33–34 on Japanese forms, including Kabuki, read through Eisenstein. Schafer indicates, moreover, his hope to complete *Patria 10*, in which his hero Wolf/Theseus will "go to the East to seek enlightenment, just as I have frequently sought it myself in oriental art and religion" (*Patria* 213). On the Catholic Mass as an "integrated ritual," see "Theatre of Confluence" 34. Schafer also cites "Eskimo," Balinese, and other "primitive" forms in "Theatre of Confluence II" 18. The *Patria* cycle itself draws directly on *The Tibetan Book of the Dead* (*Patria* 84) and on Greek, Egyptian, and other sources for mythological grounding/valorization. Schafer's general, Rousseauesque principles of primitivism are articulated in "Theatre of Confluence II" 5–7. His explanation of his use of "foreign or invented languages" is also revealing (particularly in light of his views on multiculturalism and the fact that, in *Patria 2*, Ariadne alone speaks English, while the evil doctors and nurses who attend her are linguistically constructed as Other): "The reason is that today more than ever before in history we live in a linguistic polyglot which has resulted in the polluting of all consistent linguistic paradigms. At times nothing seems to remain to us but a mass of jargon and gibberish" (*Patria* 76).

¹⁰ See also, of course, Derrida's more general theoretical critique in *Of Grammatology* 97–268 of "the privileged place . . . Rousseau occup[ies] in the history of logocentrism" (97).

[11] Schafer provides a useful synopsis of all parts, completed and in progress, in "*Patria*: The Work in Progress" (*Patria* 209–14).

[12] *Patria 4* was called *The Black Theatre of Hermes Trismegistus* when it was first produced at the Festival de Liège, Belgium, in 1989. The name was changed for the 1992 production at Union Station in Toronto as part of the DuMaurier World Stage.

[13] The structure of *Patria 6* most clearly embodies in microcosm that of the cycle as a whole. As Schafer describes it, "the form of *Ra* is tripartite, with an introduction leading to the Halls of Preparation, the descent into the Duat (Underworld), culminating in death followed by rebirth and concluding with the ascent towards the rising sun of the new dawn" (*Patria* 178).

[14] Schafer calls *Patria 7*, not yet completed, a "dance drama" in which "the apotheosis has begun" (*Patria* 157).

[15] "The clash of Dionysian and Apollonian themes is everywhere evident in the story" (*Patria* 159).

[16] This reinscription of traditional and repressive gender roles is apparent from the beginning of Schafer's theatrical career. His first work for the stage, the 1965 opera *Loving*, represents archetypally "female" or "feminine" attitudes (used interchangeably) as "vanity" (which Schafer defines as "the desire to be and remain attractive to the male"), "modesty," and "passion." The male archetypes that he employs, meanwhile, are Don Juan, the Warrior, and the Poet (*Patria* 16).

[17] Schafer intended this gallery to be two-sided, but his director, Michael Bawtree, presented him with a central pit surrounded on four sides by tiered rows of seating.

[18] I am not taking into account here a number of the ramifications of *The Greatest Show*'s relationship with its immediate community as audience, as participant, and as sponsor, ramifications that align it at once with populist disruption, local empowerment, and reification of local power structures, since these issues are similar to those covered in chapter 4. It is nevertheless worth noting these tensions, the ways in which local support for the project were marshalled through provincially and federally elected representatives and local corporations, who supported the production financially and in letters (see Adams; Domm; and Grant), circulated in the press kit for the production, about the economic benefits to the community to be gained through tourism, employment, and other opportunities for "the community's businesses and service establishments" (Grant). Schafer argued somewhat differently about what he called the social agenda of the production:

> my attempt to break down this horrible division between the professional and the amateur, the entertainer and the entertained, to find some way in which not only the actors, the musicians and the others involved in the performances, somehow in the middle between professionals and the amateurs, but also the entire audience (so called) is involved and participates. ("Text" 37)

[19] Schafer describes "the invigorating environment of this spatial variety which is never geometrical or finished off but is broken unpredictability by wing flats, soffits and coulisses, suggestive of the labyrinth which is the subtext of the entire work" (*Patria* 125).

[20] See, especially, Jonson's induction scene (*Bartholomew Fair* 9–13), in which a playwright's representative negotiates the terms of artistic judgement with the audience. It is interesting to note a similar tension in Schafer's love for football, a populist sport that is often experienced by audiences as carnival but that nevertheless depends on militaristic and masculinist strategies of planning and control. Colgrass, describing Schafer's childhood, makes the comparison:

He was an avid football player and read every book he could find on football strategy. A young team he coached in the High Park Y.M.C.A. League for five years became unbeatable, and this leadership in sports is probably relevant to his ability to direct "a cast of thousands" in his later elaborate dramas. Perhaps his love of ritual and the need to physically act out his musical ideas are also connected with his early years in sports. (33)

Schafer himself claims that "in *Patria 1* I have tried to create a work as exciting as a football game" (*Patria* 66).

[21] The script is not continuously paginated. The introduction and the scenes set at each venue begin at page 1 and proceed to the end of their own sections. My parenthetical quotations from the script will therefore indicate both section and page number.

[22] I am drawing biographical information on Liitoja from Hunt 45–46. Only one script by Liitoja has been published, *The Last Supper*, but it is not one of his environmental works and is atypical in almost every respect. My account of Liitoja and DNA is based on personal experience, secondary sources, and a videotape of a 1993 production, *The Panel*.

[23] One reviewer called Liitoja's nine-and-a-half-hour *Hamlet* "a symphonic score" (qtd. in Leonard 30), and Hunt describes the structure of *The Last Pound* as being "based on the classical sonata form (presentation of two themes, transmutation, and final recapitulation)" (46). A sample score for *Private Performances*, including Liitoja's notes, was published as "Liitoja Scores" in *Theatrum*.

[24] Liitoja also shares with his modernist predecessors a tendency to treat life — including a disturbing number of naked girls in his productions — as "raw material" for his art (Hunt 46). Hunt rightly points to "the nudity of the young girl" in *This Is What Happens in Orangeville* as "more exploitative of women than suggestive of innocence" (49).

[25] The press kit circulated by DNA includes a page entitled "Features," which outlines elements central to its productions and gives a flavour of its sensibilities:

Spectators are seated spectators throughout the performers spectators space. The spectators performance occurs spectators amongst the performers spectators spectators who are spectators performers clearly seen spectators and become spectators part of spectators the performance spectators.

1. There is much happening simultaneously at the same time.
2. Caress, blind, shout, faint, scream, Pound [sic], stop, blast, cry, flash, turn, hold, bang, flicker, jump, touch, fade, wait, stun, freeze.
3. Performers may be planted in the audience. Who is the performer?
4. Different cycles are pitted against each other.
5. Multiple repetitions.
6. Totality of the work and each performance begins before the spectator is admitted.

[26] I am indebted to Nigel Hunt's thesis "Hillar Liitoja: Chaos and Control" throughout my discussion of *This Is What Happens in Orangeville*.

[27] I am indebted to Mark Ruzylo's thesis "The Representation of AIDS in Four Canadian Plays" throughout my discussion of *The Panel*.

[28] In discussing Rose's environmental work, I am including his collaborators at Toronto's Necessary Angel Theatre, particularly playwright John Krizanc, dramaturg D.D. Kugler, and designers Dorian L. Clark and Graeme S. Thomson. Rose has worked extensively in various kinds of theatre in Canada and the United States and is by no means defined by his environmental theatre work, which was concentrated in the 1980s.

[29] For an analysis of *Tamara* and *Prague* as political plays, see Knowles, "Truth." On the different cultural work performed by *Tamara* as produced in Toronto, Los Angeles, and New York, see Knowles, "Reading Material."

[30] This paragraph is adapted from the opening of my article "Richard Rose in Rehearsal" (134).

[31] An illustration of particularly resonant environmental semiotics, and one that illustrates how site specific the cultural work performed by theatrical productions can be, occurred in the Los Angeles production of *Tamara*, performed at the Hollywood America Legion building. As Krizanc describes it,

> Early in act two, the Fascist captain, Finzi, interrogates the suspicious-looking new chauffeur, Mario:
>
> > FINZI: "Are you now, or have you ever been, a member of the communist party?"
> > MARIO: "No."
> > FINZI: "I ask again: are you a Communist?"
> > MARIO: "No."
> > FINZI: "Have you ever known a Communist?"
> > MARIO: "No."
> > FINZI: "Three times you answer no."
>
> When the scene was first rehearsed, the temperature in the room seemed to drop twenty degrees. Everyone got goose bumps. The actor playing Mario broke character and asked, "Can you feel it?"
>
> We could. Thirty years ago, the building had housed the hearings concerning the Hollywood Ten. Those words have become synonymous with McCarthyism and I had put them in the play to draw the parallel between McCarthyism and fascism. Every house has its ghosts. ("Innocents" 37–38)

[32] In fact, Marvin Carlson argues that, whatever the audience-stage relationship, "the actor remains an uncanny, disturbing 'other,' inhabiting a world with its own rules, like a space traveler within a personal capsule, which the audience, however physically close, can never truly penetrate" (*Places* 130).

[33] In an interview with Jon Kaplan, Krizanc said, "I wanted to give people more freedom than they've ever had in the theatre. I wanted to give choices back to the audience" ("*Tamara*" 137). Richard Plant, "Deconstruction" 197–98, argues that the play somewhat dangerously gives the illusion of freedom of choice to audiences whose decision making and field of vision are in fact tightly constrained, and this may account for its having been successfully appropriated by Toronto millionaire Moses Znaimer and produced as a *divertissement* for audiences of the rich and famous in New York and Los Angeles. I argue elsewhere, however, that even there "the stars, would-be stars, and star-gazers that constituted so large a percentage of *Tamara*'s American audience may have looked, at the end of the evening, at the pathetic figure of their fellow artist Gabriele d'Annunzio on his hands and knees, snorting cocaine from the feet of a corpse, and seen themselves" ("Reading Material" 275).

[34] Natalie Rewa provides a useful explication of the functioning of the setting to which I am indebted here, together with a map of the floor plan for the production by Graeme Thomson and John-Kelly Cuthbertson.

7 DIALOGIC MONOLOGUE: A DIALOGUE

[1] We would like to acknowledge the writers whose work we cite, together with those whose work and voices we have dialogically and unconsciously internalized. We quote extensively and employ extensive notes in an attempt to create a kind of critical polyphony — to admit as many voices, positions, and genres as possible into a text that, as a dialogue between two (unequal) voices and subject positions, has its own tendencies toward the monologic. A version of this chapter was first presented as a dialogue at the meetings of the Association for Canadian Theatre Research/Association de la recherche théâtrale au Canada in Calgary, 5 June 1994.

[2] Geoffrey and Jeffrey are Toronto clowns Jim Warren and Andrew Massingham, whose *Get off the Stage* satirizes Canadian theatre from the points of view of two aging British actors of the old school. The appearance of Massingham in Garnhum's *Pants on Fire* reinforced the intertextuality of the moment in which Garnhum's sign, reading "Keep off the stage," was altered to "Get off the stage" by Massingham.

[3] See Bakhtin, *Speech Genres*, especially "The Problem of Speech Genres" (60–102); and Todorov 82. Michael Gardiner provides a useful summary analysis of Bakhtin's concept of speech genres (81–85). What we are referring to as intertextuality, here and elsewhere, Bakhtin usually called "metalinguistics" or "translinguistics" (*Speech Genres* xv, 114).

[4] Todorov usefully notes that "what he [Bakhtin] described under this name [novel] is not a genre, but one or two properties of discourse, whose occurrence is not confined to a single historical moment" (91). Or, as Michael Holquist says in his introduction to Bakhtin's *The Dialogic Imagination*, "'novel' is the name Bakhtin gives to whatever force is at work within a given literary system to reveal the limits, the artificial constraints of that system" (xxxi).

[5] Sidnell argued that

the Elizabethan soliloquy and the modern monologue would appear to be more profoundly dialogic than dialogue as it is usually written, played, and understood. . . . I propose that dialogue in the theatre is a more monologic position . . . than monologue, and that novelistic polyphony has infiltrated into contemporary theatrical monologue. (5)

We are citing here a draft faxed to Ric Knowles on 27 May 1993. Paul C. Castagno has also pointed to ways in which recent monologue in the American theatre "moves from its monologic aspect . . . towards various forms of dialogism" (135).

[6] According to Volosinov/Bakhtin and his/their critique of Saussurean linguistics,

Utterance . . . is constructed between two socially organized persons. . . . The *word is oriented toward an addressee,* toward *whom* that addressee might be: a fellow member or not of the same social group, of higher or lower standing . . . , someone connected with the speaker by close social ties . . . or not. There can be no such thing as an abstract addressee. . . . *[W]ord is a two-sided act.* It is determined equally by *whose* word it is and *for whom* it is meant. As word, it is precisely *the product of the reciprocal relationship between speaker and listener, addresser and addressee.* Each and every word expresses the "one" in relation to the "other." I give myself verbal shape from the other's point of view. . . . (Volosinov, *Marxism* 85–86)

(This, together with *Freudianism: A Marxist Critique* [see note 18], is a disputed text, first published under Volosinov's name and later claimed for Bakhtin. In the areas with which we are concerned, however, the views expressed in both volumes are congruent with those of Bakhtin elsewhere, and we will treat them as his.)

It is important to note in this context that, while Bakhtin focuses here on verbal communication between speaking subjects, he elsewhere, if minimally, extends this construction of "language" to other sign systems. Also important is Luce Irigaray's extension of the implications of Bakhtin's "sociolinguistics": "'I' is sometimes truer than 'one' or 'he.' It's truer because it tells its origin" (trans. and qtd. in Schwab 58, 69).

[7] See, especially, the essay "Epic and Novel: Toward a Methodology for the Study of the Novel" (*Dialogic Imagination* 3–40).

[8] Bakhtin refers to Dostoevsky and Rabelais throughout his work, particularly of the middle period, but see, especially, *Problems*; and *Rabelais*. See also Kristeva, *Desire*. Bakhtin's concepts of degradation, abuse, and carnival inversion are of course also related to Kristeva's analysis in *Powers of Horror: An Essay on Abjection*.

[9] These concepts and coinages permeate Bakhtin's writing from beginning to end, but for some of the more idiosyncratic ones see *Problems* 196 ("word with a loophole," "cringe," and "sideways glance"), 51 (self-consciousness); *Speech Genres* 115 (indirect speaking), 120 (double voicing), 154 (hyperbole); *Dialogic Imagination* 69 ("intonational quotation marks"); and *Marxism* 141–59 ("quasi-direct speech"). "Ventriloquism," on the other hand, is a useful term introduced not by Bakhtin but by Michael Holquist in "The Politics of Representation."

[10] See also *Rabelais* 7, where Bakhtin asserts that "the absence of footlights would destroy a theatrical performance."

[11] See also *Dialogic Imagination* 266, 330, 332. It is clear that his views were based on a specific type of drama and theatre and that he failed to consider that, as Hélène Keyssar points out, "any action on stage is refracted (to use another Bakhtinian term) through the diverse points of view of writers, actors, designers and spectators" ("Drama" 89). This and other points are argued convincingly by Carlson; Keyssar 89 ff.; and Wise. Bakhtin himself discusses medieval theatre admiringly and at some length in his analyses of carnival, particularly in *Rabelais* 15, 347–49; he acknowledges "the influence of popular theatrical forms on Rabelais" (*Rabelais* 349); and he admits that, "to some extent, comedy is an exception" to his rule (*Dialogic Imagination* 405). The best example of his treatment of drama as a genre (a subject that he never addressed systematically or at length) is in *Problems* 34, but relevant passages are in *Art* 73–74, 76–78; in *Problems* 17–18, 122, 128, 188, and 239; in *Rabelais* 7–8, 39–40, 257–58, 265, and 347–49; and in *Speech Genres* 110, 122, and 126. Deborah Jacobs, writing about applications of Bakhtin to Renaissance drama, argues that "these readings 'novelize' non-novelistic materials and pre-novelistic literature; they gobble up semiotically the materials even of another culture and time, asking them questions specific to novelistic (middle-class, individualized) subjectivity as if they are the only questions in town" (74). Something might equally be argued of our present application of dialogism — Bakhtinian dialogics have tended to be gobbled up by ahistorical applications of all sorts — except, we would argue, that drama, particularly dramatic monologue in Canada, has become "novelized" in ways that make relevant questions that were previously specific to novelistic discourse, including questions of novelistic subjectivity.

[12] Robert Lepage's *Needles and Opium* and Pol Pelletier's autobiographical trilogy *Joie, Océan,* and *Or* are excellent examples of the kind of monodrama that we are interested in, but Quebec theatre and cultural production are beyond the scope of this dialogue.

[13] We don't have a copy of the script, which is as yet unpublished. The line is quoted in Wagner. Reviews consistently describe the show in dialogic terms, as when Jon Kaplan and Jill Lawless call it "a toybox of insights, paradoxes and shards of beauty both linguistic and . . . visual."

[14] Bakhtin's emphasis. Confession is problematic for Bakhtin in part, one suspects, because it is an instance in which the power relationships that always problematize dialogical space (as discussed below) are particularly apparent. As Michel Foucault says, confession is "a ritual that unfolds within a power relationship, for one does not confess without the presence (or virtual presence) of a partner who is not simply the interlocutor but the authority who requires the confession" (*History* 61). In this context, the ways in which confessional monologues in the theatre construct their audiences comprise an intriguing question but one well beyond the scope of this dialogue.

[15] Sidnell takes this one step further when he refers to "the major corollary following from the phenomenal presence of the actor, which is that the human subject is present: present to the subjects that constitute the audience. For in theatre it is commonly assumed that the physical entity is coterminous with a functional or metaphysical one" (4). Consider also his definition of performativeness: "it accepts the inextricability of the performing subject from the object of representation, yet acknowledges the impossibility of self-representation." He goes on to argue, as quoted above, that, thereby, "performance becomes, as it were, theory in action" (2).

[16] Publicity material for Toronto's Crow's Theatre-Canadian Stage production. The published script does not refer to the actor-writer's showing of his scars to the audience, but in performance the moment when Seremba rolled up his sleeves (saying "not with these wounds" [56]) was carefully orchestrated and functioned as a kind of documentary authentication.

[17] At least they did so at the premiere production at the Back Space, Tarragon Theatre, 17 March–17 April 1994.

[18] See the appendix to *Problems* (283–302).

[19] For Volosinov's/Bakhtin's discussions of subjectivity, and his quarrel with Freud, see Volosinov, *Freudianism*. See also Bakhtin, *Art* 22–23, 25–26 (on empathy), 61, and 63–80; Emerson, "Outer," especially 25–27; and Roberts, "Poetics," especially 120–24.

[20] Booth notices that Bakhtin's assumed readership is male (165–66). Bakhtin's only moderately extended discussion of gender issues is in *Rabelais* 240–41, where Rabelais is exonerated from the charge of offering a "negative, hostile attitude toward women" (241).

[21] Grotesque realism and grotesque inversion are discussed primarily in *Rabelais and His World* 303–67 and passim.

[22] There is a bumper sticker circulating in Ontario that says "ENGLISH, the universal language."

[23] From appendix 2 of *Problems of Dostoevsky's Poetics* (trans. and qtd. in Todorov 107).

[24] We are indebted to Liana Shannon-Appleford for referring us to Fischer.

[25] Bakhtin's understanding of "the dialogic encounter of two cultures" is related to his understanding of empathy, and it often sounds uncomfortably appropriative (though Bakhtin insists that it "does not result in merging or mixing"): "Each retains its own unity and *open* totality, but they are mutually enriched" (*Speech Genres* 7). It also relies heavily on a conceptualization of other cultures as "foreign":

> There exists a very strong, but one-sided and thus untrustworthy, idea that in order better to understand a foreign culture, one must enter into it, forgetting one's own, and view the world through the eyes of this foreign culture. This idea, as I said, is one-sided. Of course, a certain entry as a living being into a foreign culture, the possibility of seeing the world through its eyes, is a necessary part of the process of understanding it; but if this were the only aspect of this

understanding, it would merely be duplication and would not entail anything new or enriching. *Creative understanding* does not renounce itself, its own place in time, its own culture; and it forgets nothing. In order to understand, it is immensely important for the person who understands to be *located outside* the object of his or her creative understanding — in time, in space, in culture. . . . We raise new questions for a foreign culture, ones that it did not raise itself; we seek answers to our own questions in it; and the foreign culture responds to us by revealing to us its new aspects and new semantic depths. Without *one's own* questions one cannot creatively understand anything other or foreign. . . . (*Speech Genres* 6–7)

This passage raises, of course, the same question as do carnival and the "free" dialogic play of equal voices in discourse: how is equality ensured when such "freedoms" typically favour the powerful?

²⁶ Discussions of "linguistic carnival" in Bakhtin include (but are not limited to) *Dialogic Imagination* 33, 50, 60, 285, and 308; and *Rabelais* 473 and throughout. Sidnell provides a brief analysis of Verdecchia's use of "tongues" (5–6).

²⁷ Discussions of the hero as jester and related concepts appear frequently in *Rabelais*, but see *Dialogic Imagination* 24–25, 273–74, 402, and 404–05.

²⁸ For discussions of boundaries and borders in Bakhtin, see *Art* 274; *Problems* 287, 301; *Speech Genres* 137; Holquist, *Dialogism* 61 ("the utterance . . . is a border phenomenon"); and Kehde 27 ("the psyche . . . is a boundary phenomenon").

²⁹ See note 24. Like the visions of many left-wing cultural theorists (perhaps most notably Marcuse — see Martineau), Bakhtin's vision was ultimately utopian — in fact a "deep popular utopianism" that Bakhtin attributes to Rabelais (*Rabelais* 23) and that Verdecchia's vision of the border seems to share.

³⁰ For a useful post-colonial analysis of the way in which the play "refuses the unifying colonial gaze by creating and occupying a space *on* or *within* American borders," and thereby constructs an anticolonial discourse, see McKinnie ("Calling Off"). For an analysis of the play in the context of official policies of multiculturalism in Canada, and the tension between their constructions of "cultures" and "ethnicities," see Gomez, "Healing."

³¹ It is notable that, of the plays under discussion here, those by women tend to be less explicitly autobiographical than those by men. This difference might suggest that, for these women, the authority of the performer as a performer is less taken for granted than it is for the men. The women are thus less inclined explicitly to represent themselves autobiographically and to interrogate "themselves" in those terms. Considering the prevalence of autobiographical form in women's nondramatic writing (particularly journals, letters, and diaries), this resistance to "pure" autobiography is intriguing, suggesting that interrogation of the self's representation involves, as it does in performance, the material body, a materiality that potentially imbricates the performer in so many physical and visual phallocentric discourses and in spectatorial consumption.

³² See also Keyssar's *Feminist Theatre*, especially xiii–xiv.

³³ We have used patriarchal and ethnocentric discourses as examples here, but classist, heterosexist, scholarly, theatrical, and other authoritarian discourses may also be the objects of depriviliging or subversion by the contemporary Canadian dialogic monologue. *The Noam Chomsky Lectures*, for example, by Daniel Brooks and Guillermo Verdecchia, gains much of its impact through its theatrical interrogation of the monologism of the lecture format itself; *House* foregrounds the power relationships

inscribed in theatrical space and conventions (not to mention mental health group sessions and supermarkets); Garnhum's plays deprivilege heterosexist discourse; and so on.

[34] See also note 13.

[35] See Bernstein, especially 221.

EPILOGUE: STRUCTURING SPACETIME

[1] For accounts of quantum mechanics, including its relationship to relativity theory, see Albert; Feynam; Hawking; Herbert; Rae; and Wolf. For scientific explications of chaos theory, see Hall; Prigogine; and especially Gleick (the standard book on the field for nonscientists). The best work to date applying chaos theory to literature and culture has been by N. Katherine Hayles, particularly in her book *Chaos Bound: Orderly Disorder in Contemporary Science and Literature*, but I have also drawn on Brady and a number of the essays in Robertson et al. For complex adaptive systems, see Kauffman; and Morowitz and Singer. Hayles usefully argues that developments in literary and cultural theory and in the arts that have been identified as post-structuralist or post-modern were anticipated in the scientific and philosophical communities in prior generations but that the larger paradigm shift that I am concerned with here took hold only in the 1970s, when there was a cultural predisposition for such a shift (xii, 1–28).

[2] For analyses of Stoppard's quantum dramas that draw on "the new science," see Demastes, "Re-Inspecting" 252–53; Kremer and Kremer; and, especially, Phelan, *Unmarked* 112–29.

[3] See, however, Per Brask's whimsical closet monologue "Neils Bohr's Preamble to a Dramaturgical Theory," in which Bohr returns from the grave to take issue with Schmitt's appropriation of his work and its application to dramaturgy.

[4] It would be possible to analyse the development of new dramatic structures in the context of new developments in biology, consciousness theory, information technology (in practice, theory, and structural implications, chaos is very much the science of the computer age), and so on, and many of these fields are subject to cultural analysis in various essays in Robertson et al. The standard work on new theories of divisible consciousness, or heterophenomenology, is Dennett. I am limiting this brief chapter to works that explicitly evoke quantum mechanics and chaos as a way of gesturing toward potential new directions, of avoiding too dilettantish an appropriation of other disciplines, and of avoiding a multiplication of metaphoric applications across disciplines that can become so loose and generalized as to be meaningless.

[5] Hayles 209–35 usefully and at length explores the local/global problematic in nondeterministic science and in post-structuralism.

[6] The *interested* nature of scientific thought, including the scientist's attitude to the so-called new science, emerges clearly when Alastair Rae, having rejected a number of seemingly uncomfortable "new wave" theories concerning the measurement problem, opts for Prigogine's conceptualization of the paradigm shift on the basis that "without the possibility of change the idea of existence is meaningless, so for me at least there is no being without becoming" (117). He quotes Prigogine usefully and at length:

The classical order was: particles first, the second law [of thermodynamics — that everything tends toward increasing entropy] later — being before becoming! It is possible that this is no longer so when we come to the level of elementary particles and that here we must *first* introduce the second law before being able to define the entities. Does this mean becoming before being? Certainly this would be a radical departure from the classical way of thought. But, after all, an elementary particle, contrary to its name, is not an object that is "given"; we must construct it, and in this construction it is not unlikely that *becoming*, the participation of the particles in the evolution of the physical world, may play an essential role. (109)

⁷ Hayles engages throughout her book in productive ideological analyses of the apparently free space opened up by chaos theory and post-structuralism alike. She is at her best in her gender-based critique (171–74) of Gleick's best-selling account of *Chaos: Making a New Science*.

⁸ The Passe Muraille program also quotes at length passages from Stephen Hawking, Marcus Aurelius, and nineteenth-century British physicist James Clerk Maxwell.

⁹ I want to suggest allegory in Benjamin's sense, which concerns itself with the materiality of the sign, which cannot therefore be naturalized or mystified, and which demands *active* decoding. See Benjamin, *Origin* 166–85 and passim, and *Understanding Brecht* 17–18 and passim.

¹⁰ Jill's opening monologue to her private girls' school class also invokes social Darwinism: "Even your parents' decision to send you here to Grace can be seen as a Darwinian attempt to consolidate advantage by keeping you out of touch with an inferior gene pool. My parents certainly saw it like that" (4).

¹¹ In addition to the masculinist resonances within the play of the demand for a bigger microscope, this speech evokes Evelyn Fox Keller's history of "the biological gaze" as "literal, material transgression" or penetration in the study of embryology (107). Keller works in part from the premise that, "If we have learned anything from physics at all, it is of the impossibility, even in the physical domain, of looking without touching: the very light we shine disturbs the object at which we gaze" (117).

¹² In a telephone interview with the author and quoted in Knowles, Afterword 170–71. Krizanc explains,

> I think that one of the problems of traditional theatre — I say this because my play [*The Half of It*] deals to some extent with quantum physics — is that the Newtonian world view has us believing in the primacy of cause and effect. It is as if the initial conditions somehow set the outcome in an inevitable fashion. Quantum physics introduces a whole level of randomness. Is light a wave, or a particle? It's both. (qtd. in Burrows 3)

Burrows continues, "for Krizanc, seeing characters in terms of cause and effect is a falsification" (3).

Works Cited

Adams, Peter. Letter. n.d. Press kit, *The Greatest Show.*

Albert, David Z. *Quantum Mechanics and Experience.* Cambridge, MA: Harvard UP, 1992.

Althusser, Louis. *Lenin and Philosophy and Other Essays.* Trans. Ben Brewster. New York: Monthly Review, 1971.

Altman, Rick. "A Semantic/Syntactic Approach to Film Genre." *Cinema Journal* 23.3 (1984): 6–18.

Anderson, Benedict. *Imagined Communities: Reflections on the Origin and Spread of Nationalism.* Rev. ed. London: Verso, 1991.

The Anna Project. "Fragments: Afterthoughts." *Canadian Theatre Review* 43 (1985): 167–73.

———. *This Is for You, Anna.* Filewod, ed. 249–82.

Anthony, Geraldine, ed. *Stage Voices: Twelve Canadian Playwrights Talk about Their Lives and Work.* Toronto: Doubleday, 1978.

Appleford, Rob. "The Desire to Crunch Bone." *Canadian Theatre Review* 77 (1993): 21–26.

Aristotle. *Aristotle's Poetics.* Trans. S.H. Butcher. New York: Hill, 1961.

Armstrong, Gordon. "Theatre as a Complex Adaptive System." *New Theatre Quarterly* 13 (1997): 277–88.

Arnott, Brian. "The Passe-Muraille Alternative." Helwig, *Human Elements: Second Series* 97–111.

Aronowitz, Stanley. *Science as Power: Discourse and Ideology in Modern Society.* Minneapolis: U of Minnesota P, 1988.

Aronson, Arnold. *The History and Theory of Environmental Scenography.* Ann Arbor: UMI, 1981.

Ashley, Audrey. Rev. of *Jacob's Wake,* by Michael Cook. Conolly 189–91.

Auslander, Philip. "Live Performance in a Mediatized Culture." *Essays in Theatre/Études théâtrales* 11.1 (1992): 33–40.

———. *Presence and Resistance: Postmodernism and Cultural Politics in Contemporary American Performance.* Ann Arbor: U of Michigan P, 1994.

Bakhtin, M.M. *Art and Answerability: Early Philosophical Essays.* Ed. Michael Holquist and Vadim Liapunov. Trans. Liapunov. Austin: U of Texas P, 1990.

———. *The Dialogic Imagination.* Trans. Caryl Emerson and Michael Holquist. Austin: U of Texas P, 1981.

———. *Problems of Dostoevsky's Poetics.* Ed. and trans. Caryl Emerson. Minneapolis: U of Minnesota P, 1984.

———. *Rabelais and His World.* Trans. Helene Iswolsky. Bloomington: Indiana UP, 1984.

——. *Speech Genres and Other Late Essays*. Ed. Caryl Emerson and Michael Holquist. Trans. Vern W. McGee. Austin: U of Texas P, 1986.

Bakhtin, M.M./P.N. Medvedev. *The Formal Method in Literary Scholarship: A Critical Introduction to Sociological Poetics*. Trans. Albert J. Wehrle. Baltimore: Johns Hopkins UP, 1978.

Bank, Rosemarie. "Time, Space, Timespace, Spacetime: Theatre History in Simultaneous Universes." *Journal of Dramatic Theory and Criticism* 5.2 (1991): 65–84.

Banning, Kass. "From Didactics to Desire: Building Women's Film Culture." Tregebov 148–76.

Barber, C.L. *Shakespeare's Festive Comedy: A Study of Dramatic Form and Its Relation to Social Custom*. Princeton: Princeton UP, 1959.

Barthes, Roland. *Image-Music-Text*. Trans. Stephen Heath. New York: Hill, 1977.

——. *The Pleasure of the Text*. Trans. Richard Miller. New York: Hill, 1975.

——. *S/Z*. Trans. Richard Miller. New York: Hill, 1974.

Bauer, Dale M. *Feminist Dialogics: A Theory of Failed Community*. Albany: State U of New York P, 1988.

Bauer, Dale M., and S. Jaret McKinstry, eds. *Feminism, Bakhtin, and the Dialogic*. Albany: State U of New York P, 1991.

Bellah, Robert, et al. *Habits of the Heart: Individualism and Commitment in American Life*. Berkeley: U of California P, 1985.

Belsey, Catherine. *The Subject of Tragedy: Identity and Difference in Renaissance Drama*. London: Methuen, 1985.

Benjamin, Walter. *The Origin of German Tragic Drama*. Trans. John Osborne. London: NLB, 1977.

——. *Understanding Brecht*. Trans. Anna Bostok. London: Verso, 1973.

Bennett, Donna. "English Canada's Postcolonial Complexities." *Essays on Canadian Writing* 51–52 (1993–94): 164–210.

Bennett, Susan. "Radical (Self-) Direction and the Body: Shawna Dempsey and Lorri Millan's Performance Art." *Canadian Theatre Review* 76 (1993): 37–41.

Bennett, Tony. *Formalism and Marxism*. London: Methuen, 1979.

Benson, Eugene, and L.W. Conolly, eds. *The Oxford Companion to Canadian Theatre*. Toronto: Oxford UP, 1989.

Bernstein, Michael André. "The Poetics of *Ressentiment*." Morson and Emerson 197–223.

Bessai, Diane. "Documentary into Drama: Reaney's Donnelly Trilogy." *Essays on Canadian Writing* 24–25 (1983–84): 186–210.

——. "Documentary Theatre in Canada: An Investigation into Questions and Backgrounds." *Canadian Drama/L'Art dramatique canadien* 6.1 (1980): 9–21.

——. *Playwrights of Collective Creation*. Toronto: Simon, 1992.

——. "Sharon Pollock's Women." *Amazing Space: Writing Canadian Women Writing*. Ed. Shirley Neuman and Smaro Kamboureli. Edmonton: Longspoon-NeWest, 1986. 126–36.

Bevis, R.W. Rev. of *Leaving Home*, by David French; and *Creeps*, by David Freeman. Conolly 90–92.

Bick, Tamara. "The Interview." *Canadian Theatre Review* 77 (1993): 66–71.

Blau, Herbert. *To All Appearances: Ideology and Performance*. New York: Routledge, 1992.

Boal, Augusto. *Theatre of the Oppressed*. Trans. Charles A. McBride and Maria-Odilia Leal McBride. New York: Urizen, 1979.

Booth, Wayne C. "Freedom of Interpretation: Bakhtin and the Challenge of Feminist Criticism." Morson, ed. 145–76.

Borges, Jorge Luis. *A Universal History of Infamy.* Trans. N.T. di Giovanni. Harmondsworth, UK: Penguin, 1975.

Bradbury, Malcolm. "The Cities of Modernism." Bradbury and McFarlane 96–104.

Bradbury, Malcolm, and James McFarlane, eds. *Modernism, 1890–1930.* Harmondsworth, UK: Penguin, 1976.

Brady, Patrick. "Chaos Theory, Control Theory, and Literary Theory: Or, A Story of Three Butterflies." *Modern Language Studies* 20.4 (1990): 65–79.

Brask, Per, ed. *Contemporary Issues in Canadian Drama.* Winnipeg: Blizzard, 1995.

——. "Neils Bohr's Preamble to a Dramaturgical Theory." *Canadian Theatre Review* 92 (1997): 82–86.

Brissenden, Connie, ed. *The Factory Lab Anthology.* Vancouver: Talonbooks, 1974.

——. Introduction. Brissenden, ed. *Now* vii–ix.

——, ed. *Now in Paperback: Canadian Playwrights of the 1970s.* Toronto: Fineglow Plays, 1973.

Bristol, Michael. *Shakespeare's America, America's Shakespeare.* London: Routledge, 1990.

Brook, Peter. *The Empty Space.* Harmondsworth, UK: Penguin, 1972.

Brookes, Chris. *A Public Nuisance: A History of the Mummers Troupe.* St. John's: Institute of Social and Economic Research, Memorial U of Newfoundland, 1988.

Brooks, Daniel, and Guillermo Verdecchia. *The Noam Chomsky Lectures.* Toronto: Coach House, 1991.

Burgess, David. "Schafer's *Patria* Three: The Cycle Continues." *Canadian Theatre Review* 55 (1988): 34–42.

Burrows, Malcolm. "Necessary Theatre." *Stage Free Press* 6.2 (1989): 3.

Calderwood, James L. *Metadrama in Shakespeare's Henriad: Richard III to Henry V.* Berkeley: U of California P, 1979.

Canadian Theatre Review 90 (1997).

Carlson, Marvin. *Places of Performance: The Semiotics of Theatre Architecture.* Ithaca: Cornell UP, 1989.

——. "Theater and Dialogics." Reinelt and Roach 313–23.

Carson, Neil. "Canadian Historical Drama: Playwrights in Search of a Myth." *Studies in Canadian Literature* 2.2 (1977): 213–25.

——. "George Luscombe and the Theatre of the 'Cabotin.'" *Canadian Drama / L'Art dramatique canadien* 15.2 (1989): 149–58.

Case, Sue-Ellen. *Feminism and Theatre.* London: Macmillan, 1988.

Castagno, Paul C. "Varieties of Monologic Strategy: The Dramaturgy of Len Jenkin and Mac Wellman." *New Theatre Quarterly* 34 (1993): 134–46.

Clark, Katerina, and Michael Holquist. *Mikhail Bakhtin.* Cambridge, MA: Harvard UP, 1984.

Clark, Sally. *Jehanne of the Witches.* Hamill 7–141.

——. Letter to the editor. *Canadian Theatre Review* 66 (1991): 4.

——. "Sally Clark." Interview with Judith Rudakoff. Rudakoff and Much 74–86.

Clement, Susan, and Esther Beth Sullivan. "The Split Subject of *Blood Relations.*" Donkin and Clement 53–66.

Clifford, James. *The Predicament of Culture: Twentieth-Century Ethnography, Literature, and Art.* Cambridge, MA: Harvard UP, 1988.

Clifford, James, and George E. Marcus, eds. *Writing Culture: The Poetics and Politics of Ethnography.* Berkeley: U of California P, 1986.

Cohen, Leonard. "Anthem." *Stranger Music: Selected Poems and Songs.* Toronto: McClelland, 1993. 373.

Colgrass, Ulla. "Artistic Farming: The Many Talents of Murray Schafer." *Canadian Forum* Mar. 1989: 33–36.

Cone, Tom. *Stargazing. New Canadian Drama: I.* Ed. Neil Carson. Ottawa: Borealis, 1980. 46-68.

——. *Three Plays.* Vancouver: Arsenal Pulp, 1976.

——. "Tom Cone." Interview with Robert Wallace. Wallace and Zimmerman 31–43.

Conlogue, Ray. "A Chilling Dance of Death." *Globe and Mail* 11 Dec. 1986: C1.

Conolly, L.W., ed. *Canadian Drama and the Critics.* Rev. ed. Vancouver: Talonbooks, 1995.

Cook, Michael. *Jacob's Wake.* Vancouver: Talonbooks, 1975.

——. "Michael Cook." Anthony 207–32.

——. "Michael Cook." Interview with Robert Wallace. Wallace and Zimmerman 156–71.

Copeland, Nancy. "Imagining Aphra: Reinventing a Female Subject." *Theatre Topics* 4.2 (1994): 135–44.

Coveney, Peter. "Chaos, Entropy, and the Arrow of Time." Nina Hall 203–12.

Cowan, Cindy. "Messages in the Wilderness." *Canadian Theatre Review* 43 (1985): 100–10.

Cullen, Nancy, Alexandra Patience, and Rose Scollard, with Aphra Behn. *Aphra. Theatrum* 25 (1991): S1–11.

Cushman, Robert. Rev. of *Lion in the Streets,* by Judith Thompson. *Globe and Mail* 4 June 1990: C8.

Dafoe, Christopher. Introduction. Cone, *Three Plays* 9–13.

Davies, Paul. "Is the Universe a Machine?" Nina Hall 213–21.

Deakin, Basil. "'Collective Creation' *Another Story* Wowed Audiences in Guysborough." *Chronicle-Herald/Mail Star* [Halifax] 6 Apr. 1982: E3.

de Certeau, Michel. *The Practice of Everyday Life.* Trans. Steven Rendall. Berkeley: U of California P, 1984.

——. *The Writing of History.* Trans. Tom Conley. New York: Columbia UP, 1988.

de Lauretis, Teresa. *Alice Doesn't: Feminism, Semiotics, and Cinema.* Bloomington: Indiana UP, 1984.

——. "Oedipus Interruptus." *Wide Angle* 7.1–2 (1985): 34–40.

——. *Technologies of Gender: Essays on Theory, Film, and Fiction.* Bloomington: Indiana UP, 1987.

Deleuze, Gilles, and Felix Guattari. *Anti-Oedipus: Capitalism and Schizophrenia.* Trans. Helen R. Lane, Robert Hurley, and Mark Seem. Minneapolis: U of Minnesota P, 1983.

Demastes, William W. "Of Sciences and the Arts: From Influence to Interplay between Natural Philosophy and Drama." *Studies in the Literary Imagination* 23.2 (1991): 75–89.

——. "Re-Inspecting the Crack in the Chimney: Chaos Theory from Ibsen to Stoppard." *New Theatre Quarterly* 10 (1994): 242–54.

——. *Theatre of Chaos: Beyond Absurdism, into Orderly Disorder.* Cambridge, UK: Cambridge UP, 1998.

Dempsey, Shawna, and Lorri Millan. *Mary Medusa. Canadian Theatre Review* 76 (1993): 42–57.

Dennett, Daniel C. *Consciousness Explained.* Boston: Little, 1991.

Derrida, Jacques. *Of Grammatology.* Trans. Gayatri Chakravorty Spivak. Baltimore: Johns Hopkins UP, 1976.

Deverell, Rex. "Author's Statement." Schmalz, ed. 138–39.

———. *Beyond Batoche. Deverell of the Globe.* Ed. Don Perkins. Edmonton: NeWest, 1989. 73–134.

Deverell, Rex, and Wayne Schmalz. *The Riel Commission: An Inquiry into the Survival of a People.* Schmalz, ed. 61–79.

Diamond, Elin. "The Violence of 'We': Politicizing Identification." Reinelt and Roach 390–98.

"Difference between Lambton, Huron Farmers Is Displayed in *Farm Show.*" *Advertiser-Topic* [Petrolia, ON] 2 July 1975.

DNA Theatre. "Features." Unpublished ts., 1991.

———. *The Panel: A Devastation Concerning AIDS.* Videotape. Toronto: Buddies in Bad Times Theatre, 1990.

Dolan, Jill. *The Feminist Spectator as Critic.* Ann Arbor: U of Michigan P, 1988.

———. *Presence and Desire.* Ann Arbor: U of Michigan P, 1993.

Dollimore, Jonathan, and Alan Sinfield. "History and Ideology: The Instance of *Henry V.*" Drakakis 206–27.

———, eds. *Political Shakespeare: New Essays in Cultural Materialism.* Ithaca: Cornell UP, 1985.

Domm, Bill. Letter. 29 Feb. 1988. Press kit, *The Greatest Show.*

Donkin, Ellen, and Susan Clement, eds. *Upstaging Big Daddy: Directing Theater as if Gender and Race Matter.* Ann Arbor: U of Michigan P, 1993.

Dragland, Stan. "Afterword: Reaney's Relevance." *Essays on Canadian Writing* 23–24 (1983–84): 211–35.

———. "James Reaney's Pulsating Dance in and out of Forms." Helwig, *Human Elements: Second Series* 112–33.

Drakakis, John, ed. *Alternative Shakespeares.* London: Methuen, 1985.

Druick, Don. *Where Is Kabuki?* Toronto: Playwrights Canada, 1988.

Eagleton, Terry. *William Shakespeare.* Oxford: Blackwell, 1986.

Eliade, Mircea. *Rites and Symbols of Initiation.* Trans. Willard R. Trask. New York: Harper, 1965.

Emerson, Caryl. "The Outer Word and Inner Speech: Bakhtin, Vygotsky, and the Internalization of Language." Morson, *Bakhtin* 21–40.

———. "The Tolstoy Connection in Bakhtin." Morson and Emerson 149–70.

Endres, Robin. "Many Authors Make a Play." *Globe and Mail* 14 Mar. 1975, TV Ontario supplement.

Esslin, Martin. *The Theatre of the Absurd.* Garden City, NY: Doubleday, 1969.

Evans, Malcolm. "Deconstructing Shakespeare's Comedies." Drakakis 67–94.

Everett-Green, Robert. "Inspired by an Immigrant's Anguish." Preview of *Patria 1: The Characteristics Man,* by R. Murray Schafer, Canadian Opera Company-Shaw Festival at the Texaco Opera Theatre. *Globe and Mail* 21 Nov. 1987: C3.

———. "A Peek at Schafer's *Greatest.*" Rev. of *Patria 3: The Greatest Show,* preview version, by R. Murray Schafer, Theatre Autumn Leaf at Crary Park, Peterborough. *Globe and Mail* 10 Aug. 1987: C11.

———. "Polemics and Poetry." *Globe and Mail* 16 Feb. 1991: C8.

———. "Schafer, Peterborough Festival Embark on Long-Term Alliance." *Globe and Mail* 28 June 1989: C19.

———. "Undisciplined Script Detracts from *Patria's* Superb Music." Rev. of *Patria I: The Characteristics Man,* by R. Murray Schafer, Canadian Opera Company-Shaw Festival at the Texaco Opera Theatre. *Globe and Mail* 23 Nov. 1987: C8.

Eysteinsson, Astradur. *The Concept of Modernism*. Ithaca: Cornell UP, 1990.

Fergusson, Francis. Introduction. Aristotle 1–44.

Filewod, Alan. "Acting AIDS: Gender and Audience in Canadian Plays about HIV." Paper presented at the Association of Canadian Theatre History meetings, May 1991.

———. "Averting the Colonial Gaze: Notes on Watching Native Theatre." *Aboriginal Voices: Amerindian, Inuit, and Sami Theatre*. Ed. Per K. Brask and William Morgan. Baltimore: Johns Hopkins UP, 1992.

———. "Collective Creation: Process, Politics, and Poetics." *Canadian Theatre Review* 34 (1982): 46–58.

———. *Collective Encounters: Documentary Theatre in English Canada*. Toronto: U of Toronto P, 1987.

———. Introduction. Filewod, ed. xi–xx.

———, ed. *The CTR Anthology: Fifteen Plays from* Canadian Theatre Review. Toronto: U of Toronto P, 1993.

———. "'One Big Ontario': Nation-Building in *the Village of the Small Huts*." Brask, ed. 208–20.

Findley, Timothy. *Famous Last Words*. Toronto: Clark, 1981.

Fischer, Michael M.J. "Ethnicity and the Post-Modern Arts of Memory." Clifford and Marcus 194–223.

Fiske, John. *Understanding Popular Culture*. New York: Routledge, 1989.

Fogel, Aaron. "Coerced Speech and the Oedipus Dialogue Complex." Morson and Emerson 173–96.

Forte, Jeanie, and Christine Sumption. "Encountering *Dora*: Putting Theory into Practice." Donkin and Clement 37–52.

Foster, Dennis A. *Confession and Complicity in Narrative*. Cambridge, UK: Cambridge UP, 1987.

Foucault, Michel. *The Foucault Reader*. Ed. Paul Rabinow. New York: Pantheon, 1984.

———. *An Introduction*. Trans. Robert Hurley. New York: Vintage, 1980. Vol. 1 of *History of Sexuality*.

———. Preface. Deleuze and Guattari xi–xiv.

Fowler, Alastair. *Kinds of Literature*. Cambridge, MA: Harvard UP, 1982.

Fox, Charlie, and Mark Hamilton. *Dignity and Grace: The Story of the Eramosa Community Play* The Spirit of Shivaree. Videotape. Guelph: Hamilton-Fox Video, 1992.

Frazer, James G. *The Golden Bough: A Study in Magic and Religion*. 1890. London: Oxford UP, 1994.

French, David. "David French." Anthony 233–50.

———. "David French." Interview with Cynthia Zimmerman. Wallace and Zimmerman 304–16.

———. *Leaving Home*. Toronto: New, 1972.

———. *Of the Fields, Lately*. Toronto: New, 1975.

Freud, Sigmund. *The Ego and the Id*. Trans. Joan Riviere. Rev. and ed. James Strachey. New York: Norton, 1960.

———. *The Interpretation of Dreams*. Trans. James Strachey. Ed. Angela Richards. The Penguin Freud Library 4. Harmondsworth, UK: Penguin, 1991.

———. *On Sexuality: Three Essays on the Theory of Sexuality and Other Works*. Trans. James Strachey. Ed. Angela Richards. The Penguin Freud Library 7. Harmondsworth, UK: Penguin, 1991.

Frye, Northrop. *Anatomy of Criticism: Four Essays*. Princeton: Princeton UP, 1957.

——. "The Argument of Comedy." *Shakespeare: Modern Essays in Criticism.* Rev. ed. Ed. Leonard F. Dean. London: Oxford UP, 1967. 79–89.

——. *The Great Code: The Bible and Literature.* Toronto: Harcourt, 1983.

——. *The Myth of Deliverance.* Toronto: U of Toronto P, 1983.

——. *A Natural Perspective: The Development of Shakespearean Comedy and Romance.* New York: Columbia UP, 1965.

——. *Words with Power: Being a Second Study of the Bible and Literature.* Harmondsworth, UK: Penguin, 1990.

Fuss, Diana. *Essentially Speaking: Feminism, Nature, and Difference.* New York: Routledge, 1989.

Galloway, Myron. Rev. of *Jacob's Wake,* by Michael Cook. Conolly 188–89.

Garber, Marjorie. *Shakespeare's Ghost Writers: Literature and Uncanny Causality.* New York: Methuen, 1987.

Gardiner, Michael. *The Dialogics of Critique.* London: Routledge, 1992.

Garnhum, Ken. *Beuys Buoys Boys: A Monologue.* Wallace, ed. 59–94.

——. *Pants on Fire.* Unpublished ts., 1994.

——. *Surrounded by Water.* Sherman 11–38.

George, David. "Quantum Theatre — a New Paradigm?" *New Theatre Quarterly* 5 (1989): 171–79.

Gilbert, Sandra, and Susan Gubar. *Madwoman in the Attic: The Woman Writer and the Nineteenth-Century Literary Imagination.* New Haven: Yale UP, 1979.

Gilbert, Sky. "The Scenography of Hillar Liitoja: Childish Glee." *Canadian Theatre Review* 70 (1992): 27–28.

Gilbert, Sky, et al. "New Directions on Directing: A Panel." *Theatrum* 10 (1988): 19–27.

Gleick, James. *Chaos: Making a New Science.* New York: Penguin, 1988.

Godard, Barbara. "(Re)Appropriation as Translation." *Canadian Theatre Review* 64 (1990): 22–31.

Golding, Sue. "Quantum Philosophy, Impossible Geographies, and a Few Small Points about Life, Liberty, and the Pursuit of Sex (All in the Name of Democracy)." Keith and Pile 206–19.

Gomez, Maria Teresa. "Shifting Borders: A Project of Interculturalism in Canadian Theatre." MA thesis, U of Guelph, 1993.

Gomez, Mayte. "Healing the Border Wound: *Fronteras Americanas* and the Future of Canadian Multiculturalism." *Theatre Research in Canada/Recherches théâtrales au Canada* 16.1–2 (1995): 26–39.

Gramsci, Antonio. *Prison Notebooks.* 2 vols. New York: Columbia UP, 1991.

Grant, J.K. (Quaker Oats Company). Letter. 8 Mar. 1988. Press kit, *The Greatest Show.*

Greenland, Bill. "We Three, You and I." Brissenden, ed. *Now in Paperback.* 13–24.

Hale, Amanda. "Dialectical Drama of Facts and Fiction on the Feminist Fringe." Tregebov 77–100.

Hall, Lynda. "Bodies in Sight: Shawna Dempsey (Re)Configures Desire." *Canadian Theatre Review* 92 (1997): 10–16.

Hall, Nina, ed. *Exploring Chaos: A Guide to the New Science of Disorder.* New York: Norton, 1991.

Hamill, Tony, ed. *Big Time Women from Way Back When.* Toronto: Playwrights Canada, 1993.

Hamilton, Dale. *The Spirit of Shivaree: A Community Play for Eramosa Township.* Toronto: Playwrights Canada Compuscript, 1990.

Hancock, Geoff. "Michael Hollingsworth." Toye 362.

Handke, Peter. *Kaspar and Other Plays.* Trans. Michael Roloff. New York: Farrar, 1969.

Hart, Lynda. "Identity and Seduction." Hart and Phelan 119–37.

Hart, Lynda, and Peggy Phelan, eds. *Acting Out: Feminist Performance.* Ann Arbor: U of Michigan P, 1993.

Hawking, Stephen. *A Brief History of Time: From the Big Bang to Black Holes.* New York: Bantam, 1988.

Hay, Peter. Introduction. Simons 7–11.

Hayles, N. Katherine. *Chaos Bound: Orderly Disorder in Contemporary Science and Literature.* Ithaca: Cornell UP, 1990.

Helwig, David, ed. *The Human Elements: Critical Essays.* Toronto: Oberon, 1978.

——, ed. *The Human Elements: Second Series.* Toronto: Oberon, 1981.

Herbert, Nick. *Quantum Reality: Beyond the New Physics.* New York: Doubleday, 1985.

Herndl, Diane Price. "The Dilemmas of a Feminine Dialogic." Bauer and McKinstry 7–24.

Herrick, Marvin J. *Comic Theory in the Sixteenth Century.* Urbana: U of Illinois P, 1964.

Herst, Beth. *A Woman's Comedy.* Hamill 143–236.

——. "*A Woman's Comedy*: Male Plots or Female Experience?" *Canadian Theatre Review* 72 (1992): 76–78.

Highway, Tomson. *The Rez Sisters.* Saskatoon: Fifth House, 1988.

Hilton, Julian. "The Other Oxfordshire Theatre: The Nature of Community Art and Action." *Theatre Quarterly* 9 (1979): 53–61.

Hirschkop, Ken. "A Response to the Forum on Mikhail Bakhtin." Morson, ed. 73–80.

Hodgdon, Barbara. *The End Crowns All: Closure and Contradiction in Shakespeare's History.* Princeton: Princeton UP, 1991.

Hodkinson, Yvonne. *Female Parts: The Art and Politics of Female Playwrights.* Montreal: Black Rose, 1991.

Hollingsworth, Margaret. *Endangered Species: Four Plays.* Toronto: Act One, 1988.

——. "Margaret Hollingsworth." Interview with Judith Rudakoff. Rudakoff and Much 144–64.

——. *Willful Acts: Five Plays.* Toronto: Coach House, 1985.

Hollingsworth, Michael. *Clear Light.* Toronto: Coach House, 1973.

——. *The History of the Village of the Small Huts, Parts 1–7.* Winnipeg: Blizzard, 1994.

——. *Strawberry Fields.* Brissenden, ed. *Factory* 285–313.

Holquist, Michael. *Dialogism: Bakhtin and His World.* London: Routledge, 1990.

——. Introduction. Bakhtin, *Dialogic Imagination* xv–xxxiv.

——. "The Politics of Representation." *Allegory and Representation: Selected Papers from the English Institute, 1979–80.* Ed. Stephen J. Greenblatt. Baltimore: Johns Hopkins UP, 1981. 162–83.

Hood, Sarah B. Rev. of *"Patria" and the Theatre of Confluence*, by R. Murray Schafer. *Theatrum* 26 (1991–92): 10.

Hood, Sarah B., with C.J. Malcolm. "Ritual Abuse: The Urge for and the Effects of Re-Ritualizing the Theatre." *Theatrum* 30 (1992): 18–23.

Hopkins, Elizabeth. "Beverley Simons." Toye 758.

Howard, Tony. "Theatre of Urban Renewal: The Uncomfortable Case of Covent Garden." *Theatre Quarterly* 10 (1980): 33–46.

Hunt, Nigel. "Hillar Liitoja: Chaos and Control." *Canadian Theatre Review* 52 (1987): 45–49.

Hutcheon, Linda. "Canadian Historiographic Metafiction." *Essays on Canadian Writing* 30 (1984–85): 228–38.

——. *The Politics of Postmodernism*. London: Routledge, 1989.

——. *A Theory of Parody*. London: Methuen, 1985.

Jacobs, Deborah. "Critical Imperialism and Renaissance Drama: The Case of *The Roaring Girl*." Bauer and McKinstry 73–84.

Jameson, Fredric R. *Fables of Aggression: Wyndham Lewis the Modernist Fascist*. Berkeley: U of California P, 1979.

——. *Marxism and Form: 20th Century Dialectical Theories of Literature*. Princeton: Princeton UP, 1971.

——. *The Political Unconscious: Narrative as a Socially Symbolic Act*. Ithaca: Cornell UP, 1981.

——. *Postmodernism: Or, The Cultural Logic of Late Capitalism*. Durham: Duke UP, 1991.

Jeffery, Lawrence. *Four Plays*. Toronto: Exile, 1992.

Jellicoe, Ann. *Community Plays: How to Put Them On*. London: Methuen, 1987.

Jenkins, Anthony. "Tom Cone." Benson and Conolly 111–12.

Jewinski, Ed. "Jacob Mercer's Lust for Victimization." Conolly 92–94.

Johnson, Chris. "George F. Walker: B-Movies beyond the Absurd." *Canadian Literature* 85 (1980): 87–103.

——. "George F Walker Directs George F Walker." *Theatre History in Canada / Histoire du théâtre au Canada* 9.2 (1988): 157–72.

——. "Is That Us? Ray Lawlor's *Summer of the Seventeenth Doll* and David French's *Leaving Home*." *Canadian Drama / L'Art dramatique canadien* 6 (1980): 30–42.

Johnston, Denis W. "Playwrights and Collectives at Theatre Passe Muraille: An Historical Review." *Canadian Drama / L'Art dramatique canadien* 15.1 (1989): 63–74.

——. *Up the Mainstream: The Rise of Toronto's Alternative Theatres*. Toronto: U of Toronto P, 1991.

Jones, Manina. "'The Collage in Motion': Staging the Documentary in Reaney's *Sticks and Stones*." *Canadian Drama / L'Art dramatique canadien* 16.1 (1990): 1–22.

Jonson, Ben. *Bartholomew Fair*. 1614. Ed. E.A. Horsman. Manchester: Manchester UP, 1979.

Kane, Margo. "Moonlodge." *An Anthology of Canadian Native Literature in English*. Ed. Daniel David Moses and Terry Goldie. Toronto: Oxford UP, 1992. 278–91.

Kaplan, Jon, and Jill Lawless. "Garnhum Fired Up." *Now* 31 Mar.–6 Apr. 1994.

Kareda, Urjo. Introduction. French, *Leaving Home* v–x.

——. "R. Murray Schafer without the Panoramic Explosions." Rev. of *Patria 2: Requiem for the Party Girl*, concert version, by R. Murray Schafer, Theatre Autumn Leaf with Arraymusic at the DuMaurier Theatre Centre. *Globe and Mail* 20 Oct. 1993: C5.

Kauffman, Stuart. *At Home in the Universe: The Search for Laws of Self-Organization and Complexity*. Oxford: Oxford UP, 1995.

Kavanagh, James H. "Shakespeare and Ideology." Drakakis 144–65.

Kehde, Suzanne. "Voices from the Margin: Bag Ladies and Others." Bauer and McKinstry 25–38.

Keith, Michael, and Steve Pile, eds. *Place and the Politics of Identity*. London: Routledge, 1993.

Keller, Evelyn Fox. "The Biological Gaze." Robertson et al. 107–21.

Kelly, Thomas P. *The Black Donnellys*. Toronto: Modern Canadian Library, 1974.

Kermode, Frank. *The Sense of an Ending: Studies in the Theory of Fiction*. London: Oxford UP, 1967.

Kershaw, Baz. *The Politics of Performance: Radical Theatre as Cultural Intervention*. London: Routledge, 1992.

Keys, Janice. "Theatre Stands on Its Feet, Now It Must Move: Director." *Winnipeg Free Press* 6 Nov. 1975.

Keyssar, Helene. "Drama and the Dialogic Imagination: *The Heidi Chronicles* and *Fefu and Her Friends*." *Modern Drama* 34.1 (1991): 88–106.

——. *Feminist Theatre: An Introduction to Plays of Contemporary British and American Women*. New York: Grove, 1985.

Kirby, Michael. "Happenings: An Introduction." Sandford 1–28.

——. "The New Theatre." Sandford 29–47.

Kirby, Michael, and Richard Schechner. "An Interview with John Cage." Sandford 51–71.

Kirchhoff, H.J. "Encounters with the Nude and the Rude." Rev. of *Groove*, by Wendy Agnew and Darren O'Donnell, Pow Pow Unbound at Buddies in Bad Times Theatre. *Globe and Mail* 5 Mar. 1993: C5.

Klee, Paul. "On Modern Art." *Modern Artists on Art*. Ed. Robert L. Herbert. Englewood Cliffs, NJ: Prentice-Hall, 1964. 74–91.

Knowles, Richard Paul. Afterword. Krizanc, *The Half of It* 169–72.

——. "The Dramaturgy of the Perverse." *Theatre Research International* 17.3 (1992): 226–35.

——. "*Homo Ludens*: Canadian Theatre, Canadian Football, Shakespeare, and the NHL." *Canadian Drama/L'Art dramatique canadien* 10.1 (1984): 65–74.

——. "The Mulgrave Road Co-op: Theatre and the Community in Guysborough County, N.S." *Canadian Drama/L'Art dramatique canadien* 12.1 (1986): 18–32.

——. "Post-, 'Grapes,' Nuts and Flakes: 'Coach's Corner' as Post-Colonial Performance." *Modern Drama* 38.1 (1995): 123–30.

——. "Reading Material: Transfers, Remounts, and the Production of Meaning in Contemporary Toronto Drama and Theatre." *Essays on Canadian Writing* 51–52 (1993–94): 258–95.

——. "Replaying History: Canadian Historiographic Metadrama." *Dalhousie Review* 67 (1987): 228–43.

——. "Richard Rose in Rehearsal." *Canadian Theatre Review* 42 (1985): 134–40.

——. "'A Sense of History Here': Mary Vingoe's *Holy Ghosters, 1776*." *The Red Jeep and Other Landscapes: A Collection in Honour of Douglas Lochhead*. Ed. Peter Thomas. Fredericton: Goose Lane, 1987. 20–27.

——. "'The Truth Must Out': The Political Plays of John Krizanc." *Canadian Drama/L'Art dramatique canadien* 13.1 (1987): 27–33.

——. "Voices (off): Deconstructing the Modern English-Canadian Dramatic Canon." *Canadian Canons: Essays in Literary Value*. Ed. Robert Lecker. Toronto: U of Toronto P, 1991. 91–111.

Kremer, Prapassaree, and Jeffery Kremer. "Stoppard's *Arcadia*: Research, Time, Loss." *Modern Drama* 40.1 (1997): 1–10.

Kristeva, Julia. *Desire in Language: A Semiotic Approach*. Ed. Leon Roudiez. Trans. Thomas Gora, Alice Jardine, and Roudiez. New York: Columbia UP, 1993.

——. *Powers of Horror: An Essay on Abjection*. Trans. Leon S. Roudiez. New York: Columbia UP, 1982.

Krizanc, John. *The Half of It*. Toronto: Anansi, 1990.

——. "Innocents Abroad." *Saturday Night* Nov. 1984: 34–38.

——. *Tamara*. Toronto: Stoddart, 1989.

——. "*Tamara* Takes Off." Interview with Jon Kaplan. *Canadian Theatre Review* 44 (1985): 135–38.

Kroker, Arthur. *The Possessed Individual: Technology and Postmodernity*. London: Macmillan, 1992.

Lacan, Jacques. *Écrits: A Selection*. Trans. Alan Sheridan. New York: Norton, 1977.

Lacey, Liam. "An Exercise in Virtual Tourism." Rev. of *Sleeproom*, by Sally Clark et al., Theatre Passe Muraille. *Globe and Mail* 8 Jan. 1993: C6.

Laing, R.D. *The Divided Self*. Harmondsworth, UK: Penguin, 1965.

Lane, Harry. "Lizzie Borden and Sharon Pollock's *Blood Relations*: Metadrama and Mythologizing." Paper presented at the Association for Theatre in Higher Education, Seattle, Aug. 1991.

Lebel, Jean-Jacques. "On the Necessity of Violation." Sandford 268–84.

Lemon, Lee T., and Marion J. Reis, trans. and eds. *Russian Formalist Criticism: Four Essays*. Lincoln: U of Nebraska P, 1965.

Leonard, Paul. "The Scenography of Hillar Liitoja: Privacy and Senses." *Canadian Theatre Review* 70 (1992): 29–31.

Lévi-Strauss, Claude. *Structural Anthropology*. Trans. Claire Jacobson and Brooke Grundfest Schoepf. New York: Basic, 1963.

Liitoja, Hillar. *The Last Supper*. Toronto: ArtBiz, 1995.

——. "Liitoja Scores." *Theatrum* 8 (1987): 19–21.

——. "To Make Your Spirits Soar." Interview with Kate Taylor. *Globe and Mail* 1 May 1993: C3.

Lister, Rota. "Beverley Rosen Simons." Benson and Conolly 497.

——. "Crabdance." Benson and Conolly 118.

Little, Edward J., and R. Alex Sim. *Dramatic Action: How Eramosa Township Faced Its Problems*. Guelph: Ontario Rural Learning Association in Cooperation with the School of Rural Planning, U of Guelph, 1992.

Little, Edward J., and Ann Wilson, eds. *Canadian Theatre Review* 90 (1997).

Longhurst, Derek, ed. *Gender, Genre, and Narrative Pleasure*. London: Unwin, 1989.

Lyotard, Jean François. *The Postmodern Condition: A Report on Knowledge*. Trans. Geoff Bennington and Brian Massumi. Minneapolis: U of Minnesota P, 1984.

MacIvor, Daniel. *House/Humans*. Toronto: Coach House, 1992.

——. *See Bob Run and Wild Abandon*. Toronto: Playwrights Canada, 1990.

——. *2 Plays: Never Swim Alone and This Is a Play*. Toronto: Playwrights Canada, 1993.

——. *2-2-Tango: A Two-Man-One-Man-Show*. Wallace, ed. 189–218.

MacLeish, Archibald. *Poetry and Experience*. Cambridge, MA: Riverside, 1961.

Malone, Judy. "Memories Live in *Farm Show*." *London Free Press* 26 June 1975.

Mandelbrot, Benoit. "Fractals — a Geometry of Nature." Nina Hall 122–35.

Manguel, Alberto. Foreword. Krizanc, *Tamara* 3–7.

Marcuse, Herbert. *Negations: Essays in Critical Theory*. Boston: Beacon, 1969.

Martineau, Alain. *Herbert Marcuse's Utopia*. Montreal: Harvest House, 1986.

Massey, Doreen. "Politics and Space/Time." Keith and Pile 141–61.

McConachie, Bruce. "Approaching the 'Structure of Feeling' in Grassroots Theatre." *Theatre Topics* 8.1 (1998): 33–53.

McKinnie, Michael. "Calling Off the Border Patrol: Bhabha's 'The Other Question' and Guillermo Verdecchia's *Fronteras Americanas*." Paper presented at the Cultural Studies in Canada conference, U of Toronto, 12 May 1994.

——. "King-Maker: Reading Theatrical Presentations of Canadian Political History." *Theatre Research in Canada/Recherches théâtrales au Canada* 15.2 (1994): 164–90.

Middleton, Jesse Edgar. *A Pageant of Nursing in Canada*. Toronto: Canadian Nurses Association, 1934.

Mighton, John. *The Little Years.* Toronto: Playwrights Canada, 1995.
——. *Possible Worlds and A Short History of Night.* Toronto: Playwrights Canada, 1992.
——. *Scientific Americans.* Toronto: Playwrights Canada, 1987.
Miller, Mary Jane. "Radio's Children." *Canadian Theatre Review* 36 (1982): 30–39.
——. "Two Versions of Rick Salutin's *Les Canadiens.*" *Theatre History in Canada/Histoire du théâtre au Canada* 1.1 (1980): 57–69.
——. "The Use of Stage Metaphor in *The Donnellys.*" *Canadian Drama/L'Art dramatique canadien* 8.1 (1982): 34–41.
Mitchell, Ken. *Rebels in Time: Three Plays.* Ed. Don Kerr and Diane Bessai. Edmonton: NeWest, 1991.
Mojica, Monique. *Princess Pocahontas and the Blue Spots.* Toronto: Women's, 1991.
Mombourquette, Mary Pat. "Walker's Women in the East End Plays." MA thesis, U of Guelph, 1990.
Montrose, Louis A. "Professing the Renaissance: The Poetics and Politics of Culture." *The New Historicism.* Ed. H. Aram Veeser. London: Routledge, 1989. 15–36.
Moore, Sonia. *The Stanislavski System: The Professional Training of an Actor.* Rev. ed. Harmondsworth, UK: Penguin, 1976.
Morowitz, Harold J., and Harold L. Singer, eds. *The Mind, the Brain, and Complex Adaptive Systems.* Vol. 21. London: Addison-Wesley, 1995.
Morson, Gary Saul, ed. *Bakhtin: Essays and Dialogues on His Work.* Chicago: U of Chicago P, 1986.
——. "Who Speaks for Bakhtin?" Morson, ed. 1–19.
Morson, Gary Saul, and Caryl Emerson, eds. *Rethinking Bakhtin: Extensions and Challenges.* Evanston: Northwestern UP, 1989.
Moses, Daniel David. *Almighty Voice and His Wife.* Stratford: Williams-Wallace, 1992.
——. "Daniel David Moses." Interview with Hartmut Lutz. *Contemporary Challenges: Conversations with Canadian Native Authors.* Saskatoon: Fifth House, 1991. 155–68.
"Mother Gets Six Years for Slaying Child's Killer." *Toronto Star* 3 Mar. 1983: n. pag. Rpt. in *Canadian Theatre Review* 43 (1985): 156.
Much, Rita, ed. *Women on the Canadian Stage: The Legacy of Hrotsvit.* Winnipeg: Blizzard, 1992.
The Mulgrave Road Co-op Theatre. "The Mulgrave Road Show." Unpublished ts., 1977.
Mullaly, Edward. Rev. of *Of the Fields, Lately,* by David French. Conolly 132–33.
Mulvey, Laura. "Visual Pleasure and Narrative Cinema." *Screen* 16.3 (1975): 6–18.
The Mummers Troupe. *Buchans: A Mining Town. Canadian Drama/L'Art dramatique canadien* 13.1 (1987): 72–116.
Munday, Jenny. "The View from Inside the Electrolux." *Canadian Theatre Review* 71 (1992): 88–91.
Murray, Timothy. "The Theatricality of the Van-Guard: Ideology and Contemporary American Theatre." *Performing Arts Journal* 24 (1984): 93–99.
Murrell, John. *Waiting for the Parade.* Vancouver: Talonbooks, 1980.
Neill, Mary. "The Play-within-the-Play in R. Murray Schafer's *The Greatest Show.*" Schafer, *Patria* 216–21.
Nelson, Steve. "Redecorating the Fourth Wall: Environmental Theatre Today." *TDR* 33.3 (1989): 72–94.
Nunn, Robert C. "The Meeting of Actuality and Theatricality in *The Farm Show.*" *Canadian Drama/L'Art dramatique canadien* 8.1 (1982): 42–54.
——. "Performing Fact: Canadian Documentary Theatre." *Canadian Literature* 103 (1984): 51–62.

——. "Sharon Pollock's Plays: A Review Article." *Theatre History in Canada/Histoire du théâtre au canada* 5.1 (1984): 72–83.

O'Connor, Mary. "Subject, Voice, and Women in Some Contemporary Black American Women's Writing." Bauer and McKinstry 199–218.

Oram, John. "The Marriage of Two Minds." Colway Trust Publicity Material. Eramosa Community Play Archives, U of Guelph, n.d.

Page, Malcolm. "Sharon Pollock: Committed Playwright." *Canadian Drama/L'Art dramatique canadien* 5.2 (1979): 104–11.

Palmer, John. *Henrik Ibsen on the Necessity of Producing Norwegian Drama.* Filewod, ed. 35–46.

Parker, Brian. "On the Edge: Michael Cook's Newfoundland Trilogy." *Canadian Literature* 85 (1980): 22–43.

Parker, Gerald D. "History, Story, and Story-Style: James Reaney's *The Donnellys.*" *Canadian Drama/L'Art dramatique canadien* 4.2 (1978): 150–59.

——. *How to Play: The Theatre of James Reaney.* Toronto: ECW, 1991.

Paster, Gail Kern. "Leaky Vessels: The Incontinent Women of City Comedy." *Renaissance Drama* ns 18 (1987): 43–66.

Pater, Walter. *The Renaissance: Studies in Art and Poetry.* Ed. Donald L. Hill. Berkeley: U of California P, 1980.

Payzant, Geoffrey. Foreword. Young 7–9.

Perkyns, Richard. "*Jacob's Wake* and the European Tradition." *Canadian Drama/L'Art dramatique canadien* 15.2 (1989): 159–68.

——. *Major Plays of the Canadian Theatre 1934–1984.* Toronto: Irwin, 1984.

Phelan, Peggy. "Reciting the Citation of Others; Or, A Second Introduction." Hart and Phelan 13–31.

——. *Unmarked: The Politics of Performance.* New York: Routledge, 1993.

Phillips, Derek L. *Looking Backward: A Critical Appraisal of Communitarian Thought.* Princeton: Princeton UP, 1993.

Pinkney, Tony. "Editor's Introduction: Modernism and Cultural Theory." Williams, *Politics* 1–29.

Plant, Richard. "The Deconstruction of Pleasure: John Krizanc's *Tamara*, Richard Rose, and the Necessary Angel Theatre Company." *On-Stage and Off-Stage: English-Canadian Drama in Discourse.* Ed. Albert-Rainer Glaap. St. John's: Breakwater, 1996. 189–200.

——, ed. *The Penguin Book of Modern Canadian Drama.* Harmondsworth, UK: Penguin, 1984.

Pollock, Sharon. *Blood Relations and Other Plays.* Edmonton: NeWest, 1981.

——. *Doc.* Toronto: Playwrights Canada, 1986.

——. *Getting It Straight. Heroines: Three Plays.* Ed. Joyce Doolittle. Red Deer: Red Deer College P, 1992. 85–126.

——. *The Komagata Maru Incident.* Toronto: Playwrights Canada, 1978.

——. *The Making of Warriors. Airborne: Radio Plays by Women.* Ed. Ann Jansen. Winnipeg: Blizzard, 1991. 99–132.

——. *Walsh.* Vancouver: Talonbooks, 1973.

Prigogine, Ilya, and Isabelle Stengers. *Order out of Chaos: Man's New Dialogue with Nature.* New York: Bantam, 1984.

Rae, Alastair. *Quantum Physics: Illusion or Reality?* Cambridge, UK: Cambridge UP, 1986.

Rayner, Alice. *To Act, to Do, to Perform: Drama and the Phenomenology of Action.* Ann Arbor: U of Michigan P, 1994.

Read, Alan. *Theatre and Everyday Life: An Ethics of Performance*. London: Routledge, 1993.

Reaney, James. *The Donnellys*. Victoria: Porcèpic, 1983.

——. "An Interview with James Reaney." With Jeffrey Goffin. *Prairie Journal of Canadian Literature* 6 (1986): 3–13.

——. *King Whistle*. Brick 8 (1980): 5–48.

——. *Listen to the Wind*. Vancouver: Talonbooks, 1972.

Reinelt, Janelle G., and Joseph R. Roach, eds. *Critical Theory and Performance*. Ann Arbor: U of Michigan P, 1992.

Rewa, Natalie. "All News Newhouse." *Canadian Theatre Review* 61 (1989): 40–42.

Ridout, Denzil. *United to Serve*. Toronto: United Church of Canada, 1927.

Righter, Anne. *Shakespeare and the Idea of the Play*. Harmondsworth, UK: Penguin, 1967.

Roberts, Mathew. "Poetics Hermeneutics Dialogics: Bakhtin and Paul de Man." Morson and Emerson 115–34.

Robertson, George, et al., eds. *Future Natural: Nature, Science, Culture*. London: Routledge, 1996.

Rochefort, Christine. "Are Women Writers Still Monsters?" *New French Feminisms: An Anthology*. Ed. Elaine Marx and Isabelle de Courtivron. New York: Schocken, 1981. 183–86.

Rose, Jacqueline. "Sexuality in the Reading of Shakespeare: *Hamlet* and *Measure for Measure*." Drakakis 95–118.

Rose, Richard, and D.D. Kugler. "The Words Are Too Important." Interview with Alan Filewod. *Canadian Theatre Review* 61 (1989): 33–39.

Rubin, Don. "Celebrating the Nation: History and Canadian Theatre." *Canadian Theatre Review* 34 (1982): 12–22.

Rudakoff, Judith, and Rita Much. *Fair Play: 12 Women Speak: Conversations with Canadian Playwrights*. Toronto: Simon, 1990.

Ruzylo, Mark. "The Representation of AIDS in Four Canadian Plays." MA thesis, U of Guelph, 1993.

Ryan, Toby Gordan. *Stage Left: Canadian Theatre in the Thirties: A Memoir*. Toronto: CTR, 1981.

Said, Edward. *Orientalism*. New York: Random House, 1978.

——. *The World, the Text, and the Critic*. Cambridge, MA: Harvard UP, 1983.

Salutin, Rick. *Les Canadiens*. Vancouver: Talonbooks, 1977.

——. "Rick Salutin: The Meaning of It All." Interview with Peter Copeman. *Canadian Theatre Review* 34 (1984): 190–97.

Salutin, Rick, and Theatre Passe Muraille. *1837: The Farmers' Revolt*. Toronto: Lorimer, 1976.

Sandford, Mariellen R. *Happenings and Other Acts*. London: Routledge, 1995.

Schafer, R. Murray. *Patria 3: The Greatest Show*. Indian River, ON: Arcana, 1987.

——. *"Patria" and the Theatre of Confluence*. Indian River, ON: Arcana, 1991.

——. "The Princess of the Stars." *Canadian Theatre Review* 47 (1986): 20–28.

——. "The Text: Schafer on *The Greatest Show*." Interview with David Burgess. Burgess 37–38.

——. "The Theatre of Confluence (Note in Advance of Action)." *Open Letter* 4th ser. 4–5 (1979): 30–48.

——. "The Theatre of Confluence II." *Canadian Theatre Review* 47 (1986): 5–19.

Schechner, Richard. "The Decline and Fall of the (American) Avant-Garde." *The End of Humanism*. New York: Performing Arts Journal, 1982. 11–76.

——. *Environmental Theater: An Expanded New Edition Including "Six Axioms for Environmental Theater."* New York: Applause, 1994.

Schmalz, Wayne. Introduction. Deverell and Schmalz vi–x.

——, ed. *Studio One: Stories Made for Radio*. Regina: Coteau, 1990.

Schmitt, Natalie Crohn. *Actors and Onlookers: Theatre and Twentieth-Century Scientific Views of Nature*. Evanston: Northwestern UP, 1990.

Scholar, Michael. "*Beyond Batoche*: The Playwright in Mid-Career." *Canadian Drama/L'Art dramatique canadien* 11.2 (1985): 329–39.

Schwab, Gail M. "Irigarayan Dialogism: Play and Powerplay." Bauer and McKinstry 57–72.

Sears, Djanet. *Afrika Solo*. Toronto: Sister Vision, 1990.

Seem, Mark. Introduction. Deleuze and Guattari xv–xxiv.

Senchuck, Barbara. Rev. of *Holy Ghosters*, by Mary Vingoe, Mulgrave Road Co-op touring production. *Chronicle-Herald/Mail Star* [Halifax] 3 Nov. 1983: E3.

Seremba, George. *Come Good Rain*. Winnipeg: Blizzard, 1993.

——. Publicity material for *Come Good Rain*. Produced by Crow's Theatre/The Canadian Stage, Toronto, at 26 Berkeley Street, Upstairs, 8–26 Mar. 1994.

Sherman, Jason, ed. *Solo*. Toronto: Coach House, 1994.

Shklovsky, Victor. "Art as Technique." Lemon and Reis 3–24.

Showalter, Elaine. "Representing Ophelia: Women, Madness, and the Responsibilities of Feminist Criticism." *Shakespeare and the Question of Theory*. Ed. Patricia Parker and Geoffrey Hartman. New York: Methuen, 1985. 77–94.

Sidnell, Michael. "Ambivalences of Representation." *Canadian Theatre Review* 61 (1989): 43–44.

——. "Fronteras Theatrales." Paper presented at the Association for Canadian Theatre Research, Learned Societies, Ottawa, May 1993.

Silverman, Kaja. *The Subject of Semiotics*. New York: Oxford UP, 1983.

Simons, Beverley. *Crabdance*. Vancouver: Talonbooks, 1969.

Sinfield, Alan. *Faultlines: Cultural Materialism and the Politics of Dissident Reading*. Berkeley: U of California P, 1992.

——. "Give an Account of Shakespeare and Education, Showing Why You Think They Are Effective and What You Have Appreciated about Them. Support Your Comments with Precise References." Dollimore and Sinfield, eds. 134–57.

Smith, Barbara Herrnstein. *Poetic Closure*. Chicago: U of Chicago P, 1968.

Smyth, Donna. *Quilt*. Toronto: Women's Educational, 1982.

Sokoloski, Thom. "The Staging: A Three-Dimensional Illusion." Interview with David Burgess. Burgess 39–40.

Springate, Michael. *Dog and Crow*. Montreal: Guernica, 1990.

Stallybrass, Peter, and Allon White. *The Poetics and Politics of Transgression*. Ithaca: Cornell UP, 1986.

Standjofski, Harry. *Urban Myths: Anton and No Cycle*. Montreal: Nuage, 1992.

States, Bert O. *Great Reckonings in Little Rooms: On the Phenomenology of Theater*. Berkeley: U of California P, 1985.

Stone-Blackburn, Susan. "Feminism and Metadrama: Role-Playing in *Blood Relations*." *Canadian Drama/L'Art dramatique canadien* 15.2 (1989): 169–78.

——. "Maenadic Rites on Stage in Calgary." *Canadian Theatre Review* 69 (1991): 28–33.

Stoppard, Tom. *Arcadia*. London: Faber, 1993.

——. *Hapgood*. New York: French, 1988.

——. *The Real Thing*. London: Faber, 1982.

Surette, Leon. *The Birth of Modernism: Ezra Pound, T.S. Eliot, W.B. Yeats, and the Occult*. Montreal: McGill-Queen's UP, 1993.

Suvin, Darko. "Reflections on Happenings." Sandford 285–309.

Tancock, Martha. "Greatest Show Is Clever Conundrum." *Peterborough Examiner* 7 Aug. 1987.

Theatre Passe Muraille. *Doukhobors*. Toronto: Playwrights Co-op, 1973.

——. *The Farm Show*. Toronto: Coach House, 1976.

——. *I Love You, Baby Blue*. Erin, ON: Porcèpic, 1977.

——. *The Little Years*, by John Mighton. Program. 1995.

Thompson, Judith. *Lion in the Streets*. Toronto: Coach House, 1992.

——. *White Biting Dog*. Rev. ed. Toronto: Playwrights Canada, 1984.

Thompson, Paul. Introduction. Theatre Passe Muraille, *Doukhobors* iv–vi.

——. "Paul Thompson at Theatre Passe Muraille: Bits and Pieces." Interview with Robert Wallace. *Open Letter* 2nd ser. 7 (1974): 49–71.

Todorov, Tsvetan. *Mikhail Bakhtin and the Dialogical Principle*. Trans. Wlad Godzich. Minneapolis: U of Minnesota P, 1984.

Toye, William, ed. *The Oxford Companion to Canadian Literature*. Toronto: Oxford UP, 1983.

Tregebov, Rhea, ed. *Work in Progress: Building Feminist Culture*. Toronto: Women's, 1987.

Tremblay, Michel. *Albertine in Five Times*. Trans. John Van Burek and Bill Glassco. Vancouver: Talonbooks, 1986.

——. *Les Belles Soeurs*. Trans. John Van Burek and Bill Glassco. Vancouver: Talonbooks, 1974.

——. *The Impromptu of Outremont*. Trans. John Van Burek. Vancouver: Talonbooks, 1981.

Twenty-Fifth Street Theatre. *Paper Wheat: The Book*. Saskatoon: Western Producer Prairie, 1982.

Tyson, Brian F. "'Swallowed Up in Darkness': Vision and Division in *Of the Fields, Lately*." *Canadian Drama/L'Art dramatique canadien* 16.1 (1990): 23–31.

Usmiani, Renate. *Second Stage: The Alternative Theatre Movement in Canada*. Vancouver: UBC P, 1983.

Van Laan, Thomas F. *Role-Playing in Shakespeare*. Toronto: U of Toronto P, 1978.

Varley, Catherine M. "Speaking in (Feminist) Tongues." MA thesis, U of Guelph, 1991.

Verdecchia, Guillermo. *Fronteras Americanas*. Toronto: Coach House, 1993.

Vingoe, Mary, and Jan Kudelka. *Hooligans*. *New Canadian Drama 6: Feminist Drama*. Ed. Rita Much. Ottawa: Borealis, 1993. 1–79.

Voaden, Herman. *A Vision of Canada: Herman Voaden's Dramatic Writings 1928–1945*. Ed. Anton Wagner. Toronto: Simon, 1993.

Vogt, Gordon. "The Politics of Entertainment: George Luscombe and TWP." Helwig, *Human Elements: Second Series* 132–60.

Volosinov, V.N. *Freudianism: A Critical Sketch*. Trans. I.R. Titunik. Ed. Titunik and Neal H. Bruss. Bloomington: Indiana UP, 1986.

——. *Marxism and the Philosophy of Language*. Trans. Ladislav Matejka and I.R. Titunik. Cambridge, MA: Harvard UP, 1986.

Wagner, Vit. "*Pants on Fire* Redefines 'Roller Coaster Theatre.'" [From author's clipping file.]

Walker, George F. *Ambush at Tether's End*. Brissenden, ed. *Factory* 89–184.

——. "Looking for the Light: A Conversation with George F. Walker." With Robert Wallace. *Canadian Drama/L'Art dramatique canadien* 14.1 (1988): 22–33.

——. *Love and Anger.* Toronto: Coach House, 1990.

——. *Nothing Sacred.* Toronto: Coach House, 1988.

——. *Prince of Naples.* Brissenden, ed. *Now* 61–102.

——. Program note. *Nothing Sacred. Curtain Call Theatre Magazine,* The Elgin Winter Garden Theatre Centre (1994): 9.

——. *Three Plays: Bagdad Saloon, Beyond Mozambique, Ramona and the White Slaves.* Toronto: Coach House, 1978.

——. *Zastrozzi.* Toronto: Playwrights Co-op, 1979.

Wallace, Robert. "Holding the Focus: Paul Thompson at Theatre Passe Muraille: Ten Years Later." *Canadian Drama/L'Art dramatique canadien* 8.1 (1982): 55–65.

——, ed. *Making, Out: Plays by Gay Men.* Toronto: Coach House, 1992.

——. *Producing Marginality: Theatre and Criticism in Canada.* Saskatoon: Fifth House, 1990.

——. "Theorizing a Queer Theatre: Buddies in Bad Times." Brask, ed. 136–59.

——. "The Victor(y) of the Subject." Introduction. MacIvor, *House/Humans* 7–14.

Wallace, Robert, and Cynthia Zimmerman, eds. *The Work: Conversations with English-Canadian Playwrights.* Toronto: Coach House, 1982.

Wandor, Micheline, ed. *Plays by Women: Volume 3.* London: Methuen, 1984.

Wasserman, Jerry, ed. *Modern Canadian Plays.* 3rd ed. Vol 1. Vancouver: Talonbooks, 1993.

Weimann, Robert. *Shakespeare and the Popular Tradition in the Theatre.* Baltimore: Johns Hopkins UP, 1978.

Weiss, Peter Eliot. *The Haunted House Hamlet.* Toronto: Playwrights Union of Canada [compuscript], 1986.

Westfall, William. Rev. of *1837: William Lyon Mackenzie and the Canadian Revolution,* by Rick Salutin and Theatre Passe Muraille. *Canadian Historical Review* 59 (1978): 71–75.

White, Hayden. *The Content of the Form: Narrative Discourse and Historical Representation.* Baltimore: Johns Hopkins, 1987.

——. *Metahistory: The Historical Imagination in Nineteenth-Century Europe.* Baltimore: Johns Hopkins UP, 1973.

——. *Tropics of Discourse: Essays in Cultural Criticism.* Baltimore: Johns Hopkins UP, 1978.

White, Michèle. Introduction. Michael Hollingsworth, *History* ix–xii.

Whittaker, Herbert. Rev. of *Walsh,* by Sharon Pollock. Connolly 138–40.

Wigston, Nancy. "Nanabush in the City." *Books in Canada* Mar. 1989: 7–9.

Williams, Raymond. *Culture.* London: Fontana, 1981.

——. *The Long Revolution.* Harmondsworth, UK: Penguin, 1965.

——. *The Politics of Modernism: Against the New Conformists.* Ed. Tony Pinkney. London: Verso, 1989.

——. *Problems in Materialism and Culture.* London: Verso, 1980.

Wilson, Ann. "Bored to Distraction: Auto-Performance and the Perniciousness of Presence." *Canadian Theatre Review* 79–80 (1994): 33–37.

——. Introduction to *A Woman's Comedy.* Hamill 145–50.

——. "The Politics of the Script." *Canadian Theatre Review* 43 (1985): 174–79.

Winslow, Robert. *The Cavan Blazers.* Ennismore, ON: Ordinary, 1993.

Winter, Jack, and Cedric Smith. *Ten Lost Years.* Filewod, ed. 133–90.

Wise, Jennifer. "Marginalizing Drama: Bakhtin's Theory of Genre." *Essays in Theatre* 8.1 (1989): 15–22.

Wolf, Fred Alan. *Taking the Quantum Leap: The New Physics for Non-Scientists.* New York: Harper, 1989.

Wright, Richard, and Robin Endres, eds. *Eight Men Speak and Other Plays for the Canadian Workers' Theatre.* Toronto: New Hogtown, 1976.

Yaeger, Patricia. Afterword. Bauer and McKinstry 239–45.

Young, David. *Glenn.* Toronto: Coach House, 1992.

Young, Pamela. "Midway of Black Magic." *Maclean's* 5 Sept. 1988: 70.

Index

-oriented theatre, 110, 111, 245n6; relational, 109, 111; representation, 113, 114;
structure, 112; territorial, 109, 111, 114,
115, temporal, 109, 114, 115. *See also*
Colway Theatre Trust, Community
play.
Community play, 108, 115–16, 214; and
construction of history, 117, 246n10;
and cultural intervention, 108–9, 111,
114, 116–17; participation in, 110–13,
117, 118, 119; as process, 112, 113–14;
subject community as audience of, 85,
87, 89, 94, 96, 241n14–15, 252n18
Complex adaptive systems, 214, 215
Cone, Tom, 53, 56, 197, 237n7; *Beautiful
Tigers*, 60–61; *Cubistique*, 58–60, 61, 63
Conlogue, Ray, 38, 42
Cook, Michael, 52, 53, 56, 196–97;
autobiographical aspects of writing,
39–40; cultural position of, 42–43;
Jacob's Wake, 25, 31–32, 38–43, 233n19,
234n20; oedipal aspects of writing, 46,
48
Copeland, Nancy, 100, 249n23
Coveney, Peter, 221
Cowan, Cindy, 91, 92, 93, 94, 96,
243n27–28
Crisis, 38
Cubistique (Cone), 58–60, 61, 63
Cultural values: circulation of, 97; transmission of, 91, 93; transformation of,
95, 98
Culture: affirmation of, 36, 108, 113, 172,
173, 175, 176; consciousness of, 210;
and identity; 206; intervention in, 96,
108–9, 111, 114, 116–17; and memory,
147; products of, 98, 206; reproduction
of, 91

Dafoe, Christopher, 58–59, 61
de Certeau, Michel, 148–49, 154, 161,
189–90, 248n20
de Lauretis, Teresa, 34–35, 91, 97
Deleuze, Gilles, 47, 48, 81, 235n25
Demastes, William, 215, 218
Dempsey, Shawna: *Mary Medusa*, 80, 99,
103–5
Derrida, Jacques, 216
Desire, 82, 101, 177; displacement of, 28,
47, 89; and lack, 89, 90, 232n8; and

narrative, 35; Oedipal, 35, 39, 48;
repressed, 38–39; surplus, 30
Deverell, Rex, 138, 145, 247n9; *Beyond
Batoche*, 142–44
Dialectic, 171, 172
Dialogic monologue, 193–97, 210; auto-
biographical, 198–202; and ethnicity,
205–8; feminist, 203–5
Dialogism, 45, 64, 201, 210; and carnival,
202–3, 204, 206, 208, 209; dramaturgi-
cal, 123, 195, 197; and intertextuality,
193; politics of, 217
Diamond, Elin, 30, 230n2
Diving (Hollingsworth, Margaret), 204
DNA Theatre (Toronto), 179, 180–82, 184
Dog and Crow (Springate), 66–67
Dolan, Jill, 105
Dollimore, Jonathan, 236n2
Donnellys, The (Reaney), 124–28
Doukhobors (Theatre Passe Muraille),
84–85
Dramaturgy: dialogic, 123, 195, 197; mod-
ernist, 161, 214, 237n7; neo-
Aristotelian, 45, 226; oedipal, 28, 31, 37
Dramaturgy of the perverse, 44–49, 50–52,
64, 67–68, 71
Druick, Don, 65, 68, 71; *Where is Kabuki?*
69–70
Durang, Christopher, 124

Eagleton, Terry, 55, 231n8, 233n19
Education, 18; drama in Canadian, 25, 42,
101, 230n3; of theatre practitioners,
26–27, 44, 53–54, 58
Eliot, T.S. 54, 59, 233n16
Emerson, Caryl, 202, 203
Endres, Robin, 90
Environmental theatre, 20, 179; in Canada,
164–66, 184; spatial politics of, 163–65,
175–76, 185–86, 214, 217; semiotics of,
186, 254n31; in United States, 165, 169
Essentialism, 43, 50, 115, 172, 207, 218
Esslin, Martin, 53
Ethnocentrism, 205, 208
Evans, Malcolm, 30
Everett, Hugh, 222
Everett-Green, Robert, 166, 178

Fabre, Jan, 179
Factory Theatre Lab (Toronto), 53, 57, 101